How to
Understand the Mind

Also by Venerable Geshe Kelsang Gyatso Rinpoche

Meaningful to Behold

Clear Light of Bliss

Universal Compassion

Joyful Path of Good Fortune

The Bodhisattva Vow

Heart Jewel

Great Treasury of Merit

Introduction to Buddhism

Tantric Grounds and Paths

Ocean of Nectar

Essence of Vajrayana

Living Meaningfully, Dying Joyfully

Eight Steps to Happiness

Transform Your Life

The New Meditation Handbook

How to Solve Our Human Problems

Mahamudra Tantra

Modern Buddhism

The New Heart of Wisdom

The New Guide to Dakini Land

The Oral Instructions of Mahamudra

This book is published under the auspices of the
NKT-IKBU International Temples Project
and the profit from its sale is designated for public
benefit through this fund.
[Reg. Charity number 1015054 (England)]
Find out more:
tharpa.com/benefit-all-world-peace

VENERABLE GESHE KELSANG
GYATSO RINPOCHE

How to
Understand
the Mind

THE NATURE AND POWER
OF THE MIND

THARPA PUBLICATIONS
UK • US • CANADA
AUSTRALIA • ASIA

First published as *Understanding the Mind* in 1993
Second edition 1997; Third edition 2002
Reprinted 2004, Reset 2007, 2010, 2013
Fourth edition substantially revised and published
as *How to Understand the Mind* 2014. Reprinted 2014, 2016.

Tharpa Publications UK   Tharpa Publications US
Conishead Priory   47 Sweeney Road
Ulverston, Cumbria   Glen Spey, NY 12737
LA12 9QQ, England   USA

There are Tharpa Publications offices around the world,
and Tharpa books are published in most major languages.
See page 393 for contact details.

© New Kadampa Tradition – International Kadampa
Buddhist Union 1993, 1997, 2002, 2014

The cover image is of Venerable Geshe Kelsang Gyatso Rinpoche.
Line illustrations include images from the Wheel of Life
as well as the eight auspicious symbols.

Library of Congress Control Number: 2013949529

British Library Cataloguing in Publication Data
A catalogue record for this book is
available from the British Library.

ISBN 978-1-906665-82-1 – paperback
ISBN 978-1-906665-83-8 – ePub
ISBN 978-1-906665-84-5 – kindle

Printed and bound in the United Kingdom by Bell and Bain Ltd

Paper supplied from well-managed forests and other controlled
sources, and certified in accordance with the rules of the
Forest Stewardship Council.

Contents

Introduction

We should know that in recent years our understanding and control of the external world have increased considerably and as a result we have witnessed remarkable material progress, but there has not been a corresponding increase in human happiness. There is no less suffering in the world today, and there are no fewer problems. Indeed, it might be said that there are now more problems and greater unhappiness than ever before. This shows that the cause of happiness and the solution to our problems do not lie in knowledge or control of the external world. Happiness and suffering are feelings – parts of our mind – and so their main causes are not to be found outside the mind. If we really want to be truly happy and free from suffering we must improve our understanding of the mind.

When things go wrong in our life and we encounter difficult situations, we tend to regard the situation itself as the problem, but in reality whatever problems we experience come from our mind. If we were to respond to difficult external situations with a positive or peaceful mind they would not be problems for us; indeed we may even come to regard them as challenges or opportunities for the growth and development of our happiness. Problems arise only if we respond to difficult external situations with a negative state of mind. Therefore, if we really want to be free from problems we must learn to control our mind by controlling our desire.

By controlling our desire we can make ourself happy all the time. This is because uncontrolled desire is the source of all suffering and problems. We have strong attachment to the fulfilment of our own desires, and because of our uncontrolled desire we human beings create so many problems and dangers in the world. We experience so many problems because we are unable to control our desire. By controlling our desire we can be free from all problems.

The instructions presented in this book are methods for controlling our mind, such as our attachment to the fulfilment of our own wishes. Especially, through studying and practising the different subjects and topics presented in this book, we can improve ourself and advance from the state of an ignorant lower being to that of a higher and higher being and finally to the highest state, that of an enlightened being. We human beings have this opportunity, and it is this that makes our life very precious and meaningful. Animals such as dogs do not have this opportunity, no matter how intelligent they are. We should recognize how fortunate we are and rejoice in our good fortune.

Geshe Kelsang Gyatso
June 4th 2013

PART ONE

Follow the path to enlightenment

What is Our Mind?

We often say, 'My mind, my mind', but if someone were to ask us, 'What is your mind?', we would have no correct answer. This is because we do not understand the nature and function of the mind correctly. The nature of the mind is clarity, which means it is something that is empty like space, always lacking form, shape and colour. The mind is not actual space because produced space possesses shape and colour. During the day it can be light and during the night it can be dark, but mind never possesses shape and colour.

As I said, the mind is empty, but we should not say the mind is emptiness. What is the difference between empty and emptiness? In Buddhism, emptiness has great meaning. It is the real nature of things and is a very profound and meaningful object. If we realize emptiness directly we will attain permanent liberation from all the sufferings of this life and countless future lives; there is no greater meaning than this. So emptiness is a very meaningful object, but an empty is just empty – it has no special meaning. Therefore, we have to say that the mind is empty, which means it always lacks form, shape and colour; and we have to say that space is empty, which means it lacks obstructive contact. When we say, 'My purse is empty', this means there is no money inside it. Through this we understand that different empties have different meanings.

The function of the mind is to perceive or understand objects. We normally say, 'I see such and such'; this is because our mind sees that object. Because our mind understands things we say, 'I understand.' So our perception and under-standing are functions of our mind; without mind we are powerless to perceive and understand objects.

Also, one of the main functions of the mind is imputing things. Without names things cannot exist. A name is imputed by mind thinking, 'This is this.' So things exist only because mind imputes them. Through this we can understand that everything including the world is created by mind. There is no creator other than the mind. This truth is not difficult to understand if we check it carefully.

In conclusion, the definition of the mind is something whose nature is empty like space, always lacking form, shape and colour, and whose function is to perceive or understand objects. Through understanding the nature and function of the mind correctly, we can understand that our mind is completely different from our body, and this proves that after our death although our body will cease the mind will not. The mind leaves the body and goes to the next life like a bird leaving one nest and moving to another. Or, for example, during sleep when we are dreaming our body is as if dead, and our mind leaves the body and goes to the dream world experiencing a dream life, which is a new life. Through contemplating this alone we can understand clearly the existence of our future lives.

How the Mind is Able to Move

Our mind is like a person who possesses eyes but no legs, and so can see things but cannot move from one place to another by himself. In the same way our mind can see objects but cannot move from one object to another by itself. It can move from one object to another only through the force of a mount. The mount for the mind is the inner winds. Inner winds are the subtle winds associated with the mind, and flow through the channels of the body. It is said that there is nothing quicker than the mind. For example, our mind can reach the moon in an instant by thinking of the moon, but without inner winds this is impossible. A detailed explanation about inner winds can be found in Appendix IV of the book *Modern Buddhism*.

Cut the root of suffering

The Gross, Subtle and Very Subtle Minds

From the point of view of its different levels, the mind is divided into three: gross, subtle and very subtle.

THE GROSS MIND

During our waking life we normally use gross minds such as our eye awareness through which we can see things, ear awareness through which we can hear sounds, nose awareness through which we can smell, tongue awareness through which we can taste, body awareness through which we can experience tactile objects, and mental awareness through which we strongly think 'I' and 'mine'. These awarenesses are gross minds because they are relatively easy to recognize. Without these awarenesses we cannot communicate with others and we cannot perform our daily activities. However, these awarenesses are mistaken awarenesses. They perceive inherently existent objects, which do not exist, and therefore they cause us to experience suffering. For example, when our mental awareness thinks 'I' or 'me' through perceiving either our body or mind, we mistakenly perceive our body or mind to be our self. This is a hallucination, and because of this when our body is sick we think 'I am sick', when our body is old we think 'I am old', and when our mind experiences suffering or pain we think 'I am suffering' or 'I am in pain.' Because of this hallucination we experience suffering and problems throughout our life and in life after life without end.

This is our normal, painful situation. Understanding this we should develop renunciation, the sincere wish to liberate ourself permanently from this hallucination by realizing the true nature of things, the emptiness of all phenomena.

THE SUBTLE MIND

During sleep while we are dreaming we use subtle minds such as our dream eye awareness, ear awareness, nose awareness, tongue awareness, body awareness and mental awareness, through which we experience the appearance of various kinds of dream things. All these appearances are mistaken appearances. In the same way that all our waking appearances are mistaken appearances, Buddha says, 'You should know all phenomena are like dreams.' Dream awarenesses are called subtle minds because they are difficult to recognize.

Because the appearances in our dreams and during our waking life are all mistaken appearances and hallucinations, our normal activities both in dreams and while we are awake have no real meaning. So we should think, 'What is the real meaning of our human life?'

THE VERY SUBTLE MIND

The very subtle mind is so called because it is extremely difficult to recognize. Without the very subtle mind we would have no life because our gross and subtle minds cannot hold our life. This is because they are only temporary minds, and very unstable. They suddenly arise and quickly disappear like clouds in the sky. Therefore only our very subtle mind holds our life continuously throughout the day and night, and in life after life until we become an enlightened Buddha. When we become a Buddha our very subtle mind will become a Buddha's mind and our very subtle inner wind will become a Buddha's body. Our very subtle mind, or 'continuously residing mind', is therefore our Buddha nature. Since our very subtle inner wind, or 'continuously residing body', will never die we have a deathless body that is our own body. In truth, our present body is a part of our parents' bodies, and so it belongs to our parents and not to us.

Our very subtle mind – our Buddha nature – is very precious, like a priceless jewel, but we cannot recognize it unless we engage in special methods for recognizing it that Buddha explained in his Highest Yoga Tantra teachings. These special methods are the meditations on the central channel, indestructible drop, and indestructible wind and mind. Through these meditations we can gather and dissolve our inner winds into the central channel. When all our inner winds completely dissolve into the central channel through the force of meditation, all our gross and subtle minds will also dissolve and our very subtle mind will naturally manifest. We will then be able to recognize it through our own experience. When our very subtle mind manifests through the inner winds dissolving into the central channel, this manifest very subtle mind is called 'clear light'. It is so called because it is a clear perception and an inner light. Thus, whenever our very subtle mind manifests it is clear light. Normally, for ordinary beings, the very subtle mind manifests only during deep sleep and at the end of the death process, but Highest Yoga Tantra practitioners can manifest their very subtle mind during meditation by dissolving inner winds into the central channel through the force of meditation; this is the clear light of realization. There are three different clear lights: the clear light of sleep, the clear light of death and the clear light of realization.

When we are in deep sleep our gross and subtle inner winds and minds naturally dissolve into the central channel, and as a result our very subtle mind manifests. This manifest very subtle mind is the clear light of sleep. However, normally we cannot recognize it because during deep sleep our memory is unable to function.

At the time of our death, when we experience the death process, our inner winds naturally dissolve into the central channel. First our gross minds will dissolve and cease, and only the subtle mind remains. Then our mind becomes more and more subtle until finally, when all inner winds have completely dissolved into the central channel, our very subtle mind will manifest. This manifest very subtle mind is the clear light of death. Its nature is great bliss, it is extremely peaceful; and it perceives only emptiness, the mere absence of all phenomena. Normally we cannot recognize it because at that time our memory cannot function.

Primary Minds and
Mental Factors

From the point of view of its function, the mind can be divided into primary minds and mental factors. Primary mind, mentality and consciousness are synonyms. The definition of primary mind is a cognizer that principally apprehends the mere entity of an object. The definition of mental factor is a cognizer that principally apprehends a particular attribute of an object. These definitions were given by Maitreya.

In the case of a pot for example, the pot itself is the mere entity of the pot, and the base, sides, shape, colour, size and so forth are particular attributes of the pot. Because a distinction exists within the object, there is a corresponding distinction on the part of the mind that cognizes that object. Thus, the function of a primary mind is to apprehend the mere entity of the object, while the function of mental factors is to apprehend particular attributes of the object. As each object has only one general entity but many particular attributes, any one object has only one primary mind but many mental factors observing it. Thus, when an eye awareness perceives a pot, for example, the primary mind principally apprehends the general entity of the pot – the pot itself – and the mental factors associated with that primary mind principally apprehend the particular attributes of the pot – its various parts.

There are six types of primary mind: eye consciousness, ear consciousness, nose consciousness, tongue consciousness, body consciousness and mental consciousness. The Chittamatrins posit two more primary minds: a consciousness-basis-of-all and a deluded mentality. According to them the consciousness-basis-of-all is a stable consciousness that does not cease at death but maintains the continuity of the person from one life to the next. It is the repository of karmic potentials and the source of all other consciousnesses. The deluded mentality observes the consciousness-basis-of-all and mistakenly apprehends it as a self-supporting, substantially existent self. The Madhyamika-Prasangikas conclusively refute both the consciousness-basis-of-all and the deluded mentality. There are only six types of primary mind because there are only six types of object – forms, sounds, smells, tastes, tactile objects and phenomena. Here, 'phenomena' means phenomena that appear only to mental awareness.

The quality of a primary mind depends upon the mental factors that accompany it. If the mental factors are virtuous the primary mind is virtuous, but if the mental factors are non-virtuous or neutral the primary mind is non-virtuous or neutral. Non-virtuous mental factors cause suffering and virtuous mental factors cause peace and happiness. Thus, if we wish to experience lasting peace of mind we must make a determined effort to eliminate non-virtuous mental factors and cultivate virtuous ones.

Each primary mind is accompanied by at least five mental factors, without which it would be unable to function. These are feeling, discrimination, intention, contact and attention. They are known as the 'five all-accompanying mental factors'. Just as a car cannot function if any of its wheels is missing, so a primary mind cannot function if any of these five mental factors is absent. For example, all physical objects are composed of eight substances – the four elements (earth, water, fire and wind) and the four transformed elements (forms, smells, tastes and tactile objects) – and just as even the simplest physical object must have all eight substances, so even the most basic primary mind must have all five all-accompanying mental factors. Even very subtle primary minds have these five mental factors.

We should not think of a primary mind and its mental factors as being separate entities, like a leader and his subjects, because each mental factor is a part of a primary mind. However, although a mental factor is a part of a primary mind, it is not a primary mind, just as a hand is a part of the body but not the body.

The Tibetan word for mental factor is 'sem jung', which literally means 'arisen from mind'. Thus, a primary mind can be likened to a candle flame and its mental factors to the rays of that flame. Just as a candle flame has many rays of light, so one primary mind has many mental factors; just as the rays of light come from the flame and exist simultaneously with it, so mental factors come from the primary mind and exist simultaneously with it; and just as the flame illuminates objects by depending upon the rays of light that emanate from it, so a primary mind knows its object by depending upon its mental factors.

A primary mind and its mental factors are the same entity and possess five similarities:

1 Basis – they have the same dominant condition
2 Object – their observed object is the same
3 Aspect – their engaged object is the same
4 Time – they arise, abide and cease simultaneously
5 Substance – one primary mind has only one of each type of mental factor

The meaning of dominant condition, observed object and engaged object are explained in Part Two.

For example, when a tongue awareness tastes tea, both the primary mind and the mental factor feeling associated with it develop from the same uncommon dominant condition, the tongue sense power, and so their basis is the same. Their observed objects are the same because they both focus on the same object – the taste of the tea; their engaged objects are the same because they both apprehend the taste of the tea; and their time, or duration, is the same because they both arise, abide and cease simultaneously. They possess the fifth similarity, similarity of substance, because one primary mind can have only one mental factor feeling, one mental factor discrimination, one mental factor intention, and so forth. Similarly, one specific mental factor can be associated with only one primary mind. Sometimes we say that we have mixed feelings about something, and it may seem that in this case one primary mind has several feelings observing the same object, but this is impossible. Ordinary beings cannot have two different manifest minds observing one object at the same time. What actually happens is that we have several primary minds, each with only one feeling. For example, if we have 'mixed feelings' about a house it can either be that at one time we like the house and at another time we dislike it, or that we simultaneously have two different minds relating to the house, each focusing on a different aspect of the house.

There are fifty-one mental factors, which are divided into six groups:

1 The five all-accompanying mental factors
2 The five object-ascertaining mental factors
3 The eleven virtuous mental factors
4 The six root delusions

5 The twenty secondary delusions
6 The four changeable mental factors

Each mental factor will now be explained under three head-ings: definition, function and divisions. The first identifies the mental factor, the second shows the results of generating it, and the third deepens our understanding of it. Some of the fifty-one mental factors are quite similar, and so we need to study them carefully and discuss them with others until we have a clear understanding of each one. Although we develop these mental factors within our own mind, we still need to try to identify them precisely so that we know which ones to abandon and which ones to cultivate. Abandoning non-virtuous mental factors and cultivating virtuous ones is the essence of Dharma practice. Deluded mental factors are the cause of all negative actions and the source of all suffer-ing and danger. By identifying them and eradicating them we solve all our problems. When I studied this subject in Tibet I was very young and, although I understood the sub-ject intellectually, I did not fully appreciate how useful it is for training the mind. Now I understand this very clearly.

Attain permanent liberation from the sufferings of death

The Five All-accompanying
Mental Factors

The five all-accompanying mental factors are so called because they accompany every primary mind. If just one of them were missing, the primary mind would not be able to cognize its object. The five all-accompanying mental factors are:

1 Feeling
2 Discrimination
3 Intention
4 Contact
5 Attention

Feeling experiences an object as pleasant, unpleasant or neutral; discrimination functions to distinguish an object from other objects and thereby to identify it; intention enables the mind to move towards its object and become involved with it; contact perceives an object as pleasant, unpleasant or neutral and thereby serves as the basis for the development of feelings; and attention functions to focus the mind on a particular attribute of an object.

The need for all five of these mental factors to be present can be illustrated by considering a tongue consciousness tasting tea. Without the mental factor feeling, the tongue consciousness would not experience the taste of the tea as pleasant, unpleasant or neutral. Without discrimination, it would not be able to distinguish the taste of the tea from other objects and so would not be able to recognize it. Without intention, an internal tongue consciousness could not become involved with the taste of the tea, which is an external object. Without contact, it could not perceive the taste of the tea as pleasant, unpleasant or neutral and so there would be no basis for developing pleasant, unpleasant or neutral feelings. Without attention, it would not be able to focus on the taste of the tea.

FEELING

DEFINITION OF FEELING

The definition of feeling is a mental factor that functions to experience pleasant, unpleasant or neutral objects.

Because there are three types of object – pleasant, unpleasant and neutral – there are three types of feeling that experience these objects – pleasant feelings, unpleasant feelings and neutral feelings. It is impossible to cognize an object without experiencing it as pleasant, unpleasant or neutral.

Buddhas have only pleasant feelings; the gods of the form realm and the formless realm have pleasant and neutral feelings but do not have unpleasant feelings; and beings living in the desire realm experience all three types of feeling. During sleep most of our feelings are neutral feelings, but when we are dreaming we may also experience unpleasant and pleasant feelings.

FUNCTION OF FEELING

The general function of feeling is to experience the effects of previous actions, or karma. In the Sutras, Buddha says:

The fully ripened effects of actions ripen not on soil or stones, but only on consciousness.

This is because only consciousness has feelings, and only with feelings can we experience the ripened effects of actions. Virtuous actions result in pleasant feelings, non-virtuous actions in unpleasant feelings, and neutral actions in neutral feelings. We tend to think that pleasantness and unpleasantness are characteristics that exist from the side of the object, but in reality whether we experience an object as pleasant or unpleasant depends entirely upon our karma. Two people might eat the same food and one find it delicious while the other thinks it is revolting. If this happens it is because the first person has good karma ripening with respect to that food and the other has bad karma ripening.

More specifically, the function of contaminated feelings is to act as the basis for the three poisons – attachment, hatred and ignorance. Contaminated pleasant feelings induce attachment, contaminated unpleasant feelings induce hatred, and contaminated neutral feelings induce ignorance. In *Guide to the Bodhisattva's Way of Life* Shantideva says:

Because of feeling, craving develops.

When ordinary beings develop pleasant feelings they develop craving, or attachment. Similarly, their unpleasant feelings induce anger, and their neutral feelings induce ignorance. By closely watching our mind we can observe these automatic reactions occurring almost continuously. Contaminated feelings are like moisture germinating the seeds of delusion that we have carried from previous lives. Foe Destroyers have eradicated the seeds of delusion from their mental continuum and so even when they develop intensely pleasant feelings they do not develop desirous attachment. Being free from self-grasping, their feelings are uncontaminated and so they cannot be the cause of delusions.

All contaminated feelings are objects to be abandoned. It is easy to generate a wish to abandon unpleasant feelings, but to generate a wish to abandon contaminated pleasant and neutral feelings we need a very good understanding of the nature of samsara. Both contaminated feelings and contaminated discriminations are key links in the chain that binds us to samsara. Contaminated discriminations identify objects as pleasant, unpleasant or neutral; and contaminated feelings experience them in these ways. Contaminated feelings then give rise to the three poisons, which in turn lead us to perform contaminated actions, the principal causes of rebirth in samsara.

The function of a person – to perform actions and experience their results – is completely dependent upon feeling and discrimination. If a person lacked discriminations he or she would not be able to perform any actions, and without feelings he or she would not be able to experience the results of any actions. Feelings and discriminations are so important that when Buddha explained the five aggregates he selected them from among the fifty-one mental factors and designated them each as a separate aggregate.

DIVISIONS OF FEELING

There are several ways of dividing feeling, including the threefold division already discussed:

1 Pleasant feelings
2 Unpleasant feelings
3 Neutral feelings

There is also a twofold division from the point of view of their uncommon dominant condition:

1 Bodily feelings
2 Mental feelings

Bodily feelings are feelings associated with the five sense consciousnesses. They are generated in dependence upon a sense power possessing form. Mental feelings are feelings associated with mental consciousness, which arise in dependence upon a mental power.

There is another twofold division from the point of view of their nature:

1 Contaminated feelings
2 Uncontaminated feelings

Contaminated feelings are feelings conjoined with self-grasping, and uncontaminated feelings are feelings conjoined with wisdom directly realizing emptiness. Until we attain the path of seeing, most of our feelings are contaminated feelings.

DISCRIMINATION

DEFINITION OF DISCRIMINATION

The definition of discrimination is a mental factor that functions to apprehend the uncommon sign of an object.

Every object has features that distinguish it from other objects and enable us to recognize it. The function of the mental factor discrimination is to apprehend these uncommon features. When we look at a tree, for example, our eye consciousness knows the tree because it discerns, or discriminates, the uncommon signs of the tree. If our eye consciousness lacked the mental factor discrimination it would not be able to distinguish the tree from other objects, and so it would not be able to recognize it. To recognize an object we need to understand what are its uncommon signs, or defining characteristics. For example, a newborn baby does not understand the uncommon signs of a wristwatch, and so it cannot recognize a watch as such.

FUNCTION OF DISCRIMINATION

The function of discrimination is to distinguish an object from other objects and to identify the object as 'this' and not 'that'. Discrimination associated with conceptual minds also functions to impute, label or name objects. There are two ways of imputing: imputing by word and imputing by thought. The former is the same as naming and the latter is the same as conceiving.

The defining characteristics of an object do not exist from the side of the object but are merely imputed by the mind that apprehends them. We can understand this by considering how different people view one object. For example, observing a particular person called John, one person may identify an enemy while another identifies a friend. If the characteristics of enemy and friend existed from the side of the person there would be a contradiction here, but since these characteristics are merely imputed onto the person by different minds there is no contradiction. From his own side John does not have a fixed set of defining characteristics waiting to be discovered by various minds; what he is depends solely upon how he is identified by the minds that apprehend him. We can choose how we discriminate objects. As Dharma practitioners we should choose to discriminate only in constructive ways, in ways that are conducive to virtue.

DIVISIONS OF DISCRIMINATION

There are three ways of dividing discrimination. First, from the point of view of uncommon dominant condition there are six types of discrimination:

1 Discriminations associated with eye consciousness
2 Discriminations associated with ear consciousness
3 Discriminations associated with nose consciousness
4 Discriminations associated with tongue consciousness
5 Discriminations associated with body consciousness
6 Discriminations associated with mental consciousness

If any of the six consciousnesses lacked the mental factor discrimination it would not be able to understand its object. Discrimination associated with eye consciousness is eye awareness but not eye consciousness, because consciousness is synonymous with primary mind.

There is also a twofold division of discrimination:

1 Mistaken discriminations
2 Non-mistaken discriminations

All wrong awarenesses have mistaken discrimination, and all unskilful actions of body, speech and mind result from mistaken discrimination. We act destructively because we are under the influence of delusions, and all delusions are based upon mistaken discrimination. Anger, for example, has a discrimination of its object as inherently unpleasant, while attachment has a discrimination of its object as inherently attractive. In both cases the discrimination is mistaken because attractiveness and unattractiveness depend upon the mind and do not exist from the side of the object.

If the mental factor discrimination is mistaken, the primary mind and all the other mental factors that it accompanies are wrong awarenesses. It is precisely because self-grasping and wrong views have mistaken discrimination that they apprehend wrong objects. The sixteen wrong thoughts explained in the Lamrim teachings and listed on pages 177–178 are all based on mistaken discriminations. For example, the second of these, not wishing to take the real meaning of our precious human life, involves the mistaken discrimination that the only meaning of this life is worldly pleasure. Dharma practitioners should make prayers to be free from all these mistaken discriminations because they severely hinder our attainment of the realizations of the stages of the path. Lamrim realizations are attained by eliminating these mistaken discriminations and developing the opposite, non-mistaken discriminations.

There are many causes of mistaken discriminations, such as previous imprints, familiarity, listening to wrong teachings or advice, and contemplating wrong reasons. We all have the seeds of mistaken discriminations but whether or not they ripen and influence our life depends to a large extent upon our lifestyle. If we lead a negative, or non-virtuous, life we will tend to develop wrong thoughts as a way of justifying our behaviour; but if we lead a positive, or virtuous, life we will be much more likely to adopt correct thoughts.

The imprints of ignorance cause mistaken discriminations that apprehend an inherently existent self, even though such a self does not exist. Moreover, because of our familiarity with delusions we discriminate some people as our friends, some as enemies and some as strangers; but all these discriminations are mistaken discriminations because in reality all sentient beings are our mothers.

There is another twofold division of discrimination:

1 Clear discriminations
2 Unclear discriminations

If our discrimination is clear we will be able to learn easily and quickly. Clear and correct discrimination is a basis for improving our understanding, and it helps us to avoid unskilful actions of body, speech and mind.

As we fall asleep our discrimination becomes unclear, and so we are liable to make mistakes. To begin with, our senses are still working so that, for example, we can still hear sounds such as others talking, but we cannot clearly understand the meaning of what they are saying. People on their deathbed also have unclear discrimination and so it is difficult for them to understand instructions quickly, which is why they make many mistakes. Mental disability is also often caused by unclear discrimination.

Sometimes when we listen to teachings or read Dharma books we find them confusing and feel that they are not presented very clearly, but in reality it is our discrimination that is unclear. If our discrimination were completely clear we could understand teachings just through hand gestures!

Realizing that our feelings and discriminations stimulate delusions, some practitioners try to abandon feelings and discriminations completely by withdrawing their mind inwards through the force of concentration and thereby becoming absorbed in a subtle state where disturbing mental activity is no longer manifest. This state is known as the 'absorption without discrimination'. It is a state in which the mind is single-pointedly absorbed in nothingness, with no gross feelings or discriminations. When these practitioners die they may be reborn as non-discrimination gods of the form realm, commonly known as the 'long-life gods', where they remain in absorption without discrimination for very long periods of time.

By preventing discrimination of gross objects these meditators make it impossible for gross delusions to manifest. However, they do not actually eradicate delusions in this way and so they do not attain liberation from samsara. Although it is possible to suppress gross feelings and discriminations associated with gross levels of consciousness, and thereby temporarily to avoid all the problems that they create, it is not possible to abandon the subtle feelings and discriminations associated with the subtle mind. When we fall into a deep sleep all the mental activity of which we are normally aware ceases and it seems as if we have become mindless, like an inanimate object, but what has actually happened is that our mind has become very subtle. Some practitioners attain a similar effect through the force of meditation and mistake it for liberation. In reality, however, they are merely temporarily absorbed in a state that resembles a long, deep sleep. Eventually, when their karma to remain in that state ends, their gross mental activity will resume and they will 'wake up'.

At the time of the third Buddha, Buddha Kashyapa, two Hinayana meditators entered into absorption without discrimination, and through the power of their concentration remained in that state for millions of years without dying. It was not until after the fourth Buddha, Buddha Shakyamuni, had passed into parinirvana that these meditators were discovered beneath the ground near Varanasi. As they rose from their subtle level of consciousness and developed gross feelings and discriminations again, they asked where Buddha Kashyapa was, and Buddha Shakyamuni's disciples had to explain that Buddha Kashyapa was no longer in this world, and that even Buddha Shakyamuni had appeared and passed away! After hearing this, both meditators died. Through the force of their concentration they had managed to isolate themselves for a long time from the problems of samsara, but they had not had any opportunity to make progress in their Dharma realizations while they were absorbed. Thus, when they finally rose from meditation they had received no benefit from their prolonged absorption.

Instead of trying to stop all discriminations it is more useful to try to develop correct discriminations. If we wish to overcome delusions completely, instead of just withdrawing our mind from the objects of delusion we should clearly identify the object of self-grasping, refute it with logical reasoning, and then meditate on actual emptiness. We also need to cultivate many correct discriminations with respect to the method side of spiritual practice.

As followers of the Mahayana we should not become too interested in meditation on the absorption of feelings and discriminations because it has no long-term benefit. It does not help us to develop renunciation, compassion, bodhichitta, the correct view of emptiness or the realizations of the two Tantric stages. Sometimes it may be helpful to practise this absorption for a short time when our mind is very disturbed or anxious, but we should not regard it as our principal meditation.

INTENTION

DEFINITION OF INTENTION

The definition of intention is a mental factor that functions to focus its primary mind on an object.

It is only through the mental factor intention that our primary mind is able to focus on its object; without it our mind would be motionless. Although our body remains in our room, our mind can travel wherever it wishes because it has the mental factor intention associated with inner wind. Just as the movement of a candle flame depends upon external wind, so the movement of the mind depends upon the mental factor intention and inner wind. Our mind moves to an object by connecting with it, or becoming involved in it. For example, when we think of a distant city our mind 'moves' to that city by taking the city as its object.

FUNCTION OF INTENTION

The principal function of intention is to create karma. Of the three types of karma, or action – bodily actions, verbal actions and mental actions – intention itself is mental action. However, it is also the cause of bodily and verbal actions, because all our bodily and verbal actions are preceded by mental actions.

If a tree falls down and kills someone it does not accumulate the karma of killing because it lacks the mental factor intention. All the karma created by sentient beings depends upon intention. If our intention is virtuous we create virtuous karma, if our intention is non-virtuous we create non-virtuous karma, and if our intention is neutral we create neutral karma. Intention plans the actions that we undertake, directing our action towards a particular goal. Since the quality of our experiences depends upon the quality of our actions, and the quality of an action depends upon the quality of the intention with which it is performed, ultimately all our happiness and unhappiness depend upon the mental factor intention. Even if someone is a great scholar, if he has bad intentions his knowledge will have little value and he will experience many problems.

According to the Sautrantikas and the Chittamatrins, only the mental factor intention is karma, but according to the Madhyamika-Prasangikas and the Vaibhashikas, bodily and verbal actions are also karma. However, whether these actions are virtuous, non-virtuous or neutral depends upon the intention that motivates them.

DIVISIONS OF INTENTION

There are three types of intention:

1 Non-virtuous intentions
2 Virtuous intentions
3 Neutral intentions

There are three types of non-virtuous action – non-virtuous bodily actions, non-virtuous verbal actions and non-virtuous mental actions – and most are included within the ten non-virtuous actions. Of these, the first two are easy to recognize, but the third, non-virtuous mental actions, are more subtle and therefore more difficult to identify. The mental action covetousness, for example, is a type of desirous attachment that wishes to obtain the friends or possessions of others. Whereas desirous attachment in general may be a neutral mind, covetousness is necessarily non-virtuous. As with all complete actions, covetousness must have four conditions: the basis, intention, preparation and completion. The basis of covetousness might be someone else's partner; the intention, the wish to obtain that person motivated by desirous attachment; the preparation, planning how to obtain that person for ourself; and the completion of the action, making a definite decision to obtain that person through our chosen method. This decision is the actual non-virtuous mental action of covetousness.

The four conditions must also be present to commit the actual non-virtuous actions of harmful thought and holding wrong views. Thus, the basis of harmful thought is another person whom we see as our enemy; the intention, the wish to harm them motivated by anger; the preparation, planning how to inflict harm on them; and the completion, making a firm decision to harm them. The basis of holding wrong views is any object, such as the existence of past and future lives, that must be understood to attain liberation; the intention, the wish to deny it motivated by ignorance; the preparation, thinking of reasons to prove that it does not exist; and the completion, making a firm decision that it does not exist. It is quite difficult for Dharma practitioners to create the actual karma of holding wrong views, but we still have many imprints or tendencies of wrong views and these often function to obstruct the development of pure faith.

There are many virtuous mental actions. Meditating on compassion is both a virtuous mental action and the mental factor intention, as is meditation on love. Whenever we listen to Dharma teachings, contemplate Dharma or meditate on Dharma, we are accumulating virtuous mental karma. There are many times when we cannot accumulate bodily and verbal virtuous karma, but we can always accumulate virtuous mental karma, even while we are relaxing, eating, enjoying ourself or sleeping. Mental karma is more important than bodily or verbal karma because it is our mental intention that determines whether a bodily or verbal action is virtuous or non-virtuous. If we do not have a virtuous intention, then even if we perform positive bodily actions they will not necessarily be virtuous karma because virtuous actions must have a virtuous motivation.

There are many intentions that are neutral mental actions, such as deciding what to eat for breakfast or deciding what to wear.

Intention can also be divided from the point of view of its effect:

1 Meritorious actions
2 Non-meritorious actions
3 Unfluctuating actions

Meritorious and non-meritorious intentions can each be sub-divided into those that are throwing karma, those that are completing karma and those that are karma whose results are experienced in the same life. These three types of action are explained in detail in the book *Joyful Path of Good Fortune*.

CONTACT

DEFINITION OF CONTACT

The definition of contact is a mental factor that functions to perceive its object as pleasant, unpleasant or neutral.

Whenever our mind cognizes an object, it perceives it as pleasant, unpleasant or neutral. This is the function of the mental factor contact. If contact perceives an object as pleasant, pleasant feelings will develop, and if contact perceives the object as unpleasant, unpleasant feelings will develop. Thus, contact makes the development of feelings possible, which is why it precedes feeling in the serial order of the twelve dependent-related links.

FUNCTION OF CONTACT

Besides perceiving objects as pleasant, unpleasant or neutral, contact also functions to give rise to feelings. For example, if in the first moment of a tongue consciousness tasting tea the mental factor contact associated with that consciousness perceives the tea as pleasant, we will subsequently develop a pleasant feeling.

DIVISIONS OF CONTACT

There are six types of contact:

1 Contact associated with eye consciousness
2 Contact associated with ear consciousness
3 Contact associated with nose consciousness
4 Contact associated with tongue consciousness
5 Contact associated with body consciousness
6 Contact associated with mental consciousness

ATTENTION

DEFINITION OF ATTENTION

The definition of attention is a mental factor that functions to focus the mind on a particular attribute of an object.

An eye consciousness, for example, is moved towards the general entity of an object by the mental factor intention, but it is the mental factor attention which focuses that consciousness on a particular attribute of that object. Intention is said to be like a horse travelling along a road, while attention is said to be like the reins that direct the horse. Thus, a primary mind focuses on the general entity of its object through the power of the mental factor intention, and on particular attributes of the object through the power of attention.

FUNCTION OF ATTENTION

Attention has four functions: (1) to focus the mind on a particular object, (2) to fix the mind on that object, (3) to prevent the mind from moving from the object, and (4) to serve as a basis for mindfulness and concentration. Without the mind being focused and fixed on an object through the power of attention there is no possibility of developing mindfulness and concentration. Every mind has a certain degree of attention, though some minds, such as non-ascertaining perceivers, have very weak attention, whereas others, such as those that occur when we are in an agitated state, have unstable attention that flits from one object to another. To develop concentration we need both strong and stable attention.

DIVISIONS OF ATTENTION

There are two types of attention:

1 Correct attention
2 Incorrect attention

Correct attention is an attention whose engaged object exists, and incorrect attention is an attention whose engaged object does not exist. All wrong awarenesses have incorrect attention.

There is another twofold division of attention:

1 Appropriate attention
2 Inappropriate attention

The former is the same as correct attention and the latter is the same as incorrect attention.

*Attain permanent liberation from the sufferings
of samsaric rebirth*

The Five Object-ascertaining Mental Factors

The five object-ascertaining mental factors are:

1 Aspiration
2 Firm apprehension
3 Mindfulness
4 Concentration
5 Wisdom

They are called 'object-ascertaining' mental factors because the objects of these mental factors are necessarily particular objects.

ASPIRATION

DEFINITION OF ASPIRATION

The definition of aspiration is a mental factor that focuses on a desired object and takes an interest in it.

Aspiration, desire and wish are synonyms. Thus, we are reading this book because we developed an aspiration, a desire, or a wish to do so.

FUNCTION OF ASPIRATION

The main function of aspiration is to induce effort. For example, if we lack the aspiration to receive teachings or to meditate we will put no effort into these activities. All tasks, whether worldly or spiritual, must be preceded by aspiration if we are to apply ourself to them. The success of our actions depends upon how much effort we put into them; and the stronger our aspiration, the stronger our effort will be. If our aspiration is weak our effort will also be weak; and if we completely lack aspiration we will do nothing at all.

It is most important to cultivate appropriate aspirations. For example, at the beginning of each meditation in the Lamrim teachings there is an explanation of the benefits of doing that meditation and the disadvantages of not doing it. The purpose of these explanations is to help us to develop the aspiration to engage in the meditation.

DIVISIONS OF ASPIRATION

There are four types of aspiration:

1 Wishing to meet an object
2 Wishing not to be separated from an object
3 Wishing to obtain an object
4 Wishing to be released from an object

Each of these can be virtuous, non-virtuous or neutral, depending upon its motivation. Examples of the first are wishing to meet Spiritual Guides, Buddhas or Bodhisattvas; or wishing to meet our family and friends. Examples of the second are wishing not to be separated from our Spiritual Guides or our Dharma practice; or wishing not to be separated from our friends, our possessions or our home. Examples of the third are wishing to attain Dharma realizations such as renunciation, bodhichitta and wisdom; or wishing to obtain material possessions, high status, good reputation or other worldly achievements. Examples of the fourth are wishing to be free from samsara, the two obstructions, or self-cherishing and other non-virtuous minds; or wishing to escape from people or situations we dislike.

Every sentient being develops many aspirations each day, but they are all included within either the aspiration to obtain happiness or the aspiration to be free from unhappiness. There is no one who does not have these two aspirations; they are our basic wishes from which all our other wishes arise. Even tiny insects have these two wishes and strive to fulfil them. Unfortunately ordinary beings do not know the real causes of happiness and suffering, and so in their pursuit of happiness they often bring suffering upon themselves, and in striving to avoid suffering often increase it.

There is also a twofold division of aspiration:

1 Mistaken aspirations
2 Non-mistaken aspirations

A mistaken aspiration is any wish that is not consistent with our basic aspirations to experience happiness and avoid suffering, and a non-mistaken aspiration is one that is consistent with these basic aspirations. The difference between a wise person and a foolish person is his or her aspirations. Even if we have not studied extensively, if our aspiration is good and unmistaken we will naturally engage in virtuous actions, which will result in happiness; but if our aspirations are mistaken we will not succeed in finding happiness no matter how great our worldly intelligence. Often criminals are highly intelligent and clever but because their aspirations are mistaken they commit crimes for which they are sent to prison.

If our wishes are not good, this is a sign that we do not possess true wisdom. Some people study Dharma for many years but receive little benefit, and their understanding remains only intellectual. The main reason for this is that their aspirations are not pure. Although superficially they have some interest in Dharma, deep down their real interest is in worldly things. Other people whose aspiration is pure receive genuine experience of Dharma even though they have not studied extensively. Their correct aspirations encourage them to engage in pure, virtuous actions, and these result in pure effects. What we accomplish depends primarily upon what we wish for, and so if our wishes are pure we will obtain pure results from our practice. The most important thing, therefore, is to develop and maintain correct aspirations. The supreme aspiration is bodhichitta, the wish to attain Buddhahood for the benefit of all sentient beings. With this aspiration all our actions become causes of attaining Buddhahood.

Basically Dharma practice is quite simple because all we need to do is to receive correct Dharma teachings by listening to qualified Teachers or by reading authentic books, and then mix our mind with these teachings by meditating on them. Whenever we listen to teachings or read Dharma books we should develop a correct aspiration, or motivation, concerning each subject, and maintain this aspiration with single-pointed focus. We need to cultivate virtuous aspirations such as the wish to seize the essence of our human life, renunciation and bodhichitta. If we meditate on these aspirations continuously, eventually they will arise spontaneously in our mind. Training in this way is the very essence of Dharma practice.

FIRM APPREHENSION

DEFINITION OF FIRM APPREHENSION

The definition of firm apprehension is a mental factor that makes its primary mind apprehend its object firmly.

This mental factor is present in all realizations. If a correct awareness holds its object firmly through the force of this mental factor it necessarily realizes its object. Although some wrong awarenesses hold their objects firmly, they are not realizations because their objects do not exist and so there is no actual understanding. The reason why non-ascertaining direct perceivers do not realize their objects is that they lack this mental factor.

FUNCTION OF FIRM APPREHENSION

The main function of firm apprehension is to make its primary mind apprehend its object firmly and thereby to realize that object. It also acts as a cause of mindfulness and concentration. Unless we understand an object firmly, with certainty, it is very difficult to keep our mind on it for long. Without firm apprehension our mind is like flowing water or a leaf in the wind. The reason we find it more difficult to keep our mind on a subtle object such as emptiness than on a gross object such as our breath is that we do not yet have firm apprehension of subtle objects.

There are three special types of firm apprehension observing emptiness that are attained during our spiritual development: one on the patience level of the path of preparation, one on the path of seeing, and one on the eighth ground. These are explained in teachings on the perfection of wisdom.

DIVISIONS OF FIRM APPREHENSION

There are two types of firm apprehension:

1 Correct firm apprehensions
2 Mistaken firm apprehensions

The first includes all firm apprehensions whose engaged object exists. An example of the second is grasping very tightly to a wrong view – for example, believing with strong conviction that this world is created by Ishvara. Even if we have wrong views, if we do not hold them very strongly they will not be very harmful because they can quickly be dispelled by listening to correct teachings; but if our wrong views are made firm by mistaken firm apprehension it will be very difficult for us to overcome them.

MINDFULNESS

DEFINITION OF MINDFULNESS

The definition of mindfulness is a mental factor that functions not to forget the object realized by the primary mind.

Mindfulness can focus only on an object that has already been realized; it is not present in the first moment of realizing an object. Mindfulness maintains the continuum of the original cognition by not forgetting the object. The reason an object is not forgotten is that the primary mind does not forget it, and the reason the primary mind does not forget the object is that it possesses the mental factor mindfulness. If a primary mind lacks mindfulness it will immediately forget its object. Without mindfulness our mind is like a leaky vessel – no matter how much we study we will not be able to retain anything.

Mindfulness is essential whenever we are listening to, contemplating or meditating on Dharma teachings. It is the life-force of Dharma practice. If our mindfulness declines, our knowledge and realizations will be lost. In *Friendly Letter* Nagarjuna says:

If mindfulness degenerates, all Dharmas degenerate.

FUNCTION OF MINDFULNESS

The function of mindfulness is to prevent distractions. The more stable our mindfulness, the fewer distracting thoughts we will have. If we meditate with strong mindfulness our mind will remain on its object without distraction and we will naturally develop stable concentration. At the moment the only type of mindfulness we can use is the conceptual mindfulness associated with gross levels of consciousness. We cannot yet use subtle mindfulness associated with subtle levels of consciousness, which is why we are unable to think clearly or meditate while we are asleep. When through meditation we learn to use subtle mindfulness we will be able to meditate even during sleep.

Dharma practitioners need to make a continuous effort to improve their mindfulness, both in and out of meditation. There are some teachers, such as the eighth-century Chinese monk Hashang, who teach that the way to meditate is simply to relax and let the mind go blank. This is very harmful advice because if we emphasize this practice our mindfulness will deteriorate and we will forget all we have learnt. Our Dharma realizations will degenerate and we will become dull and stupid.

DIVISIONS OF MINDFULNESS

In the Mahamudra teachings, mindfulness is divided into:

1 New mindfulness
2 Old mindfulness

Mindfulness functions both to keep the mind on an object that has not been forgotten, and to bring back to mind an object that has been forgotten. Until we attain the fourth mental abiding we sometimes forget the object of meditation and have to make an effort to remember it. To do this we need to rely upon new mindfulness. On the fourth mental abiding the power of mindfulness is complete and we never forget the object during the meditation session. From this point onwards all our mindfulness has to do is to keep a hold of the object. This is called 'old mindfulness'.

There is another twofold division of mindfulness:

1 Mindfulness with movements of mental sinking and mental excitement
2 Mindfulness without movements of mental sinking and mental excitement

Although the power of mindfulness is completed on the fourth mental abiding, there still remain subtle mental sinking and subtle mental excitement within that state of non-forgetfulness. It is not until the eighth mental abiding that all movements of mental sinking and mental excitement cease.

Dharma texts advise us that if we wish to attain tranquil abiding we should try to do so while we are young because as we get older our powers decline and the power of our mindfulness decreases. Compared with old people, young people have clear and stable mindfulness. With stable mindfulness it is easier to develop concentration and eventually to attain tranquil abiding.

CONCENTRATION

DEFINITION OF CONCENTRATION

The definition of concentration is a mental factor that makes its primary mind remain on its object single-pointedly.

Concentration serves to focus our mind on one object. It can develop only when the object is held firmly by mindfulness. Most primary minds have a degree of concentration, but simply possessing good concentration does not mean that we have attained Dharma realizations. The concentrations that are mentioned in the Lamrim teachings are necessarily virtuous, but not all concentrations are virtuous. Sometimes concentration is neutral and sometimes it is non-virtuous. For example, when a black magician forms a curse he has strong concentration but this concentration is non-virtuous. Non-virtuous concentration should be avoided, but we need both virtuous and neutral concentration. Neutral concentration is necessary to prevent our mind from becoming distracted during mundane tasks, such as driving, sewing and cooking. For example, if we are distracted while we are driving we may have an accident, and if we are distracted while we are working we will be inefficient and make many mistakes. Without at least some concentration we could not even make a cup of tea.

Concentration is particularly important for our spiritual practice. Practices such as reciting mantras, listening, contemplating and meditating are effective only if they are done with a concentrated mind. Actions done with a distracted mind do not have much power and are subject to many errors. As Shantideva says in *Guide to the Bodhisattva's Way of Life:*

Buddha, the All Knowing One, has said
That reciting mantras and prayers, and enduring
   spiritual hardships,
Even for a long time,
Are to no avail if the mind is distracted elsewhere.

Pure concentration has four qualities: lucidity, clarity, strength and stability. When the mind is free from the clouds of distracting conceptions it becomes bright and clear, like a cloudless sky; this is known as 'lucidity'. 'Clarity' means that the object appears clearly and vividly to the mind, 'strength' that the object is held firmly by strong mindfulness, and 'stability' that the mind abides single-pointedly on its object.

FUNCTION OF CONCENTRATION

The main function of virtuous concentration is to make the mind peaceful. In *Precious Garland* Nagarjuna says:

From giving comes wealth,
From discipline comes happiness,
From patience come attractive forms,
From effort comes the fulfilment of wishes,
From concentration comes peace,
And from wisdom comes liberation.

When our mind is free from the turbulence of distracting conceptions it becomes calm and smooth. When we are enjoying internal peace and happiness our craving for external sources of pleasure naturally declines and it is easy to remain content.

Pure concentration also helps to make our body and mind comfortable, flexible and easy to use in the practice of Dharma. This serviceability of the mind, which is called 'suppleness', is one of the main benefits that come from concentration. Although at present we have a certain degree of concentration when we meditate, it is relatively weak and short-lived, and so the suppleness it produces is subtle and difficult to recognize; but as our concentration becomes stronger and more stable our suppleness will also improve.

It is not just the intensity of suppleness that is important, for suppleness must also be firm and long-lasting. If we have suppleness that lasts for twenty-four hours a day we will always find it easy to engage in virtuous actions because we will never become physically or mentally tired; and we will always be delighted to listen to, contemplate and meditate on Dharma teachings. With this joy in Dharma practice we will find no difficulty in accomplishing the five paths, the ten grounds and the realizations of the two stages of Tantra.

Suppleness is the real opponent of laziness. According to Dharma, laziness is not just attachment to sleep and physical ease – it is any mind that is disinclined to engage in virtuous activities. There is no more important spiritual task than to eliminate laziness. With suppleness, virtuous activities such as contemplation or meditation become a pleasure and there is no reluctance to engage in them. The attainment of suppleness depends upon concentration, concentration depends upon effort, effort depends upon aspiration, and aspiration depends upon recognizing the benefits of concentration. Ordinary people regard samsaric enjoyments, possessions and money as beneficial and so they put all their effort into acquiring these; but Dharma practitioners see the great benefits of concentration and strive earnestly to attain it.

Concentration gives us the freedom to accomplish whatever we wish for. Without concentration our mind has no freedom but is forced to go wherever it is led by attachment, hatred or other delusions. A person who has good, virtuous concentration has control over his mind, and his mind does what he wants it to do, like a well-trained horse that obeys its rider. By improving our concentration we can attain tranquil abiding, superior seeing, clairvoyance and miracle powers, and eventually complete all the paths to enlightenment; but if we lack concentration we will not be able to make any progress on the paths and grounds of the Mahayana, and so we will not be able to attain Buddhahood. Therefore, all mundane and supramundane attainments depend upon concentration.

We need concentration not only during formal meditation but also when we are listening to teachings or reading Dharma books. For example, if we read a book with a distracted mind we will not understand the meaning clearly. We may think that the fault lies in the book but in reality it lies in our distracted mind.

DIVISIONS OF CONCENTRATION

There are three ways of dividing virtuous concentration: from the point of view of realm, from the point of view of its effect and from the point of view of its object. There are nine levels of concentration from the point of view of realm:

1 Concentration of the desire realm
2 Concentration of the first form realm
3 Concentration of the second form realm
4 Concentration of the third form realm
5 Concentration of the fourth form realm

6 Concentration of infinite space
7 Concentration of infinite consciousness
8 Concentration of nothingness
9 Concentration of peak of samsara

In samsara there are nine realms in which sentient beings can take rebirth: the desire realm, the four form realms and the four formless realms. The desire realm has two levels: happy migrations, which include the realms of humans and gods, and unhappy migrations, which include the realms of hungry spirits, animals and hell beings.

There are nine levels of desire realm concentration:

1 Placing the mind
2 Continual placement
3 Replacement
4 Close placement
5 Controlling
6 Pacifying
7 Completely pacifying
8 Single-pointedness
9 Placement in equipoise

After we attain the ninth level, placement in equipoise, we go on to attain tranquil abiding, which marks the beginning of the concentration of the first form realm. There are four form realms: the first form realm, second form realm, third form realm and fourth form realm. There are also four formless realms: infinite space, infinite consciousness, nothingness and peak of samsara. Peak of samsara is the highest of the nine realms, and the desire realm is the lowest.

Corresponding to the nine realms there are nine levels of being, nine levels of mind and nine levels of concentration. The grossest mind is that of a desire realm being. The mind of a being of the first form realm is slightly more subtle, and so on, until the concentration of peak of samsara, which is the most subtle mind within the nine realms.

To attain a mind of the first form realm it is not necessary to take rebirth in the form realm because we can attain tranquil abiding without abandoning our human body. Compared with the minds of the desire realm, form realm minds are more subtle, peaceful and concentrated. Although form realm beings still experience attachment to inner peace they have no anger and no attachment to external objects. Desire realm minds, on the other hand, are very gross and rough, and easily give rise to strong delusions. Without training in meditation it is difficult for beings in the desire realm to develop pure, virtuous concentration because their minds are so gross and distracted. However, if we train in meditation over a long period of time our mind will gradually become more subtle, our distractions less intense, and our meditation deeper. Eventually we will attain tranquil abiding and become free from the problems of desire realm beings.

There are two types of concentration from the point of view of their effect:

1 Mundane concentrations
2 Supramundane concentrations

Mundane concentrations are concentrations that are not motivated by at least renunciation and therefore cause only samsaric happiness. If our motivation for attaining tranquil abiding is to take rebirth in the form realm, for example, our concentration will be a mundane concentration because it will cause rebirth in samsara. Concentrations that are motivated by renunciation or bodhichitta are supramundane concentrations because they lead us beyond samsara, to liberation or enlightenment.

There is another twofold division of concentration from the point of view of its object:

1 Concentrations observing conventional objects
2 Concentrations observing ultimate objects

Since there are many different types of conventional object, there are many different concentrations observing conventional objects; but since there are not different ultimate objects, from the point of view of their object there are not different concentrations observing ultimate objects.

It is also possible to divide concentrations from the point of view of their duration. Concentrations can range from a few moments of single-pointedness to an absorption that lasts forever. Once we attain tranquil abiding our concentration will be capable of remaining on an object for as long as we wish. The concentration of a Buddha never weakens but remains focused on its object forever. Foe Destroyers are also able to remain in concentration on the same object for very long periods.

WISDOM

DEFINITION OF WISDOM

The definition of wisdom is a virtuous, intelligent mind that makes its primary mind realize a meaningful object.

We need to understand or realize meaningful objects such as the existence of past and future lives, karma and emptiness. The chapter on meditation later in this book presents fourteen meditations, and the book *The New Meditation Handbook* presents twenty-one meditations. The objects of all these meditations are meaningful objects. Understanding these objects will bring great meaning to this life and to countless future lives. Many people are very intelligent in destroying their enemies, caring for their families, finding what they want and so forth, but this is not wisdom. Even animals have such intelligence. Worldly intelligence is deceptive, whereas wisdom will never deceive us. It is our inner Spiritual Guide who leads us to correct paths, and it is the divine eye through which we can see what we need to know, what we need to abandon, what we need to practise and what we need to attain. Also, it is only through wisdom that we can understand the very extensive and subtle subject of karma, the special connection between our actions in former lives and our experiences in this life.

FUNCTION OF WISDOM

In general, wisdom functions to eliminate doubts and misunderstandings, and in particular it functions to dispel ignorance. If we understand the benefits of developing wisdom we will naturally strive to attain it. The opposite of wisdom is ignorance. Nothing harms us more than ignorance – it is the source of all our problems and the root cause of all our negative actions of body, speech and mind. There is no better way to use our precious human life than to strive to overcome our ignorance, and the way to do this is to develop wisdom.

To attain enlightenment we need to eliminate ignorance and its imprints from our mind. The Tibetan word for 'Buddha' is 'sang gye', in which 'sang' means 'purified' and 'gye' means 'accomplished'. A Buddha, therefore, is someone who has completely purified his or her mind of ignorance and its imprints. At present our mind is like the sky obscured by clouds. The only reason we do not realize all phenomena is that our mind is obscured by ignorance and other delusions. Once these are eradicated our mind will naturally become the omniscient mind of a Buddha, realizing all phenomena directly and simultaneously. The way to dispel the clouds of ignorance from the sky of our mind is to cultivate wisdom; therefore there is no more important task than to increase our wisdom.

DIVISIONS OF WISDOM

There are three types of wisdom:

1 Wisdom arisen from listening or reading
2 Wisdom arisen from contemplation
3 Wisdom arisen from meditation

Wisdom arisen from listening or reading is a wisdom that arises through listening to or reading Dharma instructions. Wisdom arisen from contemplation is a wisdom that arises through contemplating Dharma instructions, and wisdom arisen from meditation is a wisdom that arises through meditating on the meaning of Dharma instructions. The third wisdom is called 'superior seeing', which means that it is superior to the other two wisdoms. All three wisdoms are necessarily valid cognizers.

In the *Vinaya Sutras* Buddha says:

You should generate wisdom in dependence upon concentration, which itself depends upon moral discipline.

This means that to develop the wisdom of superior seeing we first need to attain the concentration of tranquil abiding, and to attain tranquil abiding we need to practise pure moral discipline.

There is also a sevenfold division of wisdom:

1 Great wisdom
2 Clear wisdom
3 Quick wisdom
4 Profound wisdom
5 The wisdom of expounding Dharma
6 The wisdom of spiritual debate
7 The wisdom of composing Dharma books

All these wisdoms and special methods for accomplishing them are explained in detail in the book *Heart Jewel*.

The Eleven Virtuous
Mental Factors

The eleven virtuous mental factors are all naturally virtuous, which means that they are virtuous through their own nature and not through the force of a specific motivation. If a spoonful of sugar is stirred into a cup of tea, all the tea becomes sweet because sugar is by nature sweet. Similarly, when a virtuous mental factor is present in the mind, that entire primary mind and all its attendant mental factors also become virtuous.

The eleven virtuous mental factors are:

1 Faith
2 Sense of shame
3 Consideration for others
4 Non-attachment
5 Non-hatred
6 Non-ignorance
7 Effort
8 Mental suppleness
9 Conscientiousness
10 Equanimity
11 Non-harmfulness

FAITH

DEFINITION OF FAITH

The definition of faith is a mental factor that functions principally to eliminate non-faith.

Without understanding non-faith we cannot understand faith. There are three types of non-faith: non-faith of disbelief, non-faith of non-admiration, and non-faith of not-wishing. Non-faith of disbelief is disbelief in any correct object in which it is necessary to believe to make spiritual progress, such as the objects explained in Dharma teachings. If someone correctly explains Buddha's teachings on actions and their effects and we do not believe what they are saying, this is because the mental factor non-faith of disbelief is present in our mind. Non-faith of non-admiration is a mental factor that causes us to see faults in virtuous objects such as Dharma Teachers, the Three Jewels and other holy beings. It makes our mind unclear and confused. Non-faith of not-wishing is a mind that does not desire virtuous attainments. It prevents us from developing a wish to engage in the paths to liberation or enlightenment.

These three types of non-faith are very harmful. Disbelief prevents us from engaging in spiritual practices and attaining Dharma realizations. It is harmful even for those who are not interested in Dharma. For example, there are many diseases that doctors call cancer but which are in fact caused by spirits or by previous karma. Although these cannot be cured by ordinary medical practices, they can be cured by the healing rituals and purification practices taught by Buddha. However, for these methods to be effective we need to have faith in them. Unfortunately few people in the West have sufficient faith in these methods and so we do not have many opportunities to witness their beneficial effects.

Non-faith of non-admiration robs us of our mental peace and makes our mind turbulent and defiled. As a result, our virtuous minds decrease and we are unable to develop pure experience of Dharma. Non-faith of not-wishing harms us by preventing us from practising Dharma purely. At present, our desire to enjoy the pleasures of samsara is much stronger than our desire for spiritual attainments, and this prevents us from practising Dharma purely, undistracted by worldly concerns. The mental factor faith overcomes all three types of non-faith.

FUNCTION OF FAITH

The special function of faith is to induce virtuous aspirations. Without faith in a particular practice we will have no wish to engage in it; and without such a wish we will not put any effort into the practice and so we will not accomplish any results. Faith is the root of all spiritual attainments. If we have faith in Buddha we will develop the aspiration to become a Buddha, which will encourage us to practise the paths to enlightenment.

Faith is particularly important in the practice of Secret Mantra. An essential aspect of Tantric practice is the recitation of mantras, but success in mantra recitation depends largely upon the strength of our faith. A person who lacks faith may recite the mantra of his or her Deity for many years but fail to receive any attainments, whereas someone with pure faith may receive attainments after reciting the mantra for only a short time.

In *Lamp of the Jewel Sutra* (Skt. *Ratnalokanamadharani Sutra*) Buddha says:

Faith precedes all virtuous activities, like a mother.
It protects and increases all beneficial qualities,

Dispels hesitation, and rescues us from the four rivers.
Faith is the source of the siddhi of happiness.
It dispels mental defilements and turbulence, makes
  the mind clear,
Eliminates pride, and is the root of respect.
Faith is the supreme wealth, treasure and legs;
And is like hands with which to gather virtues.

Just as a mother gives birth to children, so faith is the source of all virtuous activities because without faith we will not engage in pure, virtuous practices. Faith prevents virtuous qualities from degenerating and causes them to increase. Believing faith dispels doubts and hesitations concerning Dharma practices. We have doubts and hesitations about Dharma because we lack faith, but when faith manifests, doubts cannot remain. Wishing faith causes us to strive to attain liberation from samsara and thereby rescues us from the 'four rivers' of birth, sickness, ageing and death. Some types of faith act as a direct antidote to the delusion-obstructions and the obstructions to omniscience. For example, it is because the vajra-like concentration of the path of meditation is conjoined with believing faith in emptiness that it can act as the direct antidote to the most subtle obstructions to omniscience.

Faith is the source of the siddhi, or attainment, of happiness, because happiness is the result of virtuous actions, and all virtuous actions are motivated by faith. Admiring faith dispels mental defilements such as bad motivations or seeing faults in holy beings such as our Spiritual Guide. By pacifying the mental turbulence caused by disturbing conceptions faith makes our mind lucid and clear. Faith overcomes our pride and is the foundation of respect for the Three Jewels and our Spiritual Guides. It is the supreme wealth because, unlike material wealth, it never deceives us. To accumulate material possessions we frequently have to endure physical and mental hardship, and even commit negative actions, and yet even if we succeed in becoming rich we still do not experience pure peace and happiness. Moreover, material wealth can be lost or stolen and can even endanger our life. Thus, external wealth is the source of much anxiety and discontent. The inner wealth of faith, on the other hand, brings only happiness. If we strengthen our faith we perform only virtuous actions, and when we are rich in faith we experience pure, lasting happiness. The wealth of faith cannot be destroyed by fire or stolen by thieves; even death cannot take it from us. Ultimately the wealth of faith leads us to liberation and great enlightenment, and so it is far superior to external wealth.

Faith is like a treasure because it is the source of inexhaustible benefit and good fortune. It is called 'supreme legs' because it enables us to traverse the ten Bodhisattva grounds and finally to reach the city of great enlightenment. Ordinary legs can take us only to samsaric places but the legs of faith can take us to Dakini Land, where we will meet Heruka and Vajrayogini, or to Sukhavati, the Pure Land of Buddha Amitabha. Faith is also like hands because it enables us to gather virtuous qualities. Just as we need hands to collect physical objects, so we need the hands of faith to gather the internal wealth of virtue.

DIVISIONS OF FAITH

There are three types of faith:

1 Believing faith
2 Admiring faith
3 Wishing faith

Believing faith is a belief in any object that is conducive to our spiritual development, such as the two basic objects (the two truths), the two paths (method and wisdom), and the three resultant bodies of a Buddha.

Admiring faith is a tranquil, lucid state of mind, free from negative conceptions, that arises when we contemplate the good qualities of virtuous objects or holy beings such as our Spiritual Guide. It is likened to a magical jewel that has the power to purify dirty water. When our mind is disturbed by negative conceptions it is like dirty water, but admiring faith causes these impure thoughts to subside and allows our primary mind to become lucid and pure, like clean, fresh water.

Wishing faith is a wish to follow any Dharma path, based on recognition of its good qualities. All virtuous aspirations are wishing faith. An example is the wish to become a Buddha based on recognition of a Buddha's good qualities. Although bodhichitta is a primary mind, not a mental factor, it has two aspirations – the aspiration to attain enlightenment and the aspiration to benefit others, both of which are wishing faith. Renunciation is also wishing faith.

Believing faith is based on admiring faith, but is much stronger and more definite. Even animals occasionally develop admiring faith, but believing faith involves consciously holding a special view. Faith pervades all virtuous minds just as space pervades all places. Every virtuous mind is mixed with faith.

SENSE OF SHAME

DEFINITION OF SENSE OF SHAME

The definition of sense of shame is a mental factor that functions to avoid inappropriate actions for reasons that concern ourself.

Sense of shame prevents us from committing negative actions by reminding us that it is not suitable for us to engage in such actions because we are a Dharma practitioner, an ordained person, a Teacher, an adult and so on. For example, if we stop ourself from squashing a mosquito that is about to bite us by thinking 'It is not right for me to kill this insect because I am a Buddhist', this motivation is sense of shame.

FUNCTION OF SENSE OF SHAME

The function of sense of shame is to serve as the foundation of moral discipline, particularly the moral discipline of restraint. If we are unable to generate sense of shame we will find it extremely difficult to practise moral discipline. Sense of shame guards us against committing negative actions by appealing to our conscience and to the standards of behaviour that we feel to be appropriate.

DIVISIONS OF SENSE OF SHAME

There are three types of sense of shame:

1 Sense of shame that restrains us from inappropriate bodily actions
2 Sense of shame that restrains us from inappropriate verbal actions
3 Sense of shame that restrains us from inappropriate mental actions

There is also a twofold division of sense of shame based on the reasons for restraint:

1 Sense of shame that restrains us from inappropriate actions out of concern simply for ourself

2 Sense of shame that restrains us from inappropriate actions out of concern for the specific undesirable results for ourself

Examples of the first type are thinking 'I should not do this because I am a Buddhist', or 'I should not do this because I am a Dharma practitioner', or 'I should not commit this action because I am a nun.' Examples of the second type are thinking 'I should not do this because it will damage my Dharma practice', or 'I should not do this because it will cause me to take rebirth in the lower realms', or 'It is inappropriate for me to commit this action because it transgresses my commitments.'

CONSIDERATION FOR OTHERS

DEFINITION OF CONSIDERATION FOR OTHERS

The definition of consideration for others is a mental factor that functions to avoid inappropriate actions for reasons that concern others.

Examples of consideration are holding back from saying something unpleasant because it will upset another person, or giving up fishing because of the suffering it causes the fish. We need to practise consideration whenever we are with other people by being mindful of how our behaviour might disturb them or harm them. Our desires are endless, and some of them would cause other people much distress if we acted them out. Therefore, before we act on a wish we should consider whether it will disturb or harm others, and if we think that it will we should not do it. If we are concerned for the welfare of others we will naturally practise consideration.

FUNCTION OF CONSIDERATION FOR OTHERS

The main function of consideration is the same as that of sense of shame – to serve as the foundation of the moral discipline of restraint. Consideration is important for Dharma practitioners and non-practitioners alike. If we are considerate, others will like us and respect us, and our relationships with our family and friends will be harmonious and long-lasting. Without consideration, however, relationships quickly deteriorate. Consideration prevents others from losing faith in us and is the basis for developing a mind of rejoicing.

Consideration for others is the foundation of the spiritual path. One of the commitments of going for refuge is not to cause harm to others, and this is the essence of the practice of consideration. If we do not practise consideration our experience of advanced practices such as tummo meditation and vajra recitation will quickly degenerate; and our aim should be to progress in our spiritual practice, not to regress.

Whether we are a good person or a bad person depends upon whether or not we have sense of shame and consideration. Without these two mental factors our daily behaviour will soon become negative and cause others to turn away from us. Sense of shame and consideration are like beautiful clothes that cause others to be attracted to us. Without them we are like a naked person whom everyone tries to avoid.

DIVISIONS OF CONSIDERATION FOR OTHERS

There are three types of consideration for others:

1 Consideration for others that restrains us from inappropriate bodily actions

2 Consideration for others that restrains us from inappropriate verbal actions
3 Consideration for others that restrains us from inappropriate mental actions

There is also a twofold division of consideration for others based on the reasons for restraint:

1 Consideration for others that restrains us from inappropriate actions out of concern simply for others
2 Consideration for others that restrains us from inappropriate actions out of concern for the specific undesirable results for others

NON-ATTACHMENT

DEFINITION OF NON-ATTACHMENT

The definition of non-attachment is a mental factor that functions as the direct opponent of attachment.

Non-attachment is not simply freedom from attachment but a mental factor that directly opposes attachment. Attachment harms us greatly by preventing us from developing the wish to escape from samsara. As long as we are attached to samsaric places, enjoyments and bodies we will not be able to develop the wish to abandon samsara, and so we will continue to accumulate contaminated karma that throws us into samsaric rebirths. To attain liberation we must first overcome attachment to this life by practising the stages of the path of initial scope, and then overcome attachment to samsara in general by practising the stages of the path of intermediate scope. In this way we develop renunciation, which is a type of non-attachment.

FUNCTION OF NON-ATTACHMENT

Non-attachment is the gateway to liberation. Attachment is like a rope that ties us to samsara. As long as we have strong attachment we have no mental freedom but are controlled by circumstances, like a puppet on a string. As soon as a pleasant object presents itself to our mind we automatically develop attachment, which causes us more problems and binds us even more tightly to samsara. To overcome this attachment and develop a genuine interest in attaining liberation from samsara we need to train in non-attachment.

To practise non-attachment it is not necessary to avoid all objects of attachment. In fact, this is impossible in our present circumstances because wherever we go we find objects of attachment. If we try to avoid places or people to whom we are attached by going elsewhere, we will soon find ourself developing attachment to new places and new friends; and if we try to abstain from all the things we presently enjoy, such as food, drink, and clothing, we will find it difficult to survive. Rather than trying to avoid objects of attachment, the way to practise non-attachment is to recognize the faults of the mind of attachment and then to try to abandon that mind. The faults of attachment are explained below in the section on attachment.

DIVISIONS OF NON-ATTACHMENT

There are three types of non-attachment:

1 Non-attachment to samsaric places
2 Non-attachment to samsaric enjoyments
3 Non-attachment to samsaric bodies

There is another threefold division:

1 Non-attachment to this life
2 Non-attachment to samsara
3 Non-attachment to solitary peace

Ordinary beings have attachment to this life and attachment to samsara, but only those who have attained tranquil abiding can develop attachment to solitary peace. Some Hinayana Foe Destroyers, for example, remain in the peace of concentration for thousands of years, during which time they do nothing to help other sentient beings. Although their attachment to peace is not an actual delusion, it is called 'attachment' to emphasize the fact that it is a major obstacle to the Bodhisattva's way of life. Bodhisattvas consider attachment to solitary peace to be more harmful than ordinary attachment. If a Bodhisattva generates attachment towards his or her family this will not necessarily cause his compassion or his wish to benefit others to diminish, but if he develops attachment to solitary peace his compassion and bodhichitta will definitely degenerate. Moreover, if he remains too long in a state of solitary peace he will transgress his commitment to benefit others. Bodhisattvas on the first and second grounds experience ordinary attachment, but this does not disturb their spiritual practice, and they are able to use it as a means of benefiting others. Just as farmers use unpleasant things such as manure to create favourable conditions for growing crops, so Bodhisattvas use their attachment as a means of helping others. The main objects to be abandoned by Bodhisattvas are attachment to solitary peace and concern for their own welfare.

We overcome these three types of attachment by training in the stages of the path of the three scopes. By practising the stages of the path of initial scope we overcome attachment to this life, by practising the stages of the path of intermediate scope we overcome attachment to samsara in general, and by practising the stages of the path of great scope we overcome attachment to solitary peace.

NON-HATRED

DEFINITION OF NON-HATRED

The definition of non-hatred is a mental factor that functions as the direct opponent of hatred.

In *Guide to the Bodhisattva's Way of Life* Shantideva says:

There is no evil greater than anger,
And no virtue greater than patience.

Hatred, or anger, is the most destructive of all non-virtuous minds. It has the power to destroy our Dharma experiences and the merit we have accumulated in the past. Unless we make an effort to practise non-hatred we will find it difficult to control our anger; and if our mind is filled with anger we will not experience peace or happiness. When we are angry we cannot enjoy life, even if we live in a luxurious house and eat the most expensive food. It is difficult to fall asleep with an angry mind, and when we do sleep we have unpleasant, disturbing dreams. When anger controls our mind we develop the intention to harm others, and we may even wish to kill ourself. We usually cherish ourself dearly, but hatred can so disturb our mind that we consider committing suicide. Shantideva said that for as long as we harbour painful thoughts of anger our mind will not experience peace.

Unless we have some experience of Dharma we will think that our enemies are other people who cause us harm, but according to Dharma our real enemies are the delusions in our mind, such as anger and attachment. If we regard other people as our enemies we will try to harm them, and this will only make the situation worse. Our relationships will deteriorate, and we will gradually accumulate more and more enemies. On the other hand, if we practise love, regarding all living beings as our kind mothers, our relationships will improve and our problems will gradually disappear. If we are going to retaliate we should do so against our delusions, for they are the source of all the harm we experience. If we succeed in destroying these inner enemies we will bring an end to all our suffering and problems, but if we show them patience and understanding they will continue to betray and harm us.

The mental factor non-hatred opposes our internal enemy of hatred. If we are about to develop hatred towards someone but counter it by thinking 'It is inappropriate for me to hate this person because hatred is like poison', we are practising non-hatred. It is most important to practise non-hatred as soon as we detect signs of anger or hatred arising in our mind. Anger is like fire. If we detect a fire as soon as it starts it will be easy to extinguish, but if we wait until it has taken hold it will be very difficult to control. In the same way, if we catch anger as soon as it arises in our mind we can easily counter it with non-hatred, but if we leave it to develop fully we will find it very difficult to stop. Therefore, as soon as we become aware that anger is about to manifest we should prevent it by reflecting on its many disadvantages. These are explained extensively in the chapter on patience in Shantideva's *Guide to the Bodhisattva's Way of Life* and in the commentary *Meaningful to Behold*.

FUNCTION OF NON-HATRED

Non-hatred has many functions. It overcomes irritation and frustration and enables us to respond to adverse conditions with a calm and positive mind. It frees us from the inner pain of hatred, and makes our mind smooth and comfortable at all times. It is the basis for generating affectionate love and all the other Mahayana realizations. When our mind is filled with non-hatred we have no enemies because everyone appears to us as kind and agreeable. As a result, we do not engage in negative actions such as fighting or killing, and so we do not have to suffer the consequences of such actions. Affectionate love, cherishing love, wishing love, compassion and patience are all the nature of non-hatred.

DIVISIONS OF NON-HATRED

There are three types of non-hatred:

1 Non-hatred towards those who harm us
2 Non-hatred towards inanimate objects that cause us suffering
3 Non-hatred towards resultant suffering

The first type is the same as the patience of not-retaliating. If someone attacks us, insults us or causes us harm in some other way, and we manage to stop ourself getting angry with them, it is the first type of non-hatred that prevents the anger from arising.

There are many inanimate objects with which we get angry. For example, we may get angry with the weather if it is too hot or too cold, with our car if it will not start, or with a piece of furniture if it falls on our foot. Some people are angered by the existence of nuclear weapons or pollution, while others become upset if their food is not to their liking. Whenever we encounter inanimate objects that cause us suffering we should remember the futility of getting angry with such things and prevent anger by practising the second type of non-hatred.

The third type of non-hatred, non-hatred towards resultant suffering, is the patience of voluntarily enduring suffering. When we are unhappy or sick we are much more prone to anger than when we are happy and healthy. People who are usually patient when they are well often develop a bad temper when they are sick. This indicates that they lack the patience of voluntarily enduring suffering. All our suffering, both physical and mental, is the result of our own negative karma. Therefore, when we are about to become angry with our suffering we should think:

This pain is the result of my own non-virtuous actions. Since I committed these negative actions I must experience their resultant suffering. Therefore, I must accept this suffering patiently.

If we are able to think like this we will not get angry or upset but will be able to endure our suffering with a peaceful mind. If our pain becomes unbearable we should try to ease it with medicines or, if our mind is strong enough, use our pain to enhance our experience of the two bodhichittas by meditating on compassion and emptiness. With a direct realization of emptiness we will not experience pain even if our limbs are cut off, because when we have seen emptiness directly we experience only peace. Even a relatively superficial experience of emptiness can ease our pain and restore our body and mind to health. We should use whatever methods we can to cure our sickness but even if these fail there is no point in becoming angry with our pain, for this will just add mental suffering to our physical suffering.

NON-IGNORANCE

DEFINITION OF NON-IGNORANCE

The definition of non-ignorance is a mental factor that functions as the direct opponent of ignorance.

Non-ignorance is a special type of wisdom that acts as the antidote to ignorance. Examples are wisdom realizing selflessness of persons and wisdom realizing selflessness of phenomena.

FUNCTION OF NON-IGNORANCE

The function of non-ignorance is to enable us to understand emptiness, the ultimate nature of phenomena. As our understanding of emptiness grows, our ignorance gradually becomes weaker, and is eventually eradicated altogether. The temporary benefit of non-ignorance is that it helps us to overcome daily problems that are caused by attachment, anger and other delusions; its long-term benefit is that it leads us to liberation and enlightenment. Our friends and family cannot solve our internal problems for us, and even our Spiritual Guides cannot remove them directly. The only way to eliminate our mental problems is to rely upon our own wisdom. Those who possess wisdom realizing emptiness can solve all their internal problems by meditating on emptiness. It is because we lack this wisdom that we need to ask others for advice when we are confronted with problems. If we had wisdom we would be able to solve all our own problems.

The benefits of wisdom realizing emptiness are inconceivable. If we had a million pounds in our pocket it would cause us much anxiety and possibly even endanger our life, but if instead of money we possessed wisdom realizing emptiness we would have no worries or problems. We would be able to use our wisdom all the time, and it would be a constant source of guidance and comfort to us. Therefore, wisdom realizing emptiness is the supreme friend and the supreme wealth.

DIVISIONS OF NON-IGNORANCE

There are four types of non-ignorance:

1 Non-ignorance arisen from listening or reading
2 Non-ignorance arisen from contemplation
3 Non-ignorance arisen from meditation
4 Non-ignorance arisen from imprints

The first three types of non-ignorance can be understood from the three wisdoms – wisdom arisen from listening or reading, wisdom arisen from contemplation, and wisdom arisen from meditation – explained previously in the section on wisdom. However, whereas the three wisdoms as presented in the previous explanation are not necessarily wisdom realizing emptiness, here, because non-ignorance is the direct opponent of ignorance, they are. The fourth type of non-ignorance is a wisdom realizing emptiness that arises naturally from imprints from past lives without the need to study emptiness in this life. It is also known as the 'wisdom attained just through the power of birth'. Some people who have meditated deeply and for a long time on emptiness in a previous life are able to carry this understanding into this present life, and as a result they are able to understand emptiness very easily without having to study or contemplate for a long time. When we eventually attain the concentration of the Dharma continuum on the path of accumulation we will not forget any Dharma that we study but will carry all our knowledge with us into the next life.

In *Training the Mind in Seven Points* Geshe Chekhawa says:

> The three objects, three poisons, and three virtuous roots
> Are the brief instruction for the subsequent attainment.

The three objects are attractive objects, unattractive objects and neutral objects; the three poisons are attachment, hatred and ignorance; and the three virtuous roots are non-attachment, non-hatred and non-ignorance. When ordinary beings encounter the three objects they automatically develop the three poisons. The essential aim of Dharma practice is to reverse this so that we automatically develop the three virtuous roots instead. When someone who has thoroughly trained their mind in Dharma meets an attractive object they develop not attachment but non-attachment; when they meet an unattractive object they develop not hatred but non-hatred; and when they meet a neutral object they develop not ignorance but non-ignorance. Since all objects are included within the three objects, those who have mastered the three virtuous roots are able to transform all their experiences into the path to enlightenment. This is why the three virtuous roots are called the 'essence of Buddhadharma'.

EFFORT

DEFINITION OF EFFORT

The definition of effort is a mental factor that makes its primary mind delight in virtue.

Effort functions to make our mind happy to engage in virtue – delighting in actions such as giving, helping others, making prostrations, making offerings, reciting prayers, reading Dharma books and listening to Dharma teachings. Effort is necessarily virtuous. Minds that strive for ordinary goals, such as business achievements, and minds that delight in non-virtue, are not effort.

The opposite of effort is laziness. There are three types of laziness: laziness arising from attachment to worldly pleasures, laziness arising from attachment to distracting activities and laziness arising from discouragement. In general, fondness for sleep is a type of laziness, but if we are able to practise the yoga of sleeping and transform sleep into a virtuous action, then the mind that enjoys sleep is effort. Similarly, if we transform other neutral actions such as eating, cooking and playing into virtuous actions by performing them with a good motivation, our enjoyment of them is also the mental factor effort.

FUNCTION OF EFFORT

The function of effort is to instigate virtue, protect virtue from degenerating, facilitate the increase of virtuous qualities and bring virtuous practices to completion. In *Ornament for Mahayana Sutras* Maitreya lists many benefits of effort:

> Among virtuous collections, effort is supreme.
> With effort we can accomplish all virtuous qualities,
> With effort we can accomplish a peaceful body and
>   mind,
> With effort we can accomplish mundane and
>   supramundane attainments,
> With effort we can obtain the pleasures of samsara,
> With effort we can take rebirth in a Pure Land,

> With effort we can be freed from delusions such as
>   the view of the transitory collection, and attain
>   liberation,
> With effort we can attain great enlightenment.

Effort is the supreme virtue because all virtuous qualities are attained through the power of effort. Effort makes both body and mind peaceful, comfortable and healthy by inducing physical and mental suppleness. When we have attained physical suppleness we do not need physical exercise to keep our body flexible and healthy. By relying upon effort we can attain both mundane and supramundane attainments, such as the Highest Yoga Tantra realizations of Deities like Heruka and Vajrayogini. Even the happiness of humans or gods depends solely upon our own effort because if we do not make an effort to practise virtuous actions we will not be able to take such rebirths in the future. Similarly, as Dharma practitioners we have the opportunity to attain rebirth in a Pure Land, but whether we succeed in doing so depends upon our own effort. If we joyfully and continually engage in the methods for attaining rebirth in a Pure Land our wishes will definitely be fulfilled.

We may be aware of the faults of delusions such as the view of the transitory collection, and we may have heard teachings on how to eliminate them and attain liberation, but we will succeed in this only if we apply strenuous effort. If we do not apply ourself to our Dharma practice no one can grant us liberation from suffering – not our spiritual friends, our Spiritual Guide, nor even all the Buddhas. We all have the seed of Buddhahood within our mental continuum, and we have the opportunity to practise the methods for ripening this seed, but our attainment of Buddhahood depends upon our own efforts. An intellectual understanding of Dharma is not sufficient to carry us to

Buddhahood – we must also overcome our laziness and put our knowledge into practice. All those who have already become Buddhas have attained enlightenment through their own effort, and all those who will become Buddhas in the future will do so through their effort. In the Sutras, Buddha says:

> If you have only effort you have all Dharmas,
> But if you have only laziness you have nothing.

A person who has no great knowledge of Dharma but who nevertheless applies effort consistently will gradually attain all virtuous qualities; but a person who knows a great deal and has only one fault – laziness – will not be able to increase his or her good qualities and gain experience of Dharma. Many other benefits of effort are mentioned in Shantideva's *Guide to the Bodhisattva's Way of Life* and Chandrakirti's *Guide to the Middle Way*.

DIVISIONS OF EFFORT

In *Guide to the Bodhisattva's Way of Life* Shantideva presents four types of effort:

1 Armour-like effort
2 Effort of non-discouragement
3 Effort of application
4 Effort of non-satisfaction

All four types of effort are very important for Dharma practitioners. The first two overcome conditions unfavourable to the practice of Dharma, the third actually engages in Dharma practice, and the fourth enables us to complete our practice.

Armour-like effort is a courageous mind that helps us to persevere in our Dharma practice no matter what hardships are involved. We can generate this effort by thinking:

I will continue to practise Dharma even if it takes me many aeons to attain great enlightenment. I will never give up my Dharma practice, no matter what difficulties I might encounter.

If we have armour-like effort we will have a long-term perspective that prevents us from being discouraged by unfavourable external conditions, and we will joyfully persevere with our practice even if it takes a long time to attain Dharma realizations. In the past when soldiers went to war they wore armour to protect their bodies; similarly when Dharma practitioners wage war against their delusions they need to wear armour-like effort to protect their minds against difficult external conditions.

We need armour-like effort at the outset because without it we may soon become discouraged by the length of time it takes to attain realizations, and as a result we may abandon our Dharma practice. Sometimes, when we find it difficult to fulfil our spiritual expectations, encounter others who are trying to dissuade us from practising or have difficulty in finding the resources to support our practice, we may consider giving up Dharma. If this happens it indicates that we lack armour-like effort. At such times we need to recall our initial enthusiasm, and strengthen our resolve by reminding ourself of the benefits of our practice.

Whereas armour-like effort protects our practice against external obstacles, the effort of non-discouragement protects us against the internal obstacle of discouragement. We may wonder 'How is it possible for someone like me who has so many delusions and so little time to practise Dharma to realize emptiness, develop bodhichitta, and attain liberation and enlightenment?' By indulging in such thoughts we may conclude that we are incapable of attaining realizations. To counteract this kind of discouragement we need to generate the effort of non-discouragement by contemplating correct reasons. For example, we can contemplate:

Sometimes my delusions are strong and sometimes they are weak. This indicates that they are impermanent. If they can be reduced temporarily, they can be eradicated altogether; so why can I not attain liberation? Buddha said that everyone has Buddha nature. If I rely sincerely upon my Spiritual Guide and practise sincerely what he or she teaches me there is no reason why I cannot attain enlightenment. With my mind empowered by my Guru's blessings I can accomplish anything.

The effort of application is a mind that engages in the practice of Dharma with delight. This effort inspires us to listen to (or read), contemplate, and meditate on Dharma teachings. It is the source of all our understanding and experience of Dharma. This effort can be either forceful or steady. Sometimes it is appropriate to use forceful effort to reach a specific goal or to overcome a particular obstacle, but it is difficult to sustain this kind of effort and it may soon lead to tiredness or discouragement. For the most part we should practise with steady effort, like a broad river flowing constantly. We should adjust our expectations and not hope for quick results, but practise steadily and constantly over a long period.

The effort of non-satisfaction encourages us continually to deepen our understanding and experience of Dharma by not being satisfied with a merely superficial experience or understanding. After having studied Dharma for two or three years we may feel contented with our understanding and feel that we have no need to listen to more teachings or to continue to meditate. Such a complacent attitude prevents us from developing deep experience and understanding. We cannot expect great results after only a few years' practice. Until we have reached the final realizations of great enlightenment we need continuously to listen to teachings and meditate on their meaning.

Bodhisattvas on the first ground are not satisfied with their realizations, even though compared to ordinary beings they have attained exalted states of mind. Spurred on by the effort of non-satisfaction they ascend to the second ground, where again the same effort prevents them from becoming complacent and urges them to strive for higher goals. In this way they progress through all ten grounds to the final goal of great enlightenment.

Great enlightenment is called the 'Path of No More Learning' because it is the only state of complete fulfilment. Before we reach this stage we still have things to learn and so our Dharma practice is not yet complete. We should not be discouraged by the fact that we will have to practise Dharma for a long time. If we abandon the path to liberation or enlightenment we will never find a better path. All other paths will lead us into samsara; and no matter how much effort we put into following samsaric paths we will never experience true happiness. In our previous lives we put great effort into accumulating material wealth, but now everything we owned has vanished; our effort was in vain. In the past we have enjoyed every conceivable samsaric pleasure, but now we have nothing to show for it. All that remain are the imprints of the negative actions we committed in fulfilling our desires. Now that we have the opportunity to follow a perfect path that definitely leads to ultimate happiness it would be a great shame if we were to abandon it for a worldly path.

In summary, at the outset of our practice we should generate armour-like effort and arm ourself with a strong determination to complete our practice, no matter how long it may take or how many external obstacles we may have to overcome. Armed with this effort we should then generate the effort of application and apply ourself steadily and confidently to our practice. To prevent ourself from becoming discouraged by the extent and duration of our practice we should develop the effort of non-discouragement; and to prevent complacency and ensure that we bring our practice to completion we should rely upon the effort of non-satisfaction.

In *Compendium of Abhidharma* Asanga presents a fivefold division of effort:

1 Armour-like effort
2 Effort of non-discouragement
3 Effort of application
4 Effort of non-satisfaction
5 Effort of irreversibility

The first four are the same as the four just explained. The fifth, the effort of irreversibility, is a type of effort that prevents harmful conditions, such as wrong advice or bad friends, from diverting us from our virtuous activities. It is called 'irreversibility' because it ensures that we continue until our goal is reached with no lessening or diversion of our energy. If we have armour-like effort and the effort of non-discouragement we will automatically have the effort of irreversibility.

In the Lamrim teachings, three types of effort are explained:

1 Armour-like effort
2 Effort of gathering virtuous Dharmas
3 Effort of benefiting others

In this classification armour-like effort is the same as that previously explained, and the other two are included within the effort of application. Because there are two types of virtuous action – gathering virtuous Dharmas and benefiting others – there are two types of effort of application that correspond to these.

Effort does not arise naturally but is generated by using special methods. In *Guide to the Bodhisattva's Way of Life* Shantideva explains four powers that are the methods for sustaining and increasing effort: the power of aspiration, the power of steadfastness, the power of joy and the power of rejection.

The power of aspiration is a strong wish to practise Dharma. This is cultivated by contemplating both the benefits of training in Dharma and the disadvantages of not training in Dharma. All our problems are the result of taking rebirth in samsara, and the reason we continue to take uncontrolled rebirth is that we do not have sufficient experience of Dharma. Since experience of Dharma depends upon training in Dharma we can say that all our problems are the result of not training in Dharma.

If we do not train in Dharma we will never find real inner peace, and we will remain ignorant of profound and important truths such as the hidden objects that are explained in Dharma. We will not be able even to identify the self-grasping mind that imprisons us in samsara, let alone abandon it. Even though many of the fifty-one mental factors manifest in our mind, if we do not train in Dharma we will not be able to recognize them, and so we will not be able to distinguish those that should be cultivated from those that should be rejected.

One of the main benefits of training in Dharma is that day by day our wisdom grows sharper and our ignorance becomes weaker. The more wisdom we have, the more peaceful our mind will be. Through training in Dharma we gradually attain all the spiritual realizations that directly protect us from suffering. All our problems are caused by desirous attachment, anger, jealousy and other negative minds. By gaining experience of virtuous minds such as love, compassion, patience and wisdom we will overcome these negative minds. These virtuous minds are our real refuge. Thus, by training in Dharma we build a refuge within our own mind. Eventually we will become a refuge for all beings, a Buddha Jewel. By contemplating these benefits of training in Dharma we develop the aspiration to practise Dharma and this makes our effort more powerful. For this reason the aspiration to practise Dharma is called a 'power'.

Having developed the power of aspiration we should practise the power of steadfastness, which means that we should make our effort in Dharma practice stable and unchangeable by developing a strong determination. In the chapter on effort in *Guide to the Bodhisattva's Way of Life* Shantideva advises us that before we commit ourself to engaging in a practice we should investigate it carefully to see whether it is suitable and whether we can sustain it; but once we have committed ourself to it we should never turn back but continue until we attain the final result. Switching from one practice to another unrelated practice not only prevents us from fulfilling our wishes in this life, but also makes it difficult for us to accomplish our goals in future lives. Moreover, it is often the cause of breaking our commitments and severing precious relationships, such as those that exist between Guru and disciple, and between spiritual friends.

We must be careful not to misunderstand the effort of non-satisfaction. Practising this effort does not mean that we should become dissatisfied with our tradition or with our main practice, and try to follow many different traditions or mix together many different practices. Every Teacher and every tradition has a slightly different approach and employs different methods. The practices taught by one Teacher will differ from those taught by another, and if we try to combine them we will become confused, develop doubts, and lose direction. If we try to create a synthesis of different traditions we will destroy the special power of each and be left only with a mishmash of our own making that will be a source of confusion and doubt. Having chosen our tradition and our daily practices we should rely upon them single-pointedly, never allowing dissatisfaction to arise. At the same time as cherishing our own tradition we should respect all other traditions and the right of each individual to follow the tradition of their choosing. This approach leads to harmony and tolerance. It is mixing different religious traditions that causes sectarianism. This is why it is said that studying non-religious subjects is less of an obstacle to our spiritual progress than studying religions of different traditions.

Once we have decided which tradition to follow and which practices to do, we should engage in them wholeheartedly with a joyful mind. This is the power of joy. Whether we are listening to Dharma teachings, reading Dharma books, reciting prayers, contemplating or meditating, we should do so with a light and happy mind, like a child at play. If we enjoy a practice we will naturally have enthusiasm for it.

We may think that renunciation, for example, is a joyless state of mind because it is so keenly aware of the suffering nature of samsara, but in fact renunciation is a light and peaceful mind that is bound for freedom. Renunciation is induced by wisdom, and wisdom never gives rise to unhappiness. Joy is called a 'power' because it sustains our effort in practising Dharma. If Dharma practice brings us no pleasure we will soon become exhausted.

The fourth power, the power of rejection, means to reject, or eliminate, tiredness. Sometimes as a result of studying, meditating or other virtuous activities, we become physically or mentally tired. If our body becomes tired, our mind can easily become unbalanced. If instead of resting we push ourself beyond our capacity, this can cause problems such as physical illness or a disinclination to practise. It is better to relax for a while and resume our practice when our body and mind are fresh and comfortable. This is particularly important when we are doing a lot of formal meditation. Knowing when to exert ourself and when to rest is essential for successful practice.

Besides the ability to know when to stop and relax, the power of rejection also includes the ability to postpone taking on more advanced practices until we have built a suitable foundation for them, and the ability to leave behind a particular stage of development and progress to higher stages.

These four powers are explained in detail in the books *Meaningful to Behold* and *Joyful Path of Good Fortune*.

MENTAL SUPPLENESS

DEFINITION OF MENTAL SUPPLENESS

The definition of mental suppleness is a flexibility of mind induced by virtuous concentration.

In general, concentration induces two types of suppleness – physical suppleness and mental suppleness – but only the latter is the mental factor suppleness. Physical suppleness is a flexible and light tactile object within our body that develops when meditation causes a pure wind to pervade the body. It purifies defiled winds and makes our body flexible and light, and this in turn induces mental suppleness.

FUNCTION OF MENTAL SUPPLENESS

Physical suppleness functions to overcome stiffness and inflexibility of the body, and makes our body feel light, comfortable and easy to use in virtuous actions. Mental suppleness removes the inflexibility, slowness and heaviness of the mind, and makes it light and easy to use in virtuous actions. The mental rigidity that is dispelled by suppleness is the basis of many delusions, and is a principal cause of resistance to and dislike of virtuous activities. By removing rigidity, suppleness overcomes laziness and other obstacles. However, only strong suppleness can do this effectively; weak, short-lived suppleness does not have the strength to overcome many obstacles.

Both physical and mental suppleness develop initially through meditation, and then function to refine and improve our concentration. Mental suppleness enables us to direct our mind wherever we wish and thus helps both analytical meditation and placement meditation. Through attaining full, authentic physical and mental suppleness we will continuously experience the physical and mental bliss of suppleness, and as a result we will feel little need to seek external sources of pleasure.

DIVISIONS OF MENTAL SUPPLENESS

There are two types of mental suppleness:

1 Subtle mental suppleness
2 Gross mental suppleness

Mental suppleness exists whenever we experience pure, virtuous concentration. However, on the first and second mental abidings the mental suppleness is so subtle that it goes unnoticed. Therefore this suppleness is called 'subtle mental suppleness'. Gross mental suppleness first develops on the third mental abiding. From then on it gradually becomes stronger and stronger until we attain tranquil abiding, at which point our suppleness is fully developed. At this stage suppleness pervades our body and mind, and we experience the bliss of suppleness without interruption. When we have attained this unchangeable suppleness we no longer experience the physical and mental discomfort that make virtuous actions difficult, and so we become completely free from laziness. With suppleness, spiritual practice is very easy because when it arises our mind naturally becomes tranquil and positive.

Initially, mental suppleness is developed through the force of concentration, but there is also a type of suppleness that is induced by wisdom. This is accomplished as a result of analytical meditation combined with tranquil abiding. The development of this type of suppleness marks the attainment of superior seeing. With superior seeing, our wisdom and concentration become mutually beneficial, and we attain the union of tranquil abiding and superior seeing.

CONSCIENTIOUSNESS

DEFINITION OF CONSCIENTIOUSNESS

The definition of conscientiousness is a mental factor that, in dependence upon effort, cherishes what is virtuous and guards the mind from delusion and non-virtue.

Conscientiousness prevents the mind from being influenced by a delusion. There are two ways to rely upon conscientiousness. The first is to keep our mind free from a delusion by preventing our mind from meeting the objects of that delusion. We can, for example, prevent ourself from getting angry with someone with whom we have had a disagreement by avoiding them and not thinking about them. The second way is to prevent our mind from developing inappropriate attention when it meets with objects of delusion. Inappropriate attention causes delusions to arise by exaggerating the good or bad qualities of an object. If we prevent inappropriate attention it is impossible for delusions to arise, even if we are directly confronted with an object of delusion. Thus, for example, if we unexpectedly meet someone with whom we normally get angry we can avoid inappropriate attention, and so prevent anger, by focusing on his or her good qualities or by remembering the faults of anger.

In *Guide to the Bodhisattva's Way of Life* Shantideva says that there is no practice more important than keeping our mind free from negativity. Normally we take great care to protect our body from injury, but it is much more important to protect our mind. For example, if we are crossing a busy street we take great care to avoid being run over, but if we were to be run over the worst that could happen would be that we would lose this one life. By contrast, if we do not take care to protect our mind from negativity when we are surrounded by so many objects of delusion there is great danger of our mind being overrun by delusions, which will inflict harm on us for many future lives. Therefore, the practice of conscientiousness is of paramount importance.

Conscientiousness should be practised in conjunction with mindfulness and alertness. With mindfulness we tie our mind to a virtuous object. A virtuous object is any object that has a positive effect on our mind, such as the objects of meditation presented later in this book and the twenty-one objects of meditation presented in the book *The New Meditation Handbook*. We should try to keep our mind on virtuous objects all the time. Alertness is a type of wisdom that understands the faults of delusions and keeps watch over our mind to check whether or not we are beginning to develop inappropriate attention. If through alertness we discover that a delusion is about to arise we should immediately prevent it by recalling the faults of delusions. This is the practice of conscientiousness. Shantideva said that when an elephant runs amok it can cause a great deal of harm, but this is nothing compared to the harm caused by the crazy elephant of an unconscientious mind, which can drag us into the deepest hell. By binding our mind to the pillar of virtuous objects with the rope of mindfulness we protect ourself from delusions, the source of all danger, and find it easy to make progress in our spiritual practice.

FUNCTION OF CONSCIENTIOUSNESS

The main function of conscientiousness is to enable us to keep pure moral discipline and to improve our concentration. Conscientiousness is so important that in *Guide to the Bodhisattva's Way of Life* Shantideva devotes an entire chapter to it.

Through practising conscientiousness we can reduce our delusions and thereby stop committing negative actions of body, speech and mind. As a result we will naturally possess pure moral discipline. If our delusions are diminished and our life becomes more disciplined we will develop far fewer distractions, and as a result we will find it easy to make progress in meditation.

If our meditation is not proceeding well we do not need to seek special advice on how to improve it – we need only to practise conscientiousness. As mentioned before, in the *Vinaya Sutras* Buddha says that through moral discipline we will attain concentration and through concentration we will attain wisdom. Since conscientiousness is the root of moral discipline it follows that concentration and wisdom also depend upon conscientiousness. By practising conscientiousness we keep our mind pure and harnessed to virtuous objects, and so our energy is not dissipated by external or internal distractions. As a result our mind becomes settled and gathered within, making it easy for us to develop virtuous concentration. Virtuous concentration makes our mind lucid and powerful, which in turn enables us to improve our wisdom.

If we plan to do long meditation retreats in the future, we need to understand conscientiousness fully and begin to train in it now. To prepare our mind for advanced levels of meditation we need to cultivate favourable internal conditions and gradually eliminate conditions that interfere with meditation. The main favourable condition is familiarity with virtuous objects, and the main obstacle is distraction. Even if we lead a busy life we can keep our mind on virtuous objects if we understand that what makes an object virtuous or non-virtuous is our attitude towards it. By applying the instructions mentioned above on generating the three virtuous roots we can transform every object we meet into a virtuous object for us.

DIVISIONS OF CONSCIENTIOUSNESS

There are two types of conscientiousness:

1 Conscientiousness that is a virtuous root of mundane paths
2 Conscientiousness that is a virtuous root of supra-mundane paths

Conscientiousness is necessarily virtuous and a cause of happiness. The first type of conscientiousness causes samsaric happiness and the second causes the happiness of liberation and enlightenment. The difference between them lies in their motivation. The first type is a conscientiousness motivated by the wish to obtain the happiness of gods or humans in future lives, and the second is a conscientiousness motivated by the wish to attain liberation or enlightenment.

EQUANIMITY

DEFINITION OF EQUANIMITY

The definition of equanimity is a mental factor that functions to keep the primary mind free from mental sinking and mental excitement.

In general there are three types of equanimity: equanimity of feeling, immeasurable equanimity and compositional equanimity. Equanimity of feeling is any neutral feeling; immeasurable equanimity is the wish for all beings equally to be free from attachment and hatred, and is a form of compassion; and compositional equanimity is the mental factor explained here.

Compositional equanimity allows our mind to abide in a balanced state, free from mental sinking and mental excitement. Since mental sinking and mental excitement are the principal obstacles to concentration, equanimity is essential if we wish to perfect our concentration. When we are meditating we should examine our mind from time to time to see if our concentration is pure. Pure concentration has three characteristics: it remains on a virtuous object single-pointedly without moving towards any other object; it holds the object firmly; and it is clear, lucid and alert. At the beginning we can sustain such pure concentration only for a moment or two, but by training we will gradually be able to increase the duration of pure concentration until eventually we attain tranquil abiding. Until we reach the eighth mental abiding there is a danger of our developing mental sinking and mental excitement, and to remain free from these interferences we need to put effort into maintaining equanimity; but after the eighth mental abiding mental sinking and mental excitement can no longer occur and equanimity arises spontaneously.

FUNCTION OF EQUANIMITY

The function of equanimity is to keep the mind in a balanced state – tranquil, clear, and undisturbed by mental sinking or mental excitement. To understand the function of equanimity fully we need a clear understanding of mental sinking and mental excitement. These are explained in detail in the books *Joyful Path of Good Fortune* and *Meaningful to Behold*.

DIVISIONS OF EQUANIMITY

There are three types of equanimity:

1 Equanimity that requires gross effort
2 Equanimity that requires subtle effort
3 Equanimity that requires no effort

The fourth through to the sixth mental abidings have equanimity that depends upon gross effort. On the seventh and eighth mental abidings gross effort is no longer needed to eliminate mental sinking and mental excitement, but we still require subtle effort to maintain equanimity. On the ninth mental abiding no effort at all is required to maintain perfect concentration because at this stage equanimity is spontaneous. Just as we need no effort to fall asleep, so at this stage the practitioner needs only to focus on the meditation object and concentration develops effortlessly.

NON-HARMFULNESS

DEFINITION OF NON-HARMFULNESS

The definition of non-harmfulness is a mental factor that wishes sentient beings not to suffer.

According to *Compendium of Abhidharma* non-harmfulness is not simply not harming others, but compassion. We must be careful to distinguish compassion from desirous attachment. Compassion is necessarily a virtuous mind whereas attachment is never virtuous. Sometimes our wish to help others arises principally from attachment. For example, a rider may wish his sick horse to get well so that he will not have to miss a riding event. At other times our concern for others is a mixture of attachment and compassion. This is often the case when we develop the wish for our friends or relatives to be free from suffering. Pure compassion, however, is completely free from attachment and is exclusively concerned with the welfare of others.

It is said that because all living beings have some compassion all living beings have Buddha seed. By gradually improving and extending our compassion we will eventually develop great compassion – the wish to protect all living beings from suffering. If we continue to improve our great compassion it will eventually transform into the omniscient wisdom of a Buddha, which has the power actually to protect all living beings. There is no better method for becoming a Buddha than to improve our compassion.

As human beings we have a perfect opportunity to develop and improve our compassion. Had we been born as gods of the form or formless realms we would not experience gross sufferings associated with a human body, and so we would find it difficult to develop concern for others who were experiencing these sufferings. Compassion is born of renunciation. If we can understand our own samsara and develop renunciation for that, we can understand the samsara of others and develop compassion for them. As humans we experience a great deal of suffering, and so it is relatively easy for us to see the faults of samsara and to develop the wish to be free from it. Then by looking around us we can see the countless sufferings experienced by other sentient beings and develop compassion for them.

FUNCTION OF NON-HARMFULNESS

The main function of non-harmfulness, or compassion, is to prevent us from harming sentient beings. A person whose mind is filled with compassion can never wish to hurt anyone. It is only because we lack compassion that we sometimes develop the intention to hurt others. Compassion and harmful intentions are like water and fire – completely incompatible. Refraining from harming others is one of the most important practices for a Buddhist. If we always practise non-harmfulness we will always be practising Dharma, even if we cannot do formal meditation.

Another function of compassion is to cause the attainment of enlightenment. Compassion is the seed of Buddhahood, and by developing and enhancing it we cause this seed to ripen and draw us closer to full enlightenment.

DIVISIONS OF NON-HARMFULNESS

There are two types of non-harmfulness, or compassion:

1 Compassion wishing sentient beings to be free from suffering

2 Compassion wishing sentient beings to be free from
   the causes of suffering

The second type of compassion is a wish for sentient beings
to be separated from contaminated karma and delusions,
which are the actual causes of suffering. Only those who
have trained in Dharma can develop this type of compassion.
When an intelligent Dharma practitioner sees the suffering
of sentient beings he or she thinks 'How wonderful it would
be if all sentient beings were free from delusions such as self-
grasping, and from karma committed under the influence of
delusions.'
   There is another twofold division of compassion:

1 Mere compassion
2 Superior compassion

Wishing sentient beings to be free from suffering is mere
compassion. Thinking 'I myself will act to free them from
suffering' is superior compassion. Thus, the superior intention explained in the instructions on the sevenfold cause and
effect is a type of superior compassion.
   In *Guide to the Middle Way* Chandrakirti presents a threefold division of compassion: compassion observing sentient
beings, compassion observing phenomena, and compassion
observing the unobservable. These are explained in the book
Ocean of Nectar.

Virtue, Non-virtue and Delusion

VIRTUE

DEFINITION OF VIRTUE

The definition of virtue is a phenomenon that functions as a main cause of happiness.

DIVISIONS OF VIRTUE

There are five types of virtue:

1 Natural virtue
2 Virtue by association
3 Virtue by motivation
4 Virtue by subsequent relation
5 Ultimate virtue

The eleven virtuous mental factors are examples of natural virtue. A primary mind that has any one of the virtuous mental factors in its retinue is a virtue by association, as are all the other mental factors associated with that primary mind. They are virtuous because they are of the same substance as a virtuous mental factor. All virtuous actions are virtues by motivation because they are performed with a virtuous motivation. The imprints left on the mental continuum by virtuous minds and virtuous actions are virtues by subsequent relation. Since all sentient beings have performed virtuous actions at some time in the past, all sentient beings have virtuous imprints. Lower schools such as the Vaibhashikas, however, assert that there are some sentient beings who have no virtuous imprints.

These four types of virtue can be understood from the following example. If we make prostrations out of faith, the mental factor faith is a natural virtue; the primary mind associated with it, as well as all its other attendant mental factors such as feeling and discrimination, are virtues by association; the bodily action of prostrating is a virtue by motivation; and the virtuous imprints left on the mental continuum by the mind of faith and the action of making prostrations are virtues by subsequent relation. The last type of virtue, ultimate virtue, refers principally to nirvana. Nirvana is ultimate virtue because when we attain nirvana we experience ultimate happiness.

NON-VIRTUE

DEFINITION OF NON-VIRTUE

The definition of non-virtue is a phenomenon that functions as a main cause of suffering.

DIVISIONS OF NON-VIRTUE

There are five types of non-virtue:

1 Natural non-virtue
2 Non-virtue by association
3 Non-virtue by motivation
4 Non-virtue by subsequent relation
5 Ultimate non-virtue

Anger, covetousness, harmful thought and wrong views are all examples of natural non-virtues because they do not depend upon a non-virtuous motivation to be non-virtuous. Examples of non-virtues by association are a primary mind and other mental factors, such as feeling, associated with anger. Examples of non-virtues by motivation are actions done with a negative motivation. Examples of non-virtues by subsequent relation are the imprints left on our mental continuum by non-virtuous minds and non-virtuous actions. We have countless non-virtuous imprints on our mindstream. Neither non-virtuous minds such as anger nor non-virtuous actions such as killing are permanent, but when they cease they leave imprints on our consciousness that, if not purified, will remain until they ripen as suffering. When we die our virtuous and non-virtuous imprints follow us like a shadow following a body.

These four types of non-virtue can be understood by considering the example of killing an insect out of anger. The mental factor anger is a natural non-virtue; the primary mind and the other mental factors associated with it, such as feeling, are non-virtues by association; the bodily action of killing is a non-virtue by motivation; and the imprints left on the mental continuum by the mind of anger and the action of killing are non-virtues by subsequent relation.

Ultimate non-virtue refers to samsara. What is samsara? According to Dharmakirti it is the five contaminated aggregates. It is because we have taken contaminated aggregates that we experience suffering continually. Human beings have to experience the suffering of humans because they have taken human aggregates, animals have to experience the suffering of animals because they have taken animal aggregates, and so on. All pain, fear, unhappiness, frustration, and all other forms of misery are experienced by the contaminated aggregate of feeling. If we did not have contaminated feelings we could not experience suffering. Our sufferings arise from our own aggregates like waves arising from the sea. If we had not taken samsaric aggregates we would have no basis for experiencing suffering. Buddha said that our contaminated aggregates are like a bundle of thorns that we carry on our back – until we abandon them we will experience uninterrupted suffering.

All our delusions arise from our contaminated aggregates, and by acting under the influence of these delusions we create the cause to take new contaminated aggregates in the future. In this way samsara is perpetuated in a vicious circle of suffering from life to life. Because contaminated aggregates are the ultimate origin of all suffering they are known as 'ultimate non-virtue'.

DELUSION

DEFINITION OF DELUSION

The definition of delusion is a mental factor that arises from inappropriate attention and that functions to make the mind unpeaceful and uncontrolled.

If we did not have delusions we would experience only peace and contentment. When our delusions are not functioning strongly our mind is relatively tranquil and contented, but as soon as anger, jealousy or desirous attachment arise they destroy our peace of mind like a sudden storm destroying the tranquillity of an ocean. Even if we are in good physical health, when delusions manifest our mind becomes ill at ease.

We should observe our mind for a day and see how often peaceful minds arise and how often deluded or neutral minds arise. If we are not well trained in Dharma it is likely that our deluded and neutral minds will far outnumber our peaceful minds. We should try gradually to increase the frequency of our peaceful minds until they remain with us all day long. When we are able to control our mind for one day we should try to control it for two days, and continue practising in this way until we can keep a peaceful mind continuously. Finally we will attain the permanent peace of liberation, or nirvana. At this point we will have completely abandoned delusions, and it will be impossible for our mind to be disturbed by anything.

The only way to attain the permanent peace of liberation is to cultivate and increase our present peaceful minds. Why is it so difficult to maintain a peaceful mind? The only reason is that we have so many delusions. External problems do not have the power to disturb our mind unless we respond to them by developing delusions. If we have no delusions, even our enemies cannot destroy our peace of mind. Because delusions are the main obstacles to our attaining liberation from samsara they are known as 'obstructions to liberation' or 'delusion-obstructions', and because they destroy our mental peace they are called 'inner enemies'.

FUNCTION OF DELUSIONS

Delusions function only to cause us harm. In *Guide to the Bodhisattva's Way of Life* Shantideva says:

> The inner enemies of hatred, attachment, and so forth
> Do not have arms and legs,
> Nor do they have courage or skill;
> So how have they made me their slave?
>
> While they remain within my mind
> They harm me at their pleasure,

And yet, without anger, I patiently endure them.
How shameful! This is no occasion for patience.

Normally we regard other people who harm us as our
enemies, but our real enemies are the delusions such as
hatred and attachment that dwell within our mind. Even
though they do not have physical bodies and are not armed
with weapons, nevertheless they are able to control us and
inflict continuous misery. It is not suitable to be patient with
delusions because if we are they will inflict even greater
suffering on us. As Shantideva says:

If all living beings, including the gods and demi-gods,
Were to rise up against me as one enemy,
They could not lead me to the fires of the deepest hell
And throw me in;

But this powerful enemy of the delusions
In an instant can cast me into that fiery place
Where even the ashes of Mount Meru
Would be consumed without a trace.

The worst harm an external enemy can inflict on us is to take
away this one life. He or she cannot harm us in future lives,
but a single delusion such as anger can, in one short instant,
cause us to take rebirth repeatedly in the deepest hells where
the suffering is utterly unbearable. Moreover, external enemies
are short-lived because sooner or later they will die of their
own accord, but the enemies of the delusions have been with
us since beginningless time, and will remain with us for ever
if we do not take steps to destroy them. As Shantideva says:

No other type of enemy
Can remain for as long a time

As can the enduring foes of my delusions,
For they have no beginning and no apparent end.

If another person is harming us and we practise patience to calm him down, he will stop harming us; but if we are patient with or tolerant towards our delusions they will simply grow stronger and continue to betray us and harm us. Thus, whereas other people who harm us can become our friends, delusions will always remain our enemies. As Shantideva says:

If I agree with external enemies and honour them,
They will eventually bring me benefit and happiness;
But if I entrust myself to delusions,
In the future they will bring me only more pain and
    suffering.

Realizing this, we should come to a very clear conclusion that all our delusions, no matter how appropriate or desirable they may seem, have only one function – to cause us harm – and we should make a firm decision not to rest until we have destroyed these inner enemies once and for all. In the words of Shantideva:

So how can I remain in samsara joyfully and without
    fear
While I readily reserve a place in my heart
For this interminable enemy of long duration
That alone is the cause of increasing all my suffering?

How can I ever be happy
While these guardians of the prison of samsara
That torture and torment me in the hells and elsewhere
Dwell like a net of iron in my mind?

Out of anger, worldly people who are filled with pride
    will not sleep
Until they have destroyed those who cause them even
    the slightest temporary harm.
In the same way, I will not abandon my efforts
Until this inner foe of mine is directly and definitely
    destroyed.

There was once a Tibetan Geshe called Geshe Ben Gungyal who used to spend all his time in his room, doing no meditation in the traditional posture, and reciting no prayers. His unorthodoxy attracted attention, and others asked him 'You do not recite prayers and you do not meditate in the usual way, so what do you do all day long in your room?' Geshe Ben Gungyal replied 'I have only one task – I am thrusting the spear of the opponents into the head of my delusions. When a delusion raises its ugly head I increase my alertness and with effort I plunge the spear straight into it. Then it leaves me in peace and I am happy. That is what I do all day long in my room.'

There are two types of opponent with which we can combat our delusions – the temporary opponents that are specific to each delusion, such as love (which is the opponent to hatred) and giving (which is the opponent to miserliness); and the ultimate opponent of wisdom realizing emptiness, which is the actual antidote to all delusions. Meditation on the specific opponents temporarily pacifies our delusions, and brings us a temporary inner peace with which we can develop the concentration and wisdom necessary to eradicate the delusions altogether by applying the ultimate opponent. To understand more fully how the different types of opponent work we first need to understand the causes of delusion.

There are six causes of delusion:

1 The seed
2 The object
3 Inappropriate attention
4 Familiarity
5 Distraction and being influenced by others
6 Bad habits

In *Treasury of Abhidharma* Vasubandhu explains that whenever the first three causes are assembled, delusion necessarily arises. The second three are conditions that encourage the development and increase of delusions.

THE SEED

The seed of a delusion is the potentiality for that delusion to arise; it is the substantial cause of the delusion. All ordinary beings have these potentialities in their mind, and they can be eradicated only by attaining wisdom directly realizing emptiness and meditating on this for a long time.

Until we have finally abandoned a delusion, the seed of that delusion will remain within our mind, even when the delusion itself is not manifest. Although the seed of a delusion is the substantial cause of that delusion and exists within us all the time, it will produce a manifest delusion only when the other necessary causes of delusion are present. For example, we have within us the seed of anger even when our mind is peaceful; but anger does not manifest in our mind until the other causes of anger, such as a disagreeable object and inappropriate attention, come together.

A Foe Destroyer has completely abandoned the seeds of all delusions. Thus, even if a Foe Destroyer meets with other causes of delusion, such as an attractive or disagree-able object, he or she will not be able to develop delusions. Foe Destroyers are so called because they have destroyed the inner foe of their delusions by eradicating their seeds. Delusions are the main obstructions to liberation because we cannot attain liberation from samsara until they are eradicated.

It is important to distinguish the seeds of delusions from the imprints of delusions. As already explained, the seeds of delusions are the substantial causes of delusions, and are obstructions to liberation. The imprints of delusions, on the other hand, are not causes of delusions but the effects of delusions. Even after we abandon the delusions by eradicating their seeds, the imprints of the delusions remain, rather as the smell of garlic lingers in a container long after the garlic has been removed from it. Because Hinayana Foe Destroyers have not abandoned the imprints of delusions, phenomena still appear to their minds as inherently existent, even though they no longer grasp at inherent existence. They are like a magician who can see an illusion he has created but is not taken in by it.

Because the imprints of delusions cause phenomena to appear as inherently existent they prevent us from directly realizing the two truths simultaneously, and so they prevent us from attaining an omniscient mind that can see all phenomena directly and simultaneously. For this reason they are known as 'obstructions to omniscience'. To remove these we must continue to meditate on emptiness on the Mahayana path of meditation. Thus, whereas the seeds of delusions – obstructions to liberation – are the principal object of abandonment for Hinayanists, the imprints of delusions – obstructions to omniscience – are the principal objects of abandonment for Mahayanists.

THE OBJECT

Delusions cannot arise without an object. For example, without seeing or recalling an attractive object we cannot develop attachment; and without seeing or recalling a disagreeable object we cannot develop anger. Thus, the fewer objects of delusion we encounter, the fewer delusions we will develop.

To reduce the number of objects of delusion they encounter, some Dharma practitioners retire to isolated places to practise in solitude. Many texts praise solitude for those who wish to engage in retreat and other forms of concentrated practice. In *The Thirty-seven Practices of the Conquerors' Sons* Thogme Zangpo mentions three benefits of relying upon solitude:

> By avoiding non-virtuous objects, delusions gradually
>   diminish;
> With no distractions, virtuous actions naturally
>   increase;
> And through the clarity of mind, a definite
>   understanding of Dharma develops;
> Therefore, relying upon solitude is a practice of the
>   Conquerors' Sons.

Also, in *Guide to the Bodhisattva's Way of Life* Shantideva advises us that if we want to develop deep experience of Dharma we should abandon our attachment to worldly activities and abide in mental and physical solitude.

Although we may be able to avoid objects of delusion to some extent by retiring to an isolated place, we will not be able to avoid such objects altogether. Even if we were to live in an isolated cave there would be some parts of the cave that would appear more attractive than other parts, and some kinds of weather that would seem more pleasant than others. We would soon find ourself preferring this sort of birdsong to that sort of birdsong, and we would still have the memories of other objects of delusion. Since we are so accustomed to finding plenty of objects of delusion wherever we go, the best way to avoid them is to practise restraining the doors of the sense powers. If we practise in this way, we will be able to prevent delusions from arising wherever we are.

INAPPROPRIATE ATTENTION

Even if our mind meets an object of delusion, a delusion will arise in our mind only if we allow inappropriate attention to develop. Generally, inappropriate attention is a mind that dwells on a contaminated object and exaggerates its apparent qualities. There are many levels of inappropriate attention, from very subtle to very gross. Whenever ordinary beings see an object they naturally apprehend it as being inherently existent. This grasping mind is itself an exaggeration and a subtle form of inappropriate attention.

As a result of grasping things as being inherently existent we exaggerate their attractiveness or unattractiveness, and thus develop desirous attachment or anger. Whereas the initial development of self-grasping is subtle inappropriate attention, the subsequent exaggeration of the good or bad qualities of the object is gross inappropriate attention. Subtle inappropriate attention can be overcome only by a direct realization of emptiness. Gross inappropriate attention is overcome by applying mindfulness, alertness and conscientiousness.

FAMILIARITY

The reason we develop delusions naturally, whereas we have to apply effort to cultivate virtuous minds, is that we are very familiar with delusions. Our minds have been acquainted with delusions since beginningless time and so deluded mental habits are very deeply ingrained. We can gradually reverse this situation by training in the various opponents of delusion and thereby becoming familiar with virtue instead of delusions. The more familiar we become with virtuous minds, the fewer delusions we will develop. Eventually we will reach the point where it is easier to develop virtuous minds than it is to develop delusions.

DISTRACTION AND BEING INFLUENCED BY OTHERS

We naturally imitate those with whom we associate. For example, if we have a close friendship with someone who disagrees with Dharma or who regularly engages in non-virtuous actions we will gradually come under his influence and begin to adopt his view and his behaviour. If our friends are very fond of drinking, smoking or engaging in reckless actions, we will soon find ourself developing the same tendencies; and if they are thieves we may even follow their example and start stealing! If someone to whom we are close gives up his Dharma practice, this may leave an impression in our mind that will lead us to follow his example in the future. If we fall under the influence of bad friends our virtuous activities diminish in strength and our delusions increase. Good friends, on the other hand, have a beneficial influence on us. Thus, if we have a friend who is a pure Dharma practitioner we will naturally find ourself adopting his or her view and behaviour, and thereby gradually developing the same good qualities.

Because we are so easily influenced by our friends it is important to choose good friends. In some ways our Dharma friends are more important than our Teacher because we are with our friends all the time but see our Teacher only occasionally. Good Dharma friends help us to reach liberation, while bad friends cause us to take rebirth in the lower realms.

There were once two friends who lived in an area of Tibet called Pembo. One of them drank heavily and often engaged in immoral actions, while the other led a blameless life. One day the good person moved to Lhasa where he took up work at an inn. Gradually he befriended the customers and as a result came under their influence. He started drinking and his general behaviour gradually deteriorated. At the same time his friend, who previously had set such a bad example, moved to Reting, a town with a famous monastery, where he became the assistant of a great Geshe. Through the influence and advice of the Geshe he finally gave up drinking and became a pure Dharma practitioner with impeccable conduct. Later when the two friends met up again they were surprised to see that their behaviour had completely reversed!

Listening to misguided teachings or advice also gives rise to delusions. Misguided teachings can cause us to develop negative thoughts towards the Three Jewels and to find fault with the Spiritual Guides in whom previously we had faith. They may even cause us to abandon Dharma. Such teachings confuse us by causing us to develop many conflicting views. For example, many teachers advocate attachment as a necessary ingredient of a healthy emotional life, or encourage us to express our anger freely, or to develop forms of self-confidence that are in fact types of deluded pride. Listening to such teachings seriously damages our Dharma practice and causes us to waste our precious human life. We must realize the danger of following such incorrect teachings and rely only upon authentic and pure teachings.

BAD HABITS

If we have bad physical habits, such as habits of killing, stealing, sexual misconduct, drinking, smoking or taking drugs; or bad verbal habits, such as habits of lying, talking meaninglessly or reading books that contradict Dharma, these will make our delusions stronger. Bad habits are the main cause of strong delusions arising in our mind.

If we think deeply about the six causes of delusions we will see that there are many temporary measures we can take to reduce their intensity and frequency. However, to abandon them altogether we need to develop the wisdom directly realizing emptiness.

DIVISIONS OF DELUSION

There are three types of delusion from the point of view of realm:

1 Delusions of the desire realm
2 Delusions of the form realm
3 Delusions of the formless realm

Of these three, the delusions of the desire realm are the grossest, the delusions of the form realm are more subtle, and the delusions of the formless realm are the most subtle. All delusions that manifest before the attainment of tranquil abiding are delusions of the desire realm. These develop more quickly and more strongly than the delusions of the upper realms. There are three levels of desire realm delusion: big, middling and small. A person with big anger, for example, will get very angry over insignificant incidents; a person with middling anger will get angry when confronted with major conditions for anger but not when encountering only slight conditions for anger; and a person with small anger will become only slightly irritated when faced with a major disturbance. The same applies to the other delusions of the desire realm. We can recognize these three levels of delusion from our own experience.

Each of the three levels of the desire realm delusions is further divided into big, middling and small; and so altogether there are nine levels of each of the delusions of the desire realm, from big-big to small-small. We begin by eliminating the grossest level of each of the delusions, and then progressively eliminate the more subtle levels. This is like putting out a fire. We cannot extinguish a large fire all at once but must gradually reduce its intensity until finally we are left with only smouldering embers to extinguish.

The form realm has four levels, known as the first, second, third and fourth form realms; and the formless realm also has four levels, called infinite space, infinite consciousness, nothingness and peak of samsara. There are therefore nine realms in which sentient beings can take rebirth: the desire realm, the four form realms and the four formless realms. Each of these nine realms has nine levels of delusion, from big-big to small-small, so altogether there are eighty-one levels of delusion. To attain liberation we need to identify and abandon all these delusions.

The grossest of the eighty-one delusions are the big-big delusions of the desire realm, and the most subtle are the small-small delusions of peak of samsara. When we have abandoned the small-small delusions of peak of samsara we have attained liberation. The first eighty levels of delusion can be abandoned temporarily, even by non-Buddhist practitioners or meditators, through the force of concentration alone; but to abandon the eighty-first level of delusion we need both authentic renunciation and the wisdom directly realizing emptiness.

There is a twofold division of delusion from the point of view of their cause:

1 Innate delusions
2 Intellectually-formed delusions

Innate delusions are delusions that arise naturally from imprints from previous lives – for example, all the delusions of animals and most of the delusions of humans, such as our normal self-grasping. Intellectually-formed delusions are delusions that arise as a result of relying upon incorrect philosophical systems or faulty reasoning. For example, some philosophical systems advocate animal sacrifice, claiming that this is a virtuous action that delights the gods. If we hold such a wrong view this is an intellectually-formed delusion. Another example of an intellectually-formed delusion is believing that war is good or spiritually justified. Buddhists are unlikely to be influenced by such wrong views but we can still develop intellectually-formed delusions through our own incorrect reasoning. For example, after several years of trying to practise Dharma we may feel that we have made little progress and conclude that Dharma does not work, or we may decide that Buddhas do not exist because we cannot see them. The lower Buddhist schools teach that phenomena are inherently existent, and as a result adherents to these schools develop intellectually-formed self-grasping. Similarly there are many intellectually-formed delusions that result from adhering to non-Buddhist traditions.

When we attain the path of seeing we abandon all intellectually-formed delusions, but the innate delusions remain. We abandon these on the path of meditation. When we abandon the small-small delusions of peak of samsara we are liberated from samsara. However, if we want to attain full enlightenment, or Buddhahood, we still need to abandon the imprints of the eighty-one levels of delusion. We abandon these on the eighth, ninth and tenth grounds of the Mahayana path of meditation. Finally, with the vajra-like concentration of the Mahayana path of meditation we eradicate the most subtle imprints of delusions, and simultaneously attain Buddhahood.

At present we develop desire realm delusions, and so it is these that we should strive to abandon first. After we have attained tranquil abiding we will develop delusions of the form and formless realms. By gradually eliminating these, eventually we will be liberated from samsara. Through understanding this process we will gain confidence in the possibility of attaining liberation, and we will see the great importance of sincere Dharma practice.

There is another twofold division of delusion from the point of view of entity:

1 Root delusions
2 Secondary delusions

These will now be explained in detail.

The Six Root Delusions

The six root delusions are the principal delusions from which all other delusions arise. They are:

1 Desirous attachment
2 Anger
3 Deluded pride
4 Ignorance
5 Deluded doubt
6 Deluded view

DESIROUS ATTACHMENT

DEFINITION OF DESIROUS ATTACHMENT

The definition of desirous attachment is a deluded mental factor that observes its contaminated object, regards it as a cause of happiness, and wishes for it.

Desirous attachment is not the same as desire. There are many non-deluded desires that it is suitable to cultivate, such as the desire to attain liberation and enlightenment, the desire to help others, or even the desire to abandon desirous attachment. Even Buddhas and Foe Destroyers have desires.

Desirous attachment develops as follows. First we perceive or remember a contaminated object and feel it to be attractive, then we focus our attention on its good qualities and exaggerate them. With an exaggerated sense of the attractiveness of the object we then hold it to be desirable and develop desire for it. Finally our desire attaches us to the object so that it feels as if we have become glued to it or absorbed into it. Only when all these stages are completed has desirous attachment occurred.

We must be careful to distinguish attachment from love. Love is a virtuous mind that creates only peace and happiness, whereas attachment is never virtuous and causes pain and problems.

DIVISIONS OF DESIROUS ATTACHMENT

There are three types of desirous attachment from the point of view of time:

1 Desirous attachment to past objects
2 Desirous attachment to present objects
3 Desirous attachment to future objects

An example of the first is recalling a friend and, out of attachment, longing to meet him or her again. We often develop this form of attachment when indulging in nostalgia, for example when remembering relatives who have died, possessions we once owned, places we used to live in or good times we have enjoyed in the past. Examples of desirous attachment to present objects are, out of attachment, wishing for the pleasures we now enjoy to last forever, or wishing never to be separated from our present friends, possessions and so forth. The anxiety we feel when we think of being separated from our partners or of losing our possessions comes from this type of desirous attachment. Examples of desirous attachment to future objects are, out of attachment, wishing to meet an attractive partner, to acquire wealth or to own a bigger house. Even though we may never acquire such objects, nevertheless due to this type of attachment we spend much time planning or daydreaming about them. Attachment to future objects is the basis for most of our discontent and disappointment.

From the point of view of entity, desirous attachment can be divided into three – big, middling and small – or into eighty-one – the nine levels of desirous attachment of each of the nine realms mentioned above. The grossest of these is the big-big desirous attachment of the desire realm, and the most subtle is the small-small desirous attachment of peak of samsara. These are all included within three:

1 Desire realm desirous attachment
2 Form realm desirous attachment
3 Formless realm desirous attachment

There is another threefold division from the point of view of its object:

1 Desirous attachment to samsaric places
2 Desirous attachment to samsaric enjoyments
3 Desirous attachment to samsaric bodies

HOW TO ABANDON DESIROUS ATTACHMENT

To eradicate attachment completely we need to develop renunciation and then meditate on emptiness until the seeds of attachment are removed from our mind. Temporarily we can abandon attachment by contemplating its faults and then applying appropriate opponents, such as meditation on impermanence or meditation on unattractiveness. The basis of all these practices is to understand why it is so important to abandon attachment by contemplating its faults, and to make a strong determination to abandon it.

What are the faults of attachment? In the Sutras, Buddha says that living beings are bound within the prison of samsara by the rope of desirous attachment. The reason we experience suffering and problems is that we remain in samsara, the reason we remain in samsara is that we have made no effort to escape, the reason we have made no effort to escape is that we have no wish to escape, and the reason we have no wish to escape is that we are so strongly attached to the places, enjoyments and bodies of samsara. Therefore, attachment is the root of all our suffering and problems.

When attachment arises in our mind it does not feel harmful; on the contrary, it usually feels beneficial. Therefore, it is important to contemplate repeatedly the faults of attachment and to recognize it as a delusion whose only function is to cause us harm. Why do criminals end up in prison? It is because they are led into committing crimes by their desirous attachment, or uncontrolled desire for the fulfilment of their own wishes. Why do we suffer from illnesses such as heart disease? It is mostly because our attachment leads us to indulge in foods and drinks that are bad for us. Why do marriages and other relationships break up so often? It is because we are led by attachment to seek other partners. Attachment is the principal cause of dissatisfaction. It never causes contentment, only restlessness and discontent. Realizing this we should make a firm decision to abandon attachment and then apply the appropriate methods.

ANGER

DEFINITION OF ANGER

The definition of anger is a deluded mental factor that observes its contaminated object, exaggerates its bad qualities, considers it to be undesirable, and wishes to harm it.

Anger can be directed towards anyone, even towards our friends. We can also become angry with inanimate objects such as bad weather, poor food or the non-fulfilment of our wishes.

DIVISIONS OF ANGER

From the point of view of entity there are nine types of anger, from big-big to small-small. However, since anger is exclusively a desire realm delusion there are not eighty-one levels of anger as there are for desirous attachment and self-grasping. Anger is a very gross and rough mind, and because beings in the form and the formless realms always have tranquil and refined minds they do not get angry.

There is another ninefold division of anger from the point of view of how it is generated:

1 Anger towards someone or something that harmed us in the past
2 Anger towards someone or something that is harming us now
3 Anger towards someone or something that might harm us in the future
4 Anger towards someone or something that harmed our friends or relatives in the past
5 Anger towards someone or something that is harming our friends or relatives now

6 Anger towards someone or something that might harm our friends or relatives in the future

7 Anger towards someone or something that helped our enemy in the past

8 Anger towards someone or something that is helping our enemy now

9 Anger towards someone or something that might help our enemy in the future

HOW TO ABANDON ANGER

As with attachment, anger can be finally eradicated only by gaining a direct realization of emptiness; but it can be temporarily abandoned by meditating on its opponents, patience and love. To practise patience we first need to contemplate the many faults of anger. Anger has no function other than to cause us harm; it is the most damaging and most destructive of all delusions. In *Tales of the Buddha* Master Vira says:

Due to the fire of anger, our beauty is lost.

Although we may have taken great pains to make ourself look attractive, as soon as we get angry our beauty disappears. When a friend whom we love is consumed with anger our love for them turns into fear. Anger prevents us from enjoying the things that normally give us pleasure. We might be lying on a soft mattress or eating delicious food but if we are angry our mind is in pain. Although our parents and Teachers have shown us nothing but kindness, if they do something we do not like we may get angry and treat them badly. Anger causes us to disregard many years of parental care, and can completely destroy our relationship with our parents.

If we constantly get angry we become unpopular and this makes it difficult for us to fulfil our wishes. When we are in a bad mood we become so unpleasant that even close friends avoid us. We use harsh and hurtful language and act in destructive, even violent, ways. When we are angry our wisdom declines and we lose our normal ability to discriminate right from wrong. Under the influence of anger we act recklessly, and even if our friends advise us to calm down we shun their advice. In short, anger makes our mind very rough and uncontrolled, robs us of our happiness, and disturbs others. Contemplating these points we should make a firm decision not to get angry.

When we wake in the morning we should remember the faults of anger and make a promise to ourself not to get angry that day. Whenever we experience misfortune or disappointment we should immediately remember our promise and calm our mind before anger develops. If we practise in this way every day, our anger will steadily decline in strength until finally nothing can make us angry. When we are free from anger others will appreciate us and respect us; and then we will know the benefits of preventing anger from our own experience.

We do not need to be sitting on a meditation cushion to practise patience or love. We can practise these at any time, combining all our daily activities with them by applying mindfulness and alertness. As long as we remain in samsara we should expect problems and difficulties. In samsara it is not possible to remain in a state of peace forever; eternal peace can be found only by escaping from samsara. While we remain in samsara it is inevitable that we will suffer because suffering is the very nature of samsara. Therefore, rather than becoming annoyed with suffering we should accept it as entirely natural. If we put our hand into a fire we would expect to be burned because it is the nature of fire to burn. In the same way, if we take rebirth in samsara we should not be surprised if we experience suffering because samsara is in the nature of suffering. Thinking like this helps us to prevent anger, even in the face of adversity. If we apply the teachings on training the mind, rather than getting angry when we experience difficulties we can use these situations to develop renunciation or compassion, to purify our negativities, and to practise patience. As Shantideva explains in *Guide to the Bodhisattva's Way of Life*, we should consider ourself extremely lucky to meet with difficult circumstances or disagreeable people because they give us an opportunity to improve our patience, and without improving our patience we cannot attain enlightenment. If we have taken Bodhisattva vows or Tantric vows we have a commitment to practise patience, so when we find an opportunity to do so we should make the best use of it. The more our patience is tested the stronger it will become, and the more quickly we will attain Buddhahood.

DELUDED PRIDE

DEFINITION OF DELUDED PRIDE

The definition of deluded pride is a deluded mental factor that, through considering and exaggerating our own good qualities or possessions, feels arrogant.

Deluded pride is an inflated view of ourself that arises as a result of considering our own qualities such as our wealth, beauty, strength, education, knowledge, status or race. Simply being aware that we have a particular quality or that we are in some respect better than other people is not necessarily deluded pride, for this may be a recognition of the truth. Deluded pride arises when our mind is 'puffed-up' with an exaggerated sense of our own importance.

There are non-deluded prides that we should cultivate, but these are not actual pride. Shantideva explains three types of non-deluded pride that are essential for completing the power of effort: pride with respect to our potential, pride in our actions and pride in thinking we can destroy our delusions. The first is based on a recognition of our spiritual potential and leads us to think 'I can and will attain Buddhahood.' The second is a strong determination to perform virtuous actions, for example a mind of superior intention thinking 'I myself will free all sentient beings from suffering.' The third is the thought 'I can conquer all my delusions; they will never conquer me.' If we lack this self-confidence we will easily be defeated by discouragement or by malevolent interferences. Another type of non-deluded pride is the divine pride that is cultivated in Secret Mantra. This differs from ordinary pride in that the I it observes is imputed in dependence upon the pure aggregates of the Deity rather than upon ordinary, contaminated aggregates. All these types of non-deluded pride make our mind peaceful and virtuous.

DIVISIONS OF DELUDED PRIDE

There are seven types of deluded pride:

1 Pride over inferiors
2 Pride over equals
3 Pride over superiors
4 Pride in identity
5 Pretentious pride

6 Emulating pride

7 Wrong pride

The first type of pride is feeling superior to someone who is in some respect inferior to ourself; the second, feeling superior to someone equal to ourself; and the third, feeling superior to someone higher than ourself. The fourth type of pride, pride in identity, is an inflated sense of self-importance based simply on our identity, such as being proud of being an English person, proud of being white, proud of being a man, or proud of being a Tantric meditator. Pretentious pride is believing that we have qualities that we do not possess, such as thinking that the slightly peaceful mind we attain in meditation is actual tranquil abiding, or thinking that we are a pure Dharma practitioner when we are largely motivated by worldly concerns. Emulating pride is feeling equal or almost equal to someone who is vastly superior to us, such as Buddhas, Bodhisattvas or our Spiritual Guide. Wrong pride is pride in inappropriate actions, such as pride at being a good marksman when shooting birds, feeling proud when we get away with shoplifting, or thinking that we are an excellent Teacher when the teachings we give are wrong.

HOW TO ABANDON PRIDE

As with all delusions, the first step in abandoning pride is to recognize its faults. The two main disadvantages of pride are that it causes us to disrespect others and that it is an obstacle to increasing our knowledge and good qualities. It is difficult for a proud person to receive much benefit from Dharma because he or she cannot listen to Dharma teachings with an open mind. This is particularly true for people who have studied other religious or philosophical traditions and who feel that they already understand certain topics. When such people hear a different view in Dharma teachings they conclude that Dharma is incorrect and of no relevance to them.

If we have been studying Dharma for a long time we may, when listening to teachings or reading a book, feel that we already know the subject and so pay only superficial attention to it. This is also a type of pride that prevents us from gaining deep experiences of Dharma. The only way to avoid such pride is to put the teachings into practice and thereby to gain some experience of their meaning. If we have a 'taste' of Dharma we will find all teachings inspiring, no matter how many times we have heard them. As the Tibetans say:

An evil person can be tamed by Dharma, but a proud person cannot.

There are several methods for eliminating pride. For example, if we are proud of our knowledge we can investigate deep and subtle topics such as those presented in the ninth chapter of the *Guide to the Bodhisattva's Way of Life*. We will soon discover that we still have much to learn, and our mind will be humbled. Another way to destroy our pride is to realize how vulnerable and unfree we are by meditating on all the unpleasant experiences we must suffer without choice, such as birth, sickness, ageing and death. At present we might be beautiful, fit, intelligent and successful, but we have no power to remain like this. Eventually, without any choice, we will have to become old, decrepit, impoverished, disabled or senile. If we compare ourself to realized beings who have perfect freedom and whose happiness cannot be destroyed by external conditions we will soon lose our pride.

IGNORANCE

DEFINITION OF IGNORANCE

The definition of ignorance is a mental factor that is confused about the nature of an object and that functions to induce wrong awareness, doubt and other delusions.

If, for example, we mistake a toy snake for a real snake we have an ignorance of the nature of that toy snake, and in dependence upon this we develop a wrong awareness that apprehends it as a real snake. Therefore, there are two distinct stages involved in the development of wrong awarenesses. First we have ignorance, which does not understand the real nature of the object, and then, as a result of this unknowing, we develop a misapprehension of the object. Thus, in the example of the toy snake, first we simply fail to realize that the long thin object is a rubber toy, and then this non-understanding causes us to misapprehend the object as a real snake.

The fundamental ignorance is ignorance of the ultimate nature of phenomena. This is the very root of samsara and the basis of all mistakes and faults. This ignorance also develops in two stages. Until we realize emptiness we are unaware of the ultimate nature of phenomena, and this unawareness is the fundamental ignorance. As a result of this unknowing we then develop actual wrong awareness – the self-grasping that misapprehends phenomena as truly existent.

Although a wrong awareness does not understand its object, it is not necessarily ignorance because ignorance is a mental factor and wrong awareness can be a primary mind. However, all wrong awarenesses possess the mental factor ignorance, and it is this that prevents the primary mind from understanding the nature of its object and makes it apprehend its object incorrectly.

The minds of all beings in the desire realm, form realm and formless realm are completely pervaded by ignorance. There is never a time when ordinary beings do not develop ignorance.

DIVISIONS OF IGNORANCE

There are two types of ignorance:

1 Ignorance of conventional truths
2 Ignorance of ultimate truths

The first is confusion about any object other than emptiness, and the second is confusion about emptiness itself. All types of ignorance are included in these two categories.

There is another twofold division of ignorance:

1 Ignorance of actions and their effects, or karma
2 Ignorance of emptiness

Whereas the first is the cause of lower rebirth in particular, the second is the cause of rebirth in samsara in general. Because we do not understand the faults of non-virtuous actions or the benefits of virtuous actions, we behave in ways that result in rebirth in unhappy migrations. When we understand actions and their effects correctly we will naturally strive to accumulate virtuous actions and abandon non-virtuous actions, and thereby protect ourself from lower rebirth. However, even if we understand the laws of karma and act accordingly, until we abandon ignorance of emptiness by realizing emptiness directly we will still perform actions that throw us into samsara. Even virtuous actions motivated by self-grasping are true origins, the source of samsaric rebirth.

HOW TO ABANDON IGNORANCE

Since all mistakes, suffering, delusions and incorrect actions arise from ignorance, we definitely need to abandon ignorance. This depends, however, upon developing wisdom, which in turn depends upon listening to or reading Dharma teachings, and contemplating and meditating on them. By doing this we will generate the wisdoms arisen from listening or reading, contemplating, and meditating, and in this way we will abandon ignorance.

The Wisdom Guru Buddha Je Tsongkhapa appeared in this world for our benefit. If we rely upon him with strong faith and continually practise the ritual prayer *Heart Jewel*, our wisdom will greatly increase. I promise this. The more our wisdom increases, the more our ignorance will become weaker until finally it will cease completely. We will thus become an Awakened One, someone who has awakened from the sleep of ignorance, and we will be permanently free from the dream of suffering and problems.

DELUDED DOUBT

DEFINITION OF DELUDED DOUBT

The definition of deluded doubt is a two-pointedness of mind that interferes with the attainment of liberation or enlightenment.

In general, doubt is a mind of uncertainty that cannot decide between two alternatives. Although we have numerous doubts, not all doubts are deluded doubts. Simply being unable to decide whether to go out or to stay in, for example, is a doubt but it is not a delusion. Deluded doubt is an uncertainty about Dharma topics that causes our faith to decline and disturbs our peace of mind. For example, if our Spiritual Guide teaches us that virtuous actions lead to happiness and non-virtuous actions to suffering, and we feel this to be probably untrue, we have developed deluded doubt. This lack of conviction in actions and their effects prevents us from practising Dharma purely, and obstructs our progress on the path to liberation. If, although we cannot come to a definite decision, we are inclined to believe Buddha's teachings on actions and their effects, this is still doubt but it is not deluded doubt because it is a step towards developing a correct belief in the laws of karma.

DIVISIONS OF DELUDED DOUBT

There are three types of doubt in general: doubts tending towards the truth, doubts tending away from the truth and balanced doubts. Any doubt about spiritually significant objects that tends away from the truth is deluded doubt. Balanced doubts with respect to these objects may or may not be deluded. For example, if a person who previously believed that Buddha does not exist hears a teaching on Buddha, and as a result starts to doubt whether Buddha exists or not, this is not a deluded doubt because it is leading him or her towards a correct belief. On the other hand, a similar doubt in the mind of someone who once believed in Buddha but whose faith is now weakening is a deluded doubt.

Doubts about Dharma are not necessarily negative. For example, people who have not met Dharma have no doubts about emptiness because it is only through listening to teachings on emptiness that we begin to wonder whether or not phenomena lack inherent existence. Such doubts impel us to think more deeply about emptiness until finally we attain a valid cognizer that realizes emptiness with complete certainty.

If we did not develop doubts about emptiness to start with, we would not subsequently gain such a deep understanding.

Although some doubts are helpful at certain stages of our development, eventually all doubts have to be abandoned. Doubts are completely abandoned only by Buddhas, whose perfect wisdom knows all phenomena exactly as they are, with no mistake or uncertainty. Hinayana Foe Destroyers have abandoned deluded doubts, but as they do not know all objects of knowledge they still have non-deluded doubts. Even tenth-ground Bodhisattvas do not fully understand the good qualities of a Buddha's body, speech and mind, and still have some doubts about them. Superior beings do not have deluded doubts because they realize emptiness directly.

HOW TO ABANDON DELUDED DOUBT

We abandon doubt by developing valid cognizers. When we develop doubts about Dharma, rather than letting them remain in our mind we should take steps to resolve them. We should think carefully about the teachings and ask others to share their understanding. We can ask questions of Teachers and read relevant books to ascertain the true meaning of the instructions. In this way we will eliminate our doubts. If we allow doubts about the teachings to remain in our mind, they will eventually turn into deluded doubts and hinder our practice. Conversely, if we are encouraged by our doubts to think more deeply about Dharma, they will help us to improve our understanding and eventually to attain valid cognizers.

In particular, we can speedily resolve doubts by developing quick wisdom. A powerful method for developing quick wisdom is to meditate on the seed-letter of Manjushri, the letter DHI. To do this we visualize at the root of our tongue an orange-coloured letter DHI, which is in essence the quick wisdom of Manjushri. We invite the quick wisdom of all the

Buddhas in the aspect of many letter DHIs to dissolve into the DHI at the root of our tongue. Then light radiates from this DHI and fills our entire body. Each atom of this light is a letter DHI and so our whole body is filled with DHIs. We recite 'DHI' as many times as possible with one breath and then, together with a little saliva, we swallow the letter DHI at our tongue. This dissolves into our root mind at our heart and we imagine that our mind transforms into the quick wisdom of all the Buddhas. If we practise this with strong faith early in the morning each day, we will definitely develop quick wisdom.

The only way finally to eliminate a doubt is to understand the object with a valid cognizer. There are two ways of knowing an object correctly: through a correct belief and through a valid cognizer. The understanding of a correct belief is useful, but is not strong or stable; and if we later listen to incorrect instructions our understanding may change into doubt, or even into wrong awareness. Valid cognizers, on the other hand, know their object clearly and thoroughly, with complete certainty. Even if we hear clever arguments that try to deny an object we know with a valid cognizer, we will not develop any doubts and our valid cognizer will be unshaken. For these reasons we should strive to understand Dharma with valid cognizers.

DELUDED VIEW

DEFINITION OF DELUDED VIEW

The definition of deluded view is a view that functions to obstruct the attainment of liberation.

In general there are two types of view: correct views and incorrect views. All deluded views are incorrect views. A correct view is a wisdom. Because human beings follow different incorrect views so many problems arise in society and in personal life. Animals are free from such problems.

DIVISIONS OF DELUDED VIEW

There are five types of deluded view:

1 View of the transitory collection
2 Extreme view
3 Holding false views as supreme
4 Holding wrong moral disciplines and conduct as supreme
5 Wrong view

VIEW OF THE TRANSITORY COLLECTION

DEFINITION OF VIEW OF THE TRANSITORY COLLECTION

The definition of view of the transitory collection is a type of self-grasping of persons that grasps our own I as being an inherently existent I.

Our mind that observes our own I or our self, which is the transitory collection, and that grasps it as being an inherently existent I is called the 'view of the transitory collection'. The view of the transitory collection is the root of samsara and the source of all delusions. In *Guide to the Middle Way* Chandrakirti says:

Wisdom sees that all delusions and all faults
Arise from the view of the transitory collection.

Because we grasp strongly at an inherently existent I we develop self-cherishing, attachment, anger and all other delusions; and these cause us to engage in contaminated actions that in turn cause us to experience the sufferings of samsara. The view of the transitory collection pervades all delusions because it functions whenever a delusion is manifest. If we wish to escape from samsara we need to eradicate this view, but before we can do this we must learn to identify it. Even though the view of the transitory collection is always manifest in the minds of ordinary beings it is not easy to recognize at first.

To recognize the view of the transitory collection we need to understand the difference between its observed object and its conceived object. For example, in the case of mistaking a toy snake for a real snake the observed object is a toy snake and the conceived object is this toy snake as a real snake. Similarly, in the case of the view of the transitory collection the observed object is the conventionally existent I, which is the I that is merely imputed in dependence upon the aggregates, and the conceived object is this conventionally existent I as an inherently existent I. The observed object of the view of the transitory collection, the mere I, exists, but the conceived object, the inherently existent I, does not.

When we think of ourself we apprehend not an I that is merely imputed upon our aggregates but an I that appears to be independent. For example, if we ask who is presently reading this book we do not think 'My body is reading this book', or 'My mind is reading this book'; we simply think 'I am reading this book', and this I appears to be independent of the body and mind. It is this independent I that is the conceived object of the view of the transitory collection, and that does not exist. Whatever exists does so in dependence upon other phenomena. The conventionally existent I, for example, exists in dependence upon the aggregates of body and mind. The conceived object of the view of the transitory collection, however, which is the I at which we habitually grasp and with which we usually identify, appears to be independent of the aggregates. Such an I could never exist.

What is the observed object of the view of the transitory collection, the conventionally existent I? Some non-Buddhist schools believe that the existent I is a permanent, indivisible entity that is a separate entity from the body and mind. Such a self is refuted by all Buddhist schools. Why is this? When our body is not healthy we say 'I am sick', and when our mind is not happy we say 'I am unhappy'; but if the I were a separate entity from the body and mind these statements would be nonsensical. If Peter becomes sick, John does not say 'I am sick', because John and Peter are separate entities. Similarly, if the I were a separate entity from the body and mind it would make no sense to say 'I am sick' just because our body was sick, or 'I am unhappy' just because our mind was unhappy.

Although no Buddhist school asserts an I that is a separate entity from the mental and physical aggregates, all the lower schools of Buddhism identify the I as existing somewhere within the aggregates. Some, such as the Vaibhashikas and some Sautrantikas, assert that the collection of the five aggregates is the I, while other Sautrantikas identify the mental consciousness as the I. The Chittamatrins say that the I is the consciousness-basis-of-all, and the Madhyamika-Svatantrikas assert that it is the continuum of the subtle mental consciousness. However, according to the highest school of Buddhism, the Madhyamika-Prasangikas, all these assertions are incorrect. The Madhyamika-Prasangikas deny that the I can be found either within the aggregates or outside them. No matter how carefully we search among the mental and physical aggregates we will never find the I. The I is just a label that is imputed in dependence upon the five aggregates. The collection of the five aggregates is the basis for imputing the I, but it is not the I itself. If we are satisfied with the I as the mere term or label 'I' that is imputed in dependence upon the aggregates we will be able to establish an I that exists and functions (the conventionally existent I); but if we search for a real I that exists 'behind' the label we will find nothing.

It is very important to identify the view of the transitory collection from our own experience by identifying it within our own mind. At first the easiest way to do this is to cause the view of the transitory collection to manifest more strongly than usual by recalling or imagining situations in which we are falsely accused, afraid, praised or embarrassed; and then to observe how the I appears at such times. We should direct most of our attention towards recreating or imagining the situation, but keep one part of our mind watching how the I appears. If we are not skilful and try to observe the I directly we will probably fail. We need to practise watching the I out of the corner of our mind and try to catch a glimpse of it surreptitiously. This is an acquired skill that requires considerable practice. Eventually we will see that the I is appearing independent of our body and mind. It seems as if our mind is 'this side' and the I is 'that side'. It is this independent I that is the conceived object of the view of the transitory collection.

By watching our mind in this way we will gain a clear generic image of the inherently existent I. Even though this I does not exist we can nevertheless have a generic image of it. For example, unicorns do not exist but we can have an image of a unicorn in our mind. Once we are able to identify the view of the transitory collection operating in extreme circumstances, such as when we are afraid or embarrassed, we should then try to identify it in less extreme circumstances. For example, we can sit down to meditate and ask ourself 'Who is meditating?', and then try to observe the inherently existent I appearing as we think 'I am meditating.'

It is very helpful to understand the etymology of the view of the transitory collection. According to the lower Buddhist school, the Sautrantika school, the view of the transitory collection is a deluded view that observes the aggregates and apprehends a self-supporting and substantially existent I. Thus, they say that the observed object of this view is the five aggregates. According to them it is the aggregates themselves that are the 'transitory collection'. They are 'transitory' because they are impermanent, and a 'collection' because there are several of them. Thus, they assert that the view of the transitory collection observes the aggregates and mistakenly apprehends a self-supporting substantially existent I within them.

According to the Madhyamika-Prasangika explanation the term 'transitory collection' refers not only to the aggregates themselves but also to the I that is imputed upon them. Buddha called the I a 'transitory collection' to counteract non-Buddhists such as the Samkhyas who assert that the I is a permanent, indivisible, independent entity. The Samkhyas say that the I is permanent because it is not destroyed at death. They believe that the I has existed since beginningless time and that in each life it takes on a different body and mind, rather as an actor puts on a different mask each time he appears on stage. Just as the actor changes appearance but remains essentially the same, so the I changes appearance from one life to the next but remains the same entity.

The Samkhyas believe that if the I were not permanent, and independent of the body and mind, there would be no rebirth because the I would cease when the body dies. Thus, they believe that the I of our previous life, which created the karma that caused this life, still exists; and will continue to exist forever. This indicates that they do not understand subtle impermanence. In reality we do not remain the same for one moment without changing, let alone for one life. Without the

I of the previous moment ceasing, the I of the next moment could not arise. The I of one moment is the cause of the I of the next moment, and a cause and its effect cannot exist at the same time. A sprout, for example, can develop only when its cause, the seed, disintegrates. It is precisely because the I disintegrates moment by moment that Buddha called the I 'transitory'. Since the I in one moment is a different entity from the I of the previous moment, it goes without saying that the I of one life is a different entity from the I of the previous life.

The Samkhyas also believe that the I is indivisible, or partless. They say that if it were not partless it could be broken down into its component parts and would therefore not be indestructible and immortal. All Buddhist schools deny this, and the Madhyamikas in particular refute such things as partless objects. It is easy to see that the body has parts, such as the limbs, the head and the trunk. The mind also has parts, such as feelings, discriminations, experiences, knowledge and appearances, as well as having past, present and future moments. Similarly, persons or selves have parts. One person may be a teacher, a father and a Dharma practitioner. These are all different parts of the same person. Similarly, one person has parts that look, listen, taste, feel, think and so forth. If we are looking at a crowd of a hundred people, for example, we have a hundred parts, each observing a different person. We can also divide a person into the past, present and future moments. From this we can see that each person has many parts, and so, rather than being a single indivisible entity, each person is the nature of a collection. It is for this reason that Buddha called the I a 'collection'.

From this explanation we can see that the term 'transitory collection' in the phrase 'view of the transitory collection' refers not only to the aggregates but also to the I. The view of the transitory collection, therefore, is a deluded view that observes the I, the transitory collection that is merely imputed in dependence upon the aggregates, and conceives it to be an inherently existent I.

DIVISIONS OF VIEW OF THE TRANSITORY COLLECTION

There are two types of view of the transitory collection:

1 View of the transitory collection conceiving I
2 View of the transitory collection conceiving mine

The first observes only the I within our continuum and conceives it to be inherently existent, and the second observes both the I and mine within our continuum and conceives mine to be inherently existent. It is important to identify the observed object of the latter view. The view of the transitory collection is necessarily a self-grasping of persons that conceives one's own I to be inherently existent, and it necessarily takes the I within one's own continuum as its observed object. The view of the transitory collection conceiving mine, therefore, must observe our own I and conceive it to be inherently existent. When we see the aspect of other things, such as our clothes or our body, we develop a sense of 'mine'. At such times we are observing our I as a possessor, as 'mine', and conceiving it to be inherently existent. Thus, 'mine' in this context refers not to the objects that are being held as mine, which is the normal use of the word, but to the subject who is being held as the possessor. If 'mine' referred to the objects, such as one's clothes or one's body, then the observed object would be a phenomenon other than persons, and the mind grasping them to be inherently existent would be a self-grasping of phenomena, not a self-grasping of persons. Even so, it is not incorrect to say that objects such as one's clothes or one's body are examples of mine.

There is another twofold division of view of the transitory collection:

1 Innate view of the transitory collection
2 Intellectually-formed view of the transitory collection

Both the view of the transitory collection conceiving I and the view of the transitory collection conceiving mine have innate and intellectually-formed types. We have had the innate view of the transitory collection since beginningless time. It arises naturally in our mind through the force of imprints, and it is manifest in the minds of ordinary beings all the time, even during sleep. It is this innate view that is the root of samsara.

Like the innate view, the intellectually-formed view of the transitory collection is also a mind that grasps at one's own I as being inherently existent, but whereas the innate view develops naturally through the force of the imprints of ignorance, the intellectually-formed view arises as a result of contemplating wrong reasons or receiving misleading teachings. We tend to fabricate such false views of the I because we are very accustomed to the innate view of the transitory collection. The innate view, therefore, is the source of all the intellectually-formed views.

In *Guide to the Middle Way* Chandrakirti lists twenty intellectually-formed views of the transitory collection, four in relation to each of the five aggregates:

(1) The view holding our aggregate of form to be an inherently existent I
(2) The view holding our aggregate of form to be possessed by an inherently existent I
(3) The view holding our aggregate of form to be the basis upon which an inherently existent I depends

(4) The view holding our aggregate of form to be dependent upon an inherently existent I

(5) The view holding our aggregate of feeling to be an inherently existent I

(6) The view holding our aggregate of feeling to be possessed by an inherently existent I

(7) The view holding our aggregate of feeling to be the basis upon which an inherently existent I depends

(8) The view holding our aggregate of feeling to be dependent upon an inherently existent I

(9) The view holding our aggregate of discrimination to be an inherently existent I

(10) The view holding our aggregate of discrimination to be possessed by an inherently existent I

(11) The view holding our aggregate of discrimination to be the basis upon which an inherently existent I depends

(12) The view holding our aggregate of discrimination to be dependent upon an inherently existent I

(13) The view holding our aggregate of compositional factors to be an inherently existent I

(14) The view holding our aggregate of compositional factors to be possessed by an inherently existent I

(15) The view holding our aggregate of compositional factors to be the basis upon which an inherently existent I depends

(16) The view holding our aggregate of compositional factors to be dependent upon an inherently existent I

(17) The view holding our aggregate of consciousness to be an inherently existent I

(18) The view holding our aggregate of consciousness to be possessed by an inherently existent I

(19) The view holding our aggregate of consciousness to be the basis upon which an inherently existent I depends

(20) The view holding our aggregate of consciousness to be dependent upon an inherently existent I.

Our aggregate of form refers to our body. Our aggregate of form is not an inherently existent I, but the first view holds it to be so; an inherently existent I does not possess our aggregate of form, but the second view holds our aggregate of form to be possessed by an inherently existent I; an inherently existent I does not depend upon our aggregate of form, but the third view holds our aggregate of form to be the basis upon which an inherently existent I depends; our aggregate of form does not depend upon an inherently existent I, but the fourth view holds our aggregate of form to be dependent upon an inherently existent I. The remaining sixteen views can be understood in the same way.

HOW TO ABANDON THE VIEW OF THE TRANSITORY COLLECTION

First we need to identify correctly and precisely the view of the transitory collection in our own experience. Then we have to realize that its conceived object, the inherently existent I, does not exist, and familiarize ourself with this knowledge for a long time in meditation. Through progressing in this meditation, eventually we will abandon this view completely.

If the inherently existent I existed we would be able to find it through investigation, but no matter how closely we investigate – whether we search within our aggregates of body and mind or elsewhere – we will never find it. From this we can safely conclude that the inherently existent I does not exist. Where previously we perceived a vividly appearing I, we now perceive a vacuity or absence, an emptiness. This emptiness is the non-existence of the inherently existent I. It is the ultimate nature of our I. By familiarizing ourself with this absence, or non-existence, of the inherently existent I, we will gradually reduce and eventually abandon altogether the view of the transitory collection grasping at such an I.

In *Commentary to Valid Cognition* Dharmakirti says:

Without its object being negated,
Self-grasping cannot be abandoned.

This means that to abandon the view of the transitory collection we need to realize the non-existence of the inherently existent self. This is like removing the fear of a snake by realizing that there is no snake. However, we should not think that in negating the conceived object of the view of the transitory collection we are driving the inherently existent I out of existence, because such an I has never existed. In this case, negating the conceived object is simply realizing that something we previously held to exist does not in fact exist.

Suppose a child is named 'Buddha' by his parents. The child would grow up thinking 'I am Buddha', but when he discovered that Buddha was someone who was free from the two obstructions he would examine his body and mind and realize he was not an actual Buddha but just an ordinary person with the name 'Buddha'. Although he might continue to call himself 'Buddha', he would know that this was merely a name and that it did not imply that he was actually a Buddha. Our situation is similar in that we have always thought of ourself as I, and assumed that, corresponding to this name, there was a real I. Like the child we should now examine our body and mind to see if this assumption is correct. If we search for this I we will not find it, either within our body and mind or outside our body and mind. Thus, we will realize that 'I' is just a name. The truly existent I we expect to find 'behind' the name does not exist at all. Thus, although we may continue to refer to ourself as 'I', we can be certain that it is just a name and that it in no way implies an inherently existent I.

Buddha explained that there are two types of self-grasping: self-grasping of persons and self-grasping of phenomena. The former is any mind that conceives a self or person to be inherently existent, and the second is any mind that conceives phenomena other than persons to be inherently existent. As mentioned before, the view of the transitory collection is a type of self-grasping of persons. Self-grasping of persons has two types: grasping at our own self as inherently existent and grasping at other persons as inherently existent, and it is only the former that is the view of the transitory collection. Both types of self-grasping of persons are the same in that they grasp at an inherently existent self, but they differ in their observed object. The first observes the self within one's own continuum and conceives it to be inherently existent, and the second observes the self of others and conceives it to be inherently existent.

How does the view of the transitory collection arise? In *Precious Garland* Nagarjuna says:

For as long as there is grasping at the aggregates
There is grasping at I.

This means that the view of the transitory collection grasping at an inherently existent I arises from grasping at our aggregates as inherently existent. When we observe our aggregates they appear as inherently existent, and we thereby develop a mind grasping at inherently existent aggregates. This is an instance of self-grasping of phenomena. In dependence upon grasping at our aggregates as inherently existent, we develop a mind grasping at our I as inherently existent – the view of the transitory collection. This is an instance of self-grasping of persons. If we understand this we will realize that to abandon the view of the transitory collection completely we must realize not only selflessness of persons but also selflessness of phenomena. For example, if a person walking through a field at dusk sees a piece of rope and mistakes it for a snake he will develop fear, but once he realizes that there is no snake his fear will subside. However, if he does not remove the piece of rope there will be a danger of making the same mistake again in the future. In the same way, in the darkness of our ignorance we observe our aggregates and mistakenly conceive an inherently existent I, and because we grasp at this I we experience all the fears and sufferings of samsara. To remove these fears and sufferings we need to remove grasping at an inherently existent I by realizing that the inherently existent I does not exist; but if we do not also remove grasping at the aggregates by realizing the emptiness of our aggregates there will be a danger of the view of the transitory collection arising again. Therefore, to attain liberation from samsara we need to realize both selflessness of persons and selflessness of phenomena.

In *Guide to the Middle Way* Chandrakirti says:

I bow down to that compassion for living beings
Who from first conceiving 'I' with respect to the self,
Then thinking 'This is mine' and generating
    attachment for things,
Are without self-control like the spinning of a well.

In this verse Chandrakirti shows how we can develop compassion for all living beings by contemplating how they are trapped in samsara by the two types of view of the transitory collection. Thus, from the view of the transitory collection conceiving I, sentient beings develop the view of the transitory collection conceiving mine. From this they develop a strong sense of 'my pleasure', 'my pain', and so forth; and in this way they develop attachment for the things that please them and hatred for the things that displease them. From these develop all other delusions that cause them to create the karma to be reborn repeatedly in samsara. Once living beings take a samsaric rebirth they have to experience suffering without any choice, just as a bucket in a well swings uncontrollably from side to side and is thereby dented, scratched and damaged. If we think deeply about this we will develop renunciation for our own samsara and compassion for others. We will see that to free ourself and others from the sufferings of samsara we must cut samsara at its root by eradicating the view of the transitory collection.

EXTREME VIEW

DEFINITION OF EXTREME VIEW

The definition of extreme view is an exaggerated incorrect view.

We know that people cause many problems through following extreme views. In general, there are two extremes: the extreme of existence and the extreme of non-existence; but neither exists because whatever exists is necessarily the middle way free from the two extremes.

DIVISIONS OF EXTREME VIEW

There are two types of extreme view: the extreme view of existence and the extreme view of non-existence. An example of the first is an extreme view that believes phenomena exist inherently, and an example of the second is an extreme view that believes phenomena do not exist at all. As our wisdom increases, extreme views will become weaker and weaker until finally they will cease completely.

HOLDING FALSE VIEWS AS SUPREME

DEFINITION OF HOLDING FALSE VIEWS AS SUPREME

The definition of holding false views as supreme is a deluded view that believes our own or others' incorrect views are supreme views.

This view is the source of wrong decisions and therefore causes many problems for ourself and others. We should avoid such views by improving our knowledge, education and wisdom.

Because we cherish ourself so strongly we naturally feel that whatever we think is correct and superior to other points of view, and we find it difficult to accept that some of our views might be mistaken. Most arguments and wars occur because each party regards their view to be superior to their opponents' view. Whenever we grasp tightly to a mistaken view, thinking that it is a correct view and the best view, we are holding false views as supreme. An example is insisting that the view of the transitory collection is the correct view.

HOLDING WRONG MORAL DISCIPLINES AND CONDUCT AS SUPREME

DEFINITION OF HOLDING WRONG MORAL DISCIPLINES AND CONDUCT AS SUPREME

The definition of holding wrong moral disciplines and conduct as supreme is a deluded view that holds any wrong moral discipline or conduct to be correct and considers it to be superior to other forms of moral discipline or conduct.

This deluded view has two types: holding wrong moral disciplines as supreme and holding wrong conduct as supreme. Some religions advocate animal sacrifice as a means of pleasing the gods and attaining liberation. Others teach that treating the body harshly helps to overcome delusions, and so the followers of these traditions jump into fires, fast for long periods of time, lacerate themselves or stand for a long time in cold water during winter. These views flourished widely in the past and still exist today. I myself saw ascetics in India who stood on one leg for three years in the belief that this would make them great Yogis. Why did they punish themselves so? It was because they believed that delusions are part of the body, and so if they could reduce the strength of the body they would be able to reduce the strength of their delusions. These are examples of views grasping at wrong moral disciplines or conduct as supreme. According to Buddhism such views are wrong paths because they do not lead to true liberation but cause us to waste our human life.

Deluded views such as these are usually the result of listening to misleading religious or philosophical teachings. We should be careful not to follow such mistaken teachings. Holding incorrect views about moral conduct and spiritual practice causes us to waste our time on inferior or perverse practices, and prevents us from making the best use of our precious human life. Some people may think that an authentic spiritual life entails living in poverty, constantly fasting, wearing poor clothing and so forth, but Buddha taught that we should treat our body with care because it is the vehicle in which we progress to enlightenment and as such is very precious. A weak or mistreated body will not be able to support our spiritual development. Therefore, without being attached to our body we should feed it, clothe it, provide adequate shelter and so on; and then concentrate our energy on training our mind. As Nagarjuna said:

Physical asceticism is of no benefit, but mental asceticism is very necessary.

By this he means that there is little purpose in enduring unnecessary physical pain, but that it is very important to endure the hardships involved in taming our mind.

WRONG VIEW

DEFINITION OF WRONG VIEW

The definition of wrong view is an intellectually-formed wrong awareness that denies the existence of an object that it is necessary to understand to attain liberation or enlightenment.

Not all wrong awarenesses are wrong views. For example, innate delusions, such as the innate view of the transitory collection, as well as all mistaken sense awarenesses, are wrong awarenesses but not wrong views. There are also many false views that are not wrong views. Denying the existence of yetis, for example, does not obstruct our progress towards liberation or enlightenment and is therefore not a wrong view. Examples of wrong views are denying the existence of past and future lives; denying the existence of the two truths; denying the existence of Buddha, Dharma and Sangha; denying the existence of the four noble truths; and denying the existence of the five paths. Such wrong views block our progress to liberation and enlightenment.

The effects of developing such wrong views are that we will become very dull and ignorant, and that we will be reborn in countries where there is no Buddhadharma or during a dark age when no Buddha has taught the doctrine. As wrong views are so harmful we should strive to overcome them by developing correct views.

It is important to realize that not all deluded views are wrong views. A wrong view is necessarily a negative mind, and is one of the ten non-virtuous actions. It consists of actively denying something that we need to believe in to attain liberation or enlightenment. Other deluded views, however, such as the innate view of the transitory collection, are neither negative states of mind nor non-virtuous actions. The innate view of the transitory collection is a neutral mind, neither negative nor positive, although it is the source of all our negative minds and of all our non-virtuous actions.

Attain permanent liberation from this cycle of samsara where there is no real happiness

The Twenty Secondary Delusions

From the six root delusions, twenty secondary delusions develop:

1 Aggression
2 Resentment
3 Spite
4 Jealousy
5 Miserliness
6 Concealment
7 Pretension
8 Denial
9 Self-satisfaction
10 Harmfulness
11 Shamelessness
12 Inconsideration
13 Dullness
14 Distraction
15 Mental excitement
16 Non-faith
17 Laziness
18 Non-conscientiousness
19 Deluded forgetfulness
20 Non-alertness

AGGRESSION

The definition of aggression is a deluded mental factor that is an increase of the root delusion anger that wishes to hurt or harm others physically or verbally.

As long as anger is hidden within our heart and cannot be detected by others it is not aggression but the root delusion anger. If this anger becomes stronger, such that we start to think of ways of harming others physically or verbally and show external signs of anger such as menacing facial expressions, and if our behaviour comes under the influence of this anger, then the anger has become aggression.

RESENTMENT

The definition of resentment is a deluded mental factor that maintains the continuum of anger without forgetting it, and wishes to retaliate.

If someone harmed us a year ago and we still bear a grudge, this is resentment. Resentment is derived from the root delusion anger. First we develop anger, and then we hold on to that anger, not allowing ourself to forget the harm we experienced. Resentment is much more harmful than the root delusion anger or the secondary delusion aggression. Due to resentment people retaliate and become involved in disputes and wars which may continue for many years. Even if we develop aggression, if we soon forget our anger this is much less harmful than bearing a grudge for many years.

SPITE

The definition of spite is a deluded mental factor that, motivated by resentment or aggression, wishes to speak harshly.

Harsh speech disturbs others' inner peace, destroys our good relationships with others, and causes others to get angry; but without the mental factor spite there would be no basis for harsh speech. Speaking harshly with a special, virtuous motivation, however, is not actual harsh speech.

JEALOUSY

The definition of jealousy is a deluded mental factor that feels displeasure when observing others' enjoyments, good qualities or good fortune.

If our neighbour buys a new car, or our friend becomes close to someone else, and we become jealous, this will make our mind very uncomfortable whenever we think about their good fortune. There are three types of jealousy: jealousy observing others' possessions; jealousy observing others' good qualities, skills, knowledge and so forth; and jealousy observing others' good reputation, fame, popularity and so forth. Jealousy is the source of much anger, discontent and disharmony. It feels like a thorn in our heart. When we are jealous our mind becomes narrow and obsessive, making it difficult for us to think of anything else or to see the situation from the other person's point of view. Jealousy is entirely futile because neither does it cause the other person's fortune or good qualities to decline, nor does it increase our own; all it does is to rob us of our own peace and happiness.

Jealousy is completely contradictory with the Bodhisattva's way of looking at things. Bodhisattvas constantly pray 'May all sentient beings possess happiness', so how can they feel displeasure when someone manages to obtain a little joy? In *Guide to the Bodhisattva's Way of Life* Shantideva says that people who are jealous of others' possessions and good qualities will never develop bodhichitta. Those with great wisdom never become jealous because they have a deep understanding of the faults of jealousy.

MISERLINESS

The definition of miserliness is a deluded mental factor that, motivated by desirous attachment, holds on to things tightly and does not want to part with them.

Due to miserliness we sometimes wish to hold on to our possessions forever, but since this is impossible we experience much suffering. If our possessions dwindle, or we are forced to give them away, we experience great pain. The more miserly we are, the more concerned we are about our possessions and the more worry and anxiety we suffer.

Miserliness is the opposite of the mind of giving. Sometimes miserliness prevents us from giving at all, and at other times it causes us to develop a sense of loss or regret when we do give. Although miserliness might appear to be a prudent attitude that ensures our material security in this life, from a long-term point of view it is very foolish. By preventing the wish to practise giving from arising, miserliness causes poverty in future lives. In the *Condensed Perfection of Wisdom Sutra* Buddha says:

Misers are reborn in the land of hungry spirits;
And when reborn as human beings they experience poverty.

And in *Friendly Letter* Nagarjuna says:

> There is no better friend for the future
> Than giving – bestowing gifts properly
> On ordained people, brahmins, the poor and friends –
> Knowing enjoyments to be transitory and essenceless.

If we want to enjoy good health, friends, relatives and material resources in future lives we must practise giving now. As a result of being generous in this life we will enjoy good conditions in future lives, so giving is our best friend for the future. To secure our well-being in this life we work very hard to accumulate material possessions, but we should not forget that to be happy in future lives we will also need material resources then. The only way to secure these resources is to practise giving now.

If we find it difficult to give, we should meditate on the impermanence and essencelessness of our possessions and enjoyments. Milarepa said:

> Since you have to depart alone, leaving everything
>   behind,
> It is more meaningful to leave everything now.

We cannot take our possessions with us when we die. No matter how tightly we hold on to them now, eventually they will all be passed on to others. If we wait until we die this will happen involuntarily and will have no meaning for us. Therefore, it is much better to give away our possessions now, while we are alive, and in this way accumulate some meaning from having owned them. In themselves samsaric objects have no essence, but by using them to practise giving they acquire meaning. If we understand the benefits of giving we will develop delight and pleasure in giving.

CONCEALMENT

The definition of concealment is a deluded mental factor that, motivated by attachment to wealth or reputation, wishes to conceal our faults from others.

Although it would be unskilful to reveal publicly all our shortcomings, nevertheless we should not develop the wish to conceal our faults from others out of attachment or with a bad motivation.

PRETENSION

The definition of pretension is a deluded mental factor that, motivated by attachment to wealth or reputation, wishes to pretend that we possess qualities that we do not possess.

Pretension causes us to engage in the non-virtuous actions of lying and deceiving others, and so causes us to experience many problems.

DENIAL

The definition of denial is a deluded mental factor that does not wish to purify non-virtuous actions that we have committed or downfalls that we have incurred.

If we commit non-virtuous actions or incur downfalls of the Pratimoksha, Bodhisattva or Tantric vows, we should immediately develop a wish to purify them by developing regret. If we do not do this, our non-virtuous actions and downfalls will increase every day and cause great obstacles to our spiritual development.

SELF-SATISFACTION

The definition of self-satisfaction is a deluded mental factor that observes our own physical beauty, wealth or other good qualities, and, being concerned only with these, has no interest in spiritual development.

In *Friendly Letter* Nagarjuna explains five different types of self-satisfaction:

(1) Self-satisfaction with respect to status
(2) Self-satisfaction with respect to physical beauty
(3) Self-satisfaction with respect to knowledge, skills and so forth
(4) Self-satisfaction with respect to youth and vitality
(5) Self-satisfaction with respect to power

These five types of self-satisfaction all deceive us eventually. Since status, beauty and so forth are impermanent, if we allow ourself to become complacent on their account we will only experience suffering when we eventually lose them.

Self-satisfaction makes our precious human life meaningless, and is the root of all non-conscientiousness. It prevents us from seeing our own faults and so makes it difficult for us to develop a wish to overcome them. For example, some people might feel that they have superior status or racial origins and therefore do not need to observe moral discipline and can do whatever they like, but the result of this way of thinking will only be that they will experience many difficulties. Self-satisfaction seriously impedes the attainment of spiritual realizations such as higher moral discipline, higher concentration and higher wisdom.

HARMFULNESS

The definition of harmfulness is a deluded mental factor that wishes other sentient beings to suffer.

Harmfulness is the opposite of compassion. A harmful intent can arise through anger, jealousy, desirous attachment or ignorance. For example, out of anger we may wish for someone to suffer, to experience problems, or even to die; out of jealousy we may find it impossible to bear the success or good fortune of others and wish for them to lose it; out of desirous attachment we may become attached to others' wealth and possessions, and even wish for them to die so that we can inherit them; and out of ignorance we may rejoice in the misfortune, or even the demise, of others. Also, out of ignorance some people hold wrong views, believing that animal sacrifice is a virtuous action, and as a result they develop the wish to kill animals. All these are examples of harmful intent.

Harmfulness is the principal object to be abandoned by Buddhists. One of the commitments of going for refuge is not to harm others. In the Sutras, Buddha says:

Those who harm others are not trainees in virtue.

This means that people who deliberately harm others are not practitioners of Buddha's teachings.

SHAMELESSNESS

The definition of shamelessness is a deluded mental factor that is the opposite of sense of shame.

Out of shamelessness we may break the commitments that we have taken in front of visualized Buddhas or our Spiritual Guide. Shamelessness leads us into non-virtuous paths, and as a result we experience suffering in this and many future lives.

INCONSIDERATION

The definition of inconsideration is a deluded mental factor that is the opposite of consideration for others.

Inconsideration and shamelessness are the basis of incurring all downfalls and of accumulating all non-virtuous karma. They lead us into lower rebirth and cause all our good qualities to degenerate. They cause many difficulties both for ourself and for others.

DULLNESS

The definition of dullness is a deluded mental factor that functions to make both the body and mind heavy and inflexible.

When dullness develops it is as if our mind has become enveloped by darkness and its object has become unclear, just as external objects become unclear when it is foggy or dark. Sometimes due to dullness Dharma teachings seem unclear to us; but in reality it is our mind that is unclear. Dullness is a cause of mental sinking and sleep, and is therefore a major obstacle to meditation. The reason we sometimes fall asleep when we are meditating is that, without being aware of it, we have developed dullness. We must be careful to distinguish dullness from mental sinking. Dullness is the cause of mental sinking and is necessarily a delusion, whereas mental sinking is not necessarily a delusion.

It is vitally important for those who are intent on making progress in meditation to overcome dullness. Without a method for counteracting dullness we will find that this mental factor will naturally develop and cause the sharpness of our intelligence to decline, and our mind to become heavy, sluggish and sleepy. As a result our body will also become heavy, our concentration will deteriorate, and we will soon forget our object of meditation. Even if we do not forget the object, our meditation will be tainted by mental sinking and our concentration will no longer be flawless.

DISTRACTION

The definition of distraction is a deluded mental factor that wanders to any object of delusion.

Distraction makes us lose our concentration on our spiritual practice by causing our mind to wander to a contaminated object, such as a samsaric place, body or enjoyment. The object of distraction can be an object of anger, an object of attachment or an object of ignorance. Distraction is the worst obstacle to our spiritual development.

MENTAL EXCITEMENT

The definition of mental excitement is a deluded mental factor that wanders to any object of attachment.

Mental excitement is closely related to attachment. It seriously interrupts both analytical and placement meditation. Because we are so familiar with objects of attachment, when we are trying to make progress in our meditation mental excitement naturally develops within our mind and destroys our concentration.

NON-FAITH

The definition of non-faith is a deluded mental factor that is the opposite of faith.

Non-faith makes our mind like a dry seed from which no sprouts of spiritual realizations can grow. However much we study Dharma, if we lack faith we will never gain any realizations. Therefore, to gain results from our Dharma study we must improve our faith in Dharma and in our Teachers.

LAZINESS

The definition of laziness is a deluded mental factor that, motivated by attachment to worldly pleasures or worldly activities, dislikes virtuous activity.

The laziness taught in Dharma and the laziness we talk of in everyday life are different. The mental factor laziness is necessarily a deluded mind. A dislike of engaging in non-virtuous actions is not a delusion but usually a virtuous mind. Similarly, a mind that lacks enthusiasm for neutral actions such as cleaning or cooking is also not necessarily deluded.

Just outside the entrance of the cave of Geshe Karakpa, one of the Kadampa Geshes, there was a thorn bush and, as the path was narrow, every time he went in and out he scratched himself. Each day he would decide to cut down the bush, but as his retreat schedule was so tight he never found time to do it. Month by month the bush grew larger until eventually it blocked the whole path. The local people thought that Geshe Karakpa was very lazy because he could not be bothered even to trim a bush, but in reality his inactivity was a sign not of laziness but of his effort in his spiritual practices.

Like non-faith, laziness is very harmful for Dharma practitioners. In this great aeon a thousand Buddhas will appear. The only difference between these Buddhas and us is that through their effort the Buddhas have attained great enlightenment, whereas we, through our laziness, remain in samsara.

NON-CONSCIENTIOUSNESS

The definition of non-conscientiousness is a deluded mental factor that wishes to engage in non-virtuous actions without restraint.

Non-conscientiousness is the opposite of conscientiousness, which functions to guard our mind against delusion and protects us from engaging in non-virtuous actions. Non-conscientiousness is the gateway to committing non-virtuous actions. It is one of the four doors of receiving downfalls. If we guard our mind by applying conscientiousness we will avoid committing non-virtuous actions, and all our actions of body, speech and mind will become pure; but if we allow non-conscientiousness to develop we will act in an unrestrained manner and happily engage in negative actions.

In *Friendly Letter* Nagarjuna says:

The Teacher, Buddha Shakyamuni said
Conscientiousness is like nectar,
Non-conscientiousness is like death.

Conscientiousness is like nectar because it causes us to experience bliss and happiness now and in the future. Non-conscientiousness is like death because it destroys the meaning of having a human life. We consider death to be the worst that could befall us, but in reality living without conscientiousness is far worse. If we waste the precious opportunities afforded by this human life by not engaging in virtuous actions we are as if already dead. As Shantideva says in *Guide to the Bodhisattva's Way of Life*, what is the meaning in taking a human rebirth if we use it only to commit evil? Death is nowhere near as unpleasant as the long-term effects of our non-virtue.

DELUDED FORGETFULNESS

The definition of deluded forgetfulness is a deluded mental factor that makes us forget a virtuous object.

Not all forgetfulness is deluded. If we forget to eat breakfast, for example, this is not a delusion. Some forgetfulness, such as forgetting objects of attachment or anger, can even be virtuous. An example of deluded forgetfulness is when we forget the object of meditation because we are distracted towards an object of attachment.

Forgetfulness is one of the major obstacles to meditation. If we forget the object of meditation we have nothing to concentrate on. One of the five obstacles to be eliminated when training in tranquil abiding is forgetting the object of meditation, and its principal opponent is mindfulness. Mindfulness is the life force of meditation, and forgetting the object is the enemy that destroys the life of meditation.

NON-ALERTNESS

The definition of non-alertness is a deluded mental factor that, being unable to distinguish faults from non-faults, causes us to develop faults.

Non-alertness is the opposite of alertness. Some people may have a strong wish to follow a spiritual path but, because they lack alertness, continue to commit non-virtuous actions. If we lack the wisdom to distinguish what is virtuous from what is non-virtuous our actions will often be faulty even though we mean well.

Alertness is a type of wisdom that knows what is a fault and what is not a fault. When we meditate, alertness acts like a spy that checks to see whether our concentration is pure. It examines the mind to see if dullness, distraction, mental excitement or mental sinking are developing. If we do not use alertness to keep a watch on our mind during meditation we will not notice dullness and mental sinking when they arise, and so there is a great danger that we will fall asleep during our meditation. Without alertness we will not be able to overcome the obstacles that occur in meditation, and so our concentration will be flawed and we will not attain tranquil abiding. Even during our daily activities, if we do not use alertness to keep a watch on our mind we may receive many downfalls.

In *Guide to the Bodhisattva's Way of Life* Shantideva says:

Moreover, for those whose minds lack alertness,
The wisdoms from listening, contemplating and
    meditating
Will not be retained by their memory,
Any more than water will remain in a leaky pot.

Even those who have much learning and faith
And who have sincerely applied great effort
Will become defiled by moral downfalls
Through the fault of lacking alertness.

There are four main causes of breaking our moral discipline, known as the 'four doors of receiving downfalls'. The first is not knowing what the downfalls are, which is non-alertness. The other three are lack of respect for Dharma, strong delusions and non-conscientiousness.

These twenty delusions are branches of the six root delusions. They are called 'secondary delusions' because they can arise from any one of the root delusions. The source of all delusions is the three poisons – desirous attachment, hatred and ignorance. These are the main objects to be abandoned by those seeking liberation.

Come under the great umbrella of Buddhism

The Four Changeable
Mental Factors

The four changeable mental factors are:

1 Sleep
2 Regret
3 Investigation
4 Analysis

Depending upon their motivation these mental factors can be virtuous, non-virtuous or neutral, which is why they are called 'changeable'.

SLEEP

The definition of sleep is a mental factor that is developed through dullness or its imprints and that functions to gather the sense awarenesses inwards.

Sleep is a subtle mind. When a subtle mind becomes manifest, gross minds such as sense awarenesses necessarily become non-manifest, which is why sleep has the function of gathering the sense awarenesses inwards. For ordinary beings sleep helps to restore the energy of the body and to bring the elements of the body into harmony, thereby making the body comfortable and prolonging life. For practitioners of Tantra the yoga of sleep helps the development of the clear light of bliss. However, if we are attached to sleep it causes us to increase our laziness.

Skilful Dharma practitioners use their understanding of sleep, dreams and waking to understand the development of death, intermediate state and rebirth, because sleep is similar to death, dreams are similar to the intermediate state and waking is similar to rebirth. Sleep is also the basis of the development of all the things we experience in dreams.

REGRET

The definition of regret is a mental factor that feels remorse for actions done in the past.

There are three types of regret: virtuous, non-virtuous and neutral. Regret for previously committed non-virtuous actions is virtuous regret because it encourages us to purify our past negative actions and acts as the first of the four opponent powers. This type of regret is developed by recognizing the faults and disadvantages of non-virtuous actions. Those who have not heard teachings on karma, however, will find it difficult to develop sincere regret, and therefore will not be able to purify their negative actions. One of the greatest gifts of Dharma is that it teaches us how to purify our past non-virtues.

We need to develop regret for past negative actions before their effects have ripened. There is no point in feeling regret for non-virtuous actions whose effects have already ripened because it is too late to do anything about them. For example, someone might have been born blind as a result of a non-virtuous action such as maliciously injuring someone's eyes in a previous life, but there is no point in their feeling regret for that action now because its effects have already ripened. Developing regret for negative actions that have already ripened only causes us to feel dejected. It is better patiently to accept our misfortune. We should think:

> *I have no choice but to experience these present effects of my past non-virtuous actions; but I will protect myself from such misfortune in the future by not accumulating any more negative karma.*

Feeling regret for previously created virtuous actions is non-virtuous regret. Some Dharma practitioners may develop this kind of regret by, for example, regretting having taken vows, or by becoming unhappy about having commitments, or by regretting having made an offering. For example, if we take the eight Mahayana precepts in the morning, and in the evening feel hungry and develop regret for having taken those precepts, this is non-virtuous regret. We should never develop such regret. Those who have taken ordination have to keep strict moral discipline and this occasionally causes them some inconvenience, but at such times they should not think that it would have been better not to have taken the vows.

Neutral regret is very common. For example, if we eat unhealthy food and then feel ill we regret having eaten it. This is neutral regret. Even though neutral regret is not non-virtuous it is generally better to avoid it because it can lead to unhappiness and serves no useful function. For example, if we start a business that subsequently fails, there is no point in our regretting having started it. Before doing anything we should carefully consider whether it is worthwhile, and whether we are able to carry the action through to completion. This is much better than acting rashly and regretting it later. There is a saying in Tibetan:

The wise person checks carefully beforehand;
The fool feels regret afterwards.

If despite careful planning our actions do not succeed, there is no need to become unhappy or to blame others. We should recognize that this is the result of our past negative actions and willingly accept it.

INVESTIGATION

The definition of investigation is a mental factor that examines an object to gain an understanding of its gross nature.

There are many ways in which we can examine, or search for, an object. For example, we can examine it superficially or in great detail. Usually if we are looking for something we stop searching as soon as we find it. For example, if we are looking for our car we know when we have found it and we do not investigate further, asking questions like 'What exactly is the car?' Only those engaged in philosophical analysis investigate an object in this way. We can all recognize our body quite easily because we have a superficial understanding of it, but only proponents of philosophical tenets who have investigated the body in depth come to conclusions about its ultimate nature. By asking questions like 'Is the body one of its parts or is it the collection of its parts?' we arrive at a conclusion about the real nature of the body. Some conclude that the body is findable, while others, notably the Madhyamika-Prasangikas, conclude that it is unfindable. Realizing the analytical unfindability of the body brings us close to realizing emptiness. This type of investigation is quite different from the investigations we conduct in everyday life.

There are two types of object to be investigated: conventional objects and ultimate objects. First we should investigate conventional objects. These are of many different types: gross, subtle and very subtle natures. For example, a car, its parts, colour and shape are all the gross nature of a car; the car depending upon its parts is the subtle nature of the car; and the car existing as mere name is the very subtle nature of the car. In *Guide to the Middle Way* Chandrakirti says:

> Nominal truths are the method for realizing ultimate truth.

Here, 'ultimate truth' refers to emptiness and 'nominal truths' to all other phenomena.

In general, we should first try to gain a rough understanding of Dharma subjects before analyzing them in great detail. If we try to make a detailed analysis of a subject before having gained a rough generic image of it through the force of investigation, we will definitely encounter difficulties. Therefore, the correct way to proceed with Dharma study is first to try to understand gross objects by relying upon investigation, and then to try to understand subtle objects by relying upon analysis.

ANALYSIS

The definition of analysis is a mental factor that examines an object to gain an understanding of its subtle nature.

After we have understood an object superficially by investigating it, we need to sharpen our wisdom by analyzing the object in greater detail. For example, having attained a rough conceptual understanding of emptiness through investigation we then need to analyze emptiness in great detail to gain a clear and precise generic image of it. With this we can then go on to attain a yogic direct perceiver realizing emptiness.

When we begin to meditate on any object we perceive only a very rough mental image of it, but by continuing to meditate on it with analytical and placement meditation we gradually perceive the object more clearly until eventually we attain complete clear appearance of the object. This occurs when the generic image ceases and our mind transforms into a yogic direct perceiver. By continuing to meditate on the object, this yogic direct perceiver will eventually transform into the uncontaminated mind of a Buddha. The only way to progress from our initial superficial conceptual understanding of an object to the perfect wisdom of a Buddha is to depend upon investigation and analysis.

If we do not engage in analysis our understanding will remain at the level of a correct belief, which is not completely reliable and can be reversed. Therefore, we must engage in analysis to transform our correct beliefs into valid cognizers, and eventually into yogic direct perceivers.

PART TWO

Maintain harmony and joy all the time

Conceptual and
Non-conceptual Minds

From the point of view of how they engage their objects, minds can be divided into two types: conceptual minds and non-conceptual minds. Whereas non-conceptual minds engage their objects directly, conceptual minds engage their objects through the medium of a generic image. Until we become a Buddha we need both conceptual and non-conceptual minds. Even the highest Bodhisattvas, for example, realize the two truths simultaneously only with their conceptual minds.

Some people believe that all conceptual thoughts are bad and should be abandoned. This mistaken view was taught by the eighth-century Chinese monk Hashang, who misunderstood what Buddha taught in the *Perfection of Wisdom Sutras* and believed that the way to meditate on emptiness was simply to empty the mind of all conceptual thoughts. This view still has many adherents today, but if we hold this view we will have no opportunity to progress on the spiritual paths. For one thing, if we prevent conceptual minds from arising we will not be able to remember anything, and as a result all our spiritual development will cease. Moreover, conceptual realizations are the main causes of the realizations of yogic direct perceivers, and without these the attainment of liberation is impossible.

CONCEPTUAL MIND

DEFINITION OF CONCEPTUAL MIND

The definition of conceptual mind is a thought that apprehends its object through a generic image.

Although other scholars have different explanations, this definition is explained by Khedrubje in *Ornament of the Seven Sets*. When we think of or remember an object, say an elephant, there appears to our conceptual mind an object that is the opposite of non-elephant. This appearance is the generic image of elephant. Even though there is no actual elephant in front of us, nevertheless there is a generic image of elephant appearing to our mind. Thus our conceptual mind apprehends elephant through the generic image of elephant. We can apply this to all other phenomena.

There are five types of object: appearing object, observed object, engaged object, apprehended object and conceived object. When we see a table with our eye awareness, for example, that table is the appearing object of our eye awareness because it appears directly to our eye awareness. The table is also the observed object, engaged object and apprehended object of our eye awareness because at that time our eye awareness is focused on the table, understands the table and apprehends the table. However, the table is not a conceived object of our eye awareness because only conceptual minds have conceived objects. For us, non-conceptual minds cannot conceive an object.

When our eye awareness sees a table we may develop the thought 'This is a table.' This thought is a conceptual mind that apprehends the table through a generic image of the table. For this conceptual mind, the table is the observed object, the engaged object, the apprehended object and the conceived object. However, it is not the appearing object of this mind because the appearing object of this conceptual mind is a generic image of the table, not the table itself.

The definition of generic image is the appearing object of a conceptual mind. Although other texts give a different explanation, this definition is Khedrubje's intention. A generic image of an object is like a reflection of that object. When we look in a mirror we see directly the reflection of our face, and through this we know what our actual face looks like. In a similar way, conceptual minds know their object through the appearance of a generic image of that object, not by seeing the object directly. If we speak precisely, we must say that table appears to a conceptual mind apprehending table because the general aspect of table appears to that mind. The general aspect of table and the generic image of table are synonyms. However, table is not the appearing object of a conceptual mind apprehending table. This can be applied to all other objects.

As with other types of mind, the nature of conceptual mind is clarity that completely lacks form and possesses the power to perceive objects. However, its function is different from that of other types of mind. The principal function of conceptual mind is to impute names by thinking 'This is a table', 'This is a chair', 'I am Peter', 'He is John', and so on. All phenomena are merely imputed by conceptual mind in this way.

Another function of conceptual mind is to find the object of meditation. Whenever we meditate we first need to find the object on which we are going to meditate. This means trying to perceive clearly the generic image of the object of meditation, and this is achieved by conceptual mind. Moreover, the root of meditation is to maintain mindfulness, which means to hold the object without forgetting it, and for us this is also a function of conceptual thought because our non-conceptual mind cannot do this.

When we first realize the ultimate nature of phenomena, emptiness, we do so with our conceptual mind. If we then meditate repeatedly on this conceptual realization, eventually we will realize emptiness directly. At that time our conceptual realization will transform into a yogic direct perceiver realizing emptiness directly, which is the direct antidote to the delusions. It is through this yogic direct perceiver that we will be released from the ocean of samsaric sufferings.

DIVISIONS OF CONCEPTUAL MIND

There are three types of conceptual mind:

1 Conceptual minds that perceive the generic image of an object mainly through the force of listening or reading
2 Conceptual minds that perceive the generic image of an object mainly through the force of contemplating the meaning of that object
3 Conceptual minds that perceive the generic image of an object mainly through the force of previous imprints

An example of the first type is a thought perceiving an appearance of the opposite of non-yeti that develops mainly through the force of listening to someone else explaining about yetis. Other examples can be understood from this. An example of the second type is a thought perceiving an appearance of the opposite of non-yeti that develops mainly through the force of our own contemplation of yetis after listening to an explanation about them. Again, other examples can be understood from this. Examples of the third type are all natural conceptual thoughts, such as innate self-grasping and other innate delusions.

There is also a twofold division of conceptual mind:

1 Correct conceptual minds
2 Wrong conceptual minds

The first includes all conceptual minds whose conceived objects exist, such as conceptual minds conceiving pen, paper and so forth; and the second includes all conceptual minds whose conceived objects do not exist, such as a conceptual mind conceiving a reflection of a face to be an actual face, a mind of self-grasping, or a conceptual mind conceiving karma, reincarnation or enlightened beings to be non-existent.

GENERATION OF CONCEPTUAL MINDS

There are three ways in which conceptual minds are generated: through the force of hearing names, through the force of contemplating and through the force of previous imprints. These can be understood from the previous explanation of the three types of conceptual mind.

APPLICATION OF CONCEPTUAL MINDS TO DHARMA PRACTICE

It is very important to distinguish conceptual minds that are harmful and to be abandoned from those that are beneficial and to be cultivated. Although there are countless wrong thoughts and attitudes, there are sixteen in particular that we should know and strive to abandon because they directly prevent realizations of the stages of the path. They are:

(1) Disliking or having disrespect for our Spiritual Guide
(2) Not wishing to take the real meaning of our precious human life

(3) Not remembering death

(4) Being attached to the pleasures and happiness of this life alone

(5) Not fearing rebirth in the lower realms

(6) Not wishing to go for refuge to the Three Jewels

(7) Not having faith or conviction in the laws of karma

(8) Seeking to accumulate non-virtuous actions and not virtuous actions

(9) Regarding samsara as having the nature of happiness

(10) Wishing to increase delusions and contaminated actions

(11) Being uninterested in attaining liberation

(12) Not wanting to practise the three higher trainings, which are the causes of liberation

(13) Forsaking mother living beings

(14) Self-cherishing

(15) Self-grasping

(16) Disliking the practice of Secret Mantra

Corresponding to these there are sixteen correct thoughts and attitudes that we need to cultivate:

(1) Relying faithfully upon and having respect for our Spiritual Guide

(2) Wishing to take the real meaning of our precious human life

(3) Remembering death

(4) Not being attached to the pleasures and happiness of this life

(5) Fearing rebirth in the lower realms

(6) Wishing to go for refuge to the Three Jewels

(7) Having faith and conviction in the laws of karma

   (8) Seeking to accumulate virtuous actions and not non-virtuous actions

   (9) Regarding samsara as having the nature of suffering

  (10) Wishing to abandon delusions and contaminated actions, which are the causes of samsaric rebirth

  (11) Being determined to attain liberation

  (12) Wanting to practise the three higher trainings

  (13) Cherishing all mother living beings

  (14) Forsaking self-cherishing

  (15) Realizing selflessness

  (16) Liking the practice of Secret Mantra

We should try to understand all these conceptual minds well by studying authentic explanations such as those given in *Joyful Path of Good Fortune*, and then, based on this understanding, make a strong determination to abandon the sixteen wrong thoughts and cultivate the sixteen correct thoughts. Then we should put this determination into practice.

NON-CONCEPTUAL MIND

DEFINITION OF NON-CONCEPTUAL MIND

The definition of non-conceptual mind is a cognizer to which its object appears clearly without being mixed with a generic image.

DIVISIONS OF NON-CONCEPTUAL MIND

There are two types of non-conceptual mind:

1 Sense awarenesses
2 Non-conceptual mental awarenesses

All sense awarenesses are non-conceptual minds, but mental awarenesses can be either conceptual or non-conceptual. Conceptual mental awareness and conceptual mind are synonyms.

There are three types of non-conceptual mental awareness:

1 Non-conceptual mental direct perceivers
2 Yogic direct perceivers
3 Non-conceptual mental awarenesses that are neither of these two

An example of the first is a mental direct perceiver to which a form appears clearly without being mixed with a generic image, such as eye clairvoyance. An example of the second is a direct perceiver realizing emptiness. An example of the third is a dream eye awareness that apprehends a dream mountain as an actual mountain. This is not an actual eye awareness because eye awareness does not exist during sleep. As Chandrakirti says in *Guide to the Middle Way:*

> Because eye awareness is impossible in sleep, it does
>   not exist;
> Only mental awareness exists.

This means that since there can be no sense awareness, such as eye awareness, during sleep, dream objects that are objects of sense awareness do not exist. Only mental awareness exists during sleep. Therefore, dream eye awareness, ear awareness, nose awareness, tongue awareness and body awareness are mental awarenesses; and because their objects appear clearly to them, without being mixed with a generic image, they are non-conceptual mental awarenesses.

It should be noted at this point that if an object appears clearly to a mind, that mind is not necessarily non-conceptual.

For example, some conceptual minds that are clear and strong concentrations perceive their object clearly but, because they are conceptual minds, their object is perceived through the medium of a generic image of that object.

There is another twofold division of non-conceptual mind:

1 Correct non-conceptual minds
2 Wrong non-conceptual minds

A correct non-conceptual mind is a non-conceptual mind whose apprehended object exists. All sense direct perceivers are correct non-conceptual minds. Also, in general, dream eye, ear, nose, tongue and body awarenesses are correct non-conceptual minds because they are non-conceptual minds and their apprehended objects exist. For non-conceptual minds, apprehended object and appearing object are synonyms. A dream mountain that appears to a dream eye awareness, therefore, exists. It is a form that is a phenomena source, and is like a reflection of a mountain. Dream things cannot be objects of sense awareness but only of mental awareness; therefore they are phenomena sources.

Non-conceptual minds such as an eye awareness apprehending a toy snake as a real snake, or an ear awareness apprehending an echo as the actual sound of speech, are wrong non-conceptual minds because they are non-conceptual minds and their apprehended objects do not exist.

GENERATION OF NON-CONCEPTUAL MINDS

All non-conceptual minds are included within sense awarenesses and non-conceptual mental awarenesses. All five sense awarenesses are generated from their own previous continuum and the meeting of their particular sense power with a corresponding sense object. Non-conceptual mental awarenesses are generated from their own previous continuum and their dominant condition, the mental power.

APPLICATION OF NON-CONCEPTUAL MINDS TO DHARMA PRACTICE

At present we cannot use our non-conceptual mental awareness in our daily activities. The only non-conceptual awarenesses we can use are our sense awarenesses. Although our sense awarenesses are not our I, nevertheless when they see a form, hear a sound, and so on, we say 'I saw such and such', 'I heard such and such', and so on. If we use our sense awarenesses for virtuous activities we will experience beneficial results and develop good qualities, but if we use them for non-virtuous activities we will experience suffering and problems. Knowing this, we should make a determination not to use our sense awarenesses for non-virtuous purposes but to use them only for virtuous purposes. Then we should put this determination into practice.

One special way of using our sense awarenesses for virtuous purposes that is explained in the *Perfection of Wisdom Sutras* is, whenever we see visual forms, hear sounds, smell odours, experience tastes or touch tactile objects, immediately to recognize that these sense objects lack true existence. By familiarizing ourself with this recognition we will gradually reduce our attachment, anger and other delusions, and especially our self-grasping.

Sense and Mental Awarenesses

From the point of view of their uncommon dominant condition, minds can be divided into two types: sense awarenesses and mental awarenesses.

SENSE AWARENESS

DEFINITION OF SENSE AWARENESS

The definition of sense awareness is an awareness that is developed in dependence upon its uncommon dominant condition, a sense power possessing form.

As with other minds, the nature of sense awareness is clarity, but it has different functions from other types of mind. The principal functions of sense awareness are seeing visual forms, hearing sounds, and experiencing odours, tastes and tactile objects. There are five sense awarenesses, which are called the 'awarenesses of the five doors'. The five doors are the eyes, ears, nose, tongue and body. In dependence upon their respective doors, eye awareness sees visual forms, ear awareness hears sounds, and so on.

Insofar as they permit us to read and listen to Dharma instructions, sense awarenesses are useful for our Dharma practice, but from the point of view of their obstructing our meditation and concentration they are quite harmful. If a sense awareness manifests when we are meditating on an object single-pointedly it immediately disturbs our concentration by causing distraction to other objects. It is like a sharp thorn sticking into our flesh. This is why many meditators who are emphasizing the attainment of tranquil abiding develop renunciation for sense awarenesses.

As a result of having developed renunciation for sense awarenesses in their previous lives, form and formless realm beings have no sense awarenesses of their own. Form realm beings, for example, can see forms and hear sounds, but they do so by using desire realm eye awareness and ear awareness in much the same way as we see distant forms by using binoculars and hear distant sounds by using a telephone. They have no need of nose awareness, tongue awareness or body awareness at all because they do not need to enjoy smells, taste food and drink, or experience tactile objects. Instead they derive continuous enjoyment from the inner food of the suppleness of concentration.

DIVISIONS OF SENSE AWARENESS

There are five types of sense awareness: eye awareness, ear awareness, nose awareness, tongue awareness and body awareness. There are also five sense objects: visual forms, sounds, smells, tastes and tactile objects. The definition of eye awareness is an awareness that is developed in dependence upon its uncommon dominant condition, an eye sense power. This definition can be applied to the other four sense awarenesses by changing the uncommon dominant condition to the ear sense power, the nose sense power, the tongue sense power, or the body sense power.

The eye sense power is an inner energy power abiding in the very centre of the eye organ that functions directly to generate eye awareness. The ear sense power is an inner energy power abiding in the very centre of the ear organ that functions directly to generate ear awareness. The remaining sense powers can be understood in the same way. The eye sense power itself is not form, but it possesses form. This is similar to a person. Persons are not form but they possess form, namely their form aggregate, their body.

It is said that the eye sense power is a very hidden object. The Buddhist schools of the Vaibhashikas and the Sautrantikas believe that it is form. They say that it is a very clear lucid form located in the centre of the eye organ in which visual forms are reflected. However, the Madhyamika schools reject this assertion.

Sense consciousnesses are primary minds. Their retinues of secondary minds, or mental factors, are sense awarenesses but not sense consciousnesses. Consciousness and primary mind are synonyms.

GENERATION OF SENSE AWARENESSES

Sense awarenesses are generated in dependence upon two conditions – their dominant condition and their immediate condition.

The definition of dominant condition of sense awareness is that which principally assists in the development of a sense awareness. There are two types of dominant condition: common dominant condition and uncommon dominant condition. For our eye awareness the common dominant condition is light. We cannot see any objects with our eye awareness if it is dark, therefore light is a necessary condition for eye awareness. It is called a 'common dominant condition' because it is common to everyone. The uncommon dominant condition of eye awareness is the eye sense power. This is said to be uncommon because it is specific to each person.

Different types of being have different types of eye sense power. For example, a human eye sense power needs a considerable amount of light to function well, whereas a cat's eye sense power functions equally well in both light and dark, and an owl's eye sense power is particularly suited to the dark.

A particular sense power can give rise only to its particular sense awareness. Thus, the eye sense power, for example, can give rise only to eye awareness. However, in *Close Placement of Mindfulness Sutra* Buddha says that snakes have a special eye sense power that enables them to hear sounds with their eye awareness. Light is not a necessary condition for hearing, and so even though they use their eyes to hear, they can hear in the dark. The eye awareness of a Buddha can see, hear, taste, smell and touch.

The immediate condition of an eye awareness apprehending a form is a mental consciousness that develops immediately before that eye awareness and that is the same continuum as that eye awareness. It exists simultaneously with the eye sense power.

According to the Sautrantikas, sense and mental awarenesses also have an observed object condition, which must be both an observed object of that awareness and a cause of that awareness. For them, blue is both the observed object of an eye awareness apprehending blue and a cause of that awareness, and so blue is the observed object condition of an eye awareness apprehending blue.

The Chittamatrins do not assert observed object conditions because they believe that a mind and its object arise simultaneously from the same seed. Thus, they say that an object cannot be a cause of the mind that apprehends it because it is the same entity as that mind. According to the schools that assert observed object conditions, an object is a cause of the mind that apprehends it and is therefore a different entity to that mind, but for the Chittamatrins this difference in entity between an object and the mind that apprehends it is the principal object to be negated.

APPLICATION OF SENSE AWARENESSES
TO DHARMA PRACTICE

This can be understood from the previous explanation of the application of non-conceptual minds to Dharma practice.

MENTAL AWARENESS

DEFINITION OF MENTAL AWARENESS

The definition of mental awareness is an awareness that is developed in dependence upon its uncommon dominant condition, a mental power.

The definition of mental power is a mentality that principally functions directly to produce the uncommon aspect of a mental awareness. For example, after the last moment of an eye consciousness apprehending blue we usually develop a mental direct perceiver directly apprehending blue. This is a mental awareness. Its dominant condition, a mental power, is the last moment of the eye consciousness apprehending blue. This eye consciousness is a mentality because it is a primary mind. It directly produces the uncommon aspect of a mental direct perceiver directly apprehending blue, which is its apprehending blue and not non-blue. After the last moment of the mental direct perceiver directly apprehending blue we usually develop a conceptual awareness thinking 'This is blue.' The dominant condition of this conceptual mental awareness is the last moment of the mental direct perceiver directly apprehending blue. All other mental awarenesses can be understood in the same way.

DIVISIONS OF MENTAL AWARENESS

There are two types of mental awareness:

1 Conceptual mental awarenesses
2 Non-conceptual mental awarenesses

Conceptual mental awareness and conceptual mind are synonymous. Examples of non-conceptual mental awareness are dream sense awarenesses apprehending dream objects and a wisdom directly realizing emptiness.

There is also a threefold division of mental awareness:

1 Non-virtuous mental awarenesses
2 Virtuous mental awarenesses
3 Neutral mental awarenesses

Within mental awareness, deluded mental awarenesses – such as covetousness, harmful thought, wrong view, anger and jealousy – are non-virtuous mental awarenesses. All non-virtue arises from delusions, and delusions arise from four causes: the root, the seed, the object and inappropriate attention. The root of all delusions is self-grasping; the seed of a delusion is a potential left on the mental continuum by similar delusions in the past that acts as the substantial cause of that delusion; the object is any contaminated object; and inappropriate attention is a mental factor that focuses on the object in a mistaken way and acts as a co-operative cause of delusions. For a delusion to arise, all four causes are necessary.

Some people believe that delusions are caused by bodily vigour because their delusions seem to be stronger when their vital energies increase, and so to reduce their delusions they try to weaken their body by engaging in harsh ascetic practices such as fasting and exposing their body to extremes of heat and cold. In reality, however, the causes of delusions exist within the mind, not the body. For this reason Nagarjuna said that physical asceticism is not very important. To overcome delusions we need the mental asceticism of practices such as meditation and patience.

The easiest way to prevent delusions from arising is to stop inappropriate attention by not allowing our mind to dwell on and exaggerate the attractive or unattractive features of contaminated objects. In this way we will be able temporarily to prevent delusions. However, to eradicate them completely we must abandon their root, self-grasping, by attaining a yogic direct perceiver realizing emptiness. Once we have attained a direct realization of emptiness, we will gradually eradicate the seeds of all the delusions. We eradicate the seeds of all intellectually-formed delusions on the path of seeing, and the seeds all innate delusions on the path of meditation.

Nagarjuna said that minds can be like writing in stone, writing in sand, or writing in water. Minds that are like writing in stone are deeply ingrained and difficult to remove; those that are like writing in sand can be removed more easily; and those that are like writing in water disappear naturally almost as soon as they arise. At present, our deluded minds are like writing in stone and our virtuous minds are like writing in water. We should try to reverse this situation. It is difficult to stop delusions completely but if we conscientiously apply their opponents we can gradually weaken them so that they are no longer engraved in our mind like writing in stone. At first they will become like writing in sand, which can be removed with little effort, and then gradually as their strength continues to diminish they will become like writing in water. Eventually they will disappear altogether.

As for virtuous mental awarenesses, these include all the stages of the path to enlightenment from respect for our Spiritual Guide to superior seeing. All virtuous minds arise from four causes: imprints, the object, appropriate attention and the empowering blessings of the Buddhas. Although all sentient beings have at least some virtuous imprints, those who have very few find it extremely difficult to generate virtuous minds, while those who have very rich imprints develop virtuous minds naturally. The objects from which virtuous minds develop are the Three Jewels and their representations – such as our Spiritual Guide and our spiritual friends. Appropriate attention is a mental factor attention possessing a special way of thinking that acts as a co-operative cause for a virtuous mind. The fourth cause, the empowering blessings of the Buddhas, is a little more difficult to understand. It is said that all the virtuous minds of sentient beings are the result of the enlightened activities of the Buddhas. The two principal ways in which Buddhas help sentient beings are by giving teachings and by blessing their minds. Without the blessings of the Buddhas it is impossible for a virtuous mind to arise. All sentient beings have at some time or another received Buddha's blessings. It is almost impossible for animals to develop virtuous thoughts on their own but there are many cases of animals naturally developing virtuous thoughts as a result of receiving Buddha's blessings. If this happens at the time of their death they will take a rebirth in one of the higher realms. As with deluded minds, all four causes are necessary for a virtuous mind to develop.

A neutral mental awareness is a thought with neither a virtuous nor a non-virtuous motivation – for example simply wishing to eat or to go for a walk.

GENERATION OF MENTAL AWARENESSES

Mental awareness is generated in dependence upon two conditions: the dominant condition and the immediate condition. The dominant condition of a mental awareness is a mental power. The immediate condition of a mental awareness is an awareness whose principal function is to produce directly the nature of a mental awareness. For example, the nature of a mental awareness apprehending blue is the clarity of that awareness. This nature is produced by its immediate condition, which is the same continuum as that awareness. In summary, mental awareness is generated from the meeting of its dominant condition and its immediate condition.

APPLICATION OF MENTAL AWARENESSES TO
DHARMA PRACTICE

The practice of meditation depends almost entirely upon mental awareness because we cannot contemplate or meditate with our sense awarenesses. Initially our meditation is conceptual mental awareness but gradually it becomes non-conceptual mental awareness. Moreover, all virtuous actions of body and speech are initiated by virtuous mental awareness. We should practise the methods for cultivating virtuous mental awarenesses that are explained in the Lamrim teachings. In this way we will be able to reduce, and eventually completely abandon, all non-virtuous mental awarenesses.

Take the precious jewels of wisdom and compassion
from the treasure vase of Kadam Dharma

Direct Perceivers

The mind can also be divided into seven types:

1 Direct perceivers
2 Subsequent cognizers
3 Re-cognizers
4 Correct beliefs
5 Non-ascertaining perceivers
6 Non-deluded doubt
7 Wrong awarenesses

All minds are included in this sevenfold division. The main purpose of explaining this is to enable us to understand how we can become a Superior being, a Yogi, by attaining yogic direct perceivers.

DIRECT PERCEIVERS

DEFINITION OF DIRECT PERCEIVER

The definition of direct perceiver is a cognizer that apprehends its object correctly and directly.

All sense awarenesses and mental awarenesses that apprehend their objects correctly and directly are direct perceivers.

DIVISIONS OF DIRECT PERCEIVER

There are three types of direct perceiver:

1 Sense direct perceivers
2 Mental direct perceivers
3 Yogic direct perceivers

SENSE DIRECT PERCEIVERS

DEFINITION OF SENSE DIRECT PERCEIVER

The definition of sense direct perceiver is a direct perceiver that is generated in dependence upon its uncommon dominant condition, a sense power possessing form.

Examples of sense direct perceivers are an eye consciousness seeing blue, an ear consciousness hearing a sound, and so on. Although all sense awarenesses are non-conceptual minds, they are not necessarily sense direct perceivers. For example, wrong sense awarenesses such as an eye awareness that, under the influence of the drug datura, sees the earth as yellow, or one that due to an eye disease sees snowy mountains as having a bluish colour, are not sense direct perceivers.

DIVISIONS OF SENSE DIRECT PERCEIVER

Because there are five types of sense object, there are five types of sense direct perceiver: eye sense direct perceivers, ear sense direct perceivers, and so on. These are distinguished by their uncommon dominant condition and their object. Eye sense direct perceivers, for example, are produced from an eye sense power as their uncommon dominant condition and have visual forms as their objects; ear sense direct perceivers are generated in dependence upon an ear sense power and have sounds as their objects; and so on. The remaining types of sense direct perceiver can be understood in the same way.

There is also a threefold division of sense direct perceiver:

1 Sense direct perceivers that are valid cognizers but not re-cognizers
2 Sense direct perceivers that are both valid cognizers and re-cognizers
3 Sense direct perceivers that are non-ascertaining perceivers

An example of the first type is the first moment of a sense awareness apprehending any of the five sense objects – forms, sounds, smells, tastes and tactile objects. Such minds are not re-cognizers because they realize their object through their own power. All Buddhas' sense and mental direct perceivers are valid cognizers that are not re-cognizers because Buddhas have no re-cognizers. Examples of the second type are the second and subsequent moments of a sense awareness apprehending any of the five sense objects. These are re-cognizers because they realize their object through the power of the first moment of that awareness. The object of the first, second and subsequent moments of such a sense direct perceiver is the same, but the way of realizing it is different. Examples of the third type, sense direct perceivers that are non-ascertaining perceivers, are the eye awareness of a new-born baby seeing its father's face, and an eye awareness seeing unfamiliar faces in a crowd.

GENERATION OF SENSE DIRECT PERCEIVERS

All phenomena are included within both the twelve sources and the eighteen elements. The twelve sources are the six object sources – visual form source, sound source, smell source, taste source, tactile object source and phenomena source; and the six power sources – eye source, ear source, nose source, tongue source, body source and mentality source. These twelve are called 'sources' because generally they are the sources of consciousness. The first six are objects that are sources of consciousness, and the second six are powers, or uncommon dominant conditions, that are sources of consciousness. Within the six object sources, phenomena source comprises objects that appear only to mental awareness.

The eighteen elements are the twelve sources plus their effects, the six consciousnesses – eye consciousness, ear consciousness, nose consciousness, tongue consciousness, body consciousness and mental consciousness. When a visual form source and an eye source meet, an eye consciousness develops; when a sound source and an ear source meet, an ear consciousness develops; when a phenomena source and a mentality source meet, mental consciousness develops; and so on.

An ear consciousness, for example, develops only when a sound and an ear sense power meet. If someone shoots a pistol in the distance we do not hear the shot as soon as it is fired because it takes time for the sound to reach us. Thus, we do not develop an ear consciousness apprehending that sound until the sound and the ear sense power have met. Similarly, if we look at the moon, an eye consciousness apprehending the moon develops when light from the moon meets our eye sense power. For mental awareness to develop it is not necessary for an object and the mental power to meet. Thus, we can think of the moon without the moon being present before us. Distance does not prevent an object from appearing clearly to a mental awareness, but to perceive distant things clearly with a sense awareness we need to use special devices such as telescopes, or to have clairvoyance.

Due to karma, sentient beings have different sense powers and can therefore perceive different objects. Thus, beings of the desire realm have contaminated sense powers with which they experience the five contaminated objects of desire – forms, sounds, and so on. We can enjoy these objects only because we have these sense powers. If we purify our sense powers we can attain certain types of clairvoyance, such as the clairvoyance of the fleshly eye, with which subtle and distant visual forms beyond the range of ordinary vision can be seen with the eyes.

To develop a sense direct perceiver a non-defective sense power and a non-deceptive sense object must meet. An example of a defective sense power is the eye sense power of a person suffering from jaundice that causes that person to see things as yellow. An example of a deceptive object is a whirling incense stick that appears to be a circle of light. If both the object and the sense power are free from such faults, a sense direct perceiver will be generated when they meet.

APPLICATION OF SENSE DIRECT PERCEIVERS TO DHARMA PRACTICE

Whenever our eye sense direct perceivers see attractive, un-attractive or neutral forms, or our ear sense direct perceivers hear pleasant, unpleasant or neutral remarks, and so on, we must prevent attachment, anger and confusion from arising within our mind by not allowing inappropriate attention to develop with respect to these objects. This is a great Dharma practice that we can practise during our daily activities. It is called 'restraining the sense doors'. It is very important to emphasize this practice if we want to be able to meditate without distractions.

MENTAL DIRECT PERCEIVERS

DEFINITION OF MENTAL DIRECT PERCEIVER

The definition of mental direct perceiver is a direct perceiver that is generated in dependence upon its uncommon dominant condition, a mental power.

DIVISIONS OF MENTAL DIRECT PERCEIVER

There are three types of mental direct perceiver:

1 Mental direct perceivers induced by sense direct perceivers
2 Mental direct perceivers induced by meditation
3 Mental direct perceivers that are induced neither by sense direct perceivers nor by meditation

There are five types of mental direct perceiver induced by sense direct perceivers: these are mental direct perceivers apprehending forms, sounds, smells, tastes and tactile objects. These five mental direct perceivers are very hidden phenomena, and because their duration is just one instant they are extremely difficult to recognize. For example, after an eye awareness apprehending blue has developed we usually develop a conceptual mind that thinks 'This is blue', and between these two minds we also develop a mental direct perceiver apprehending blue. This mental direct perceiver is induced by a sense direct perceiver, but it is difficult to recognize because its duration is just one instant.

An example of a mental direct perceiver induced by meditation is a mental direct perceiver that realizes emptiness directly.

Mental direct perceivers that are induced neither by sense direct perceivers nor by meditation are types of clairvoyance that because of karma see things beyond ordinary sight, hear very distant sounds or see some future things.

APPLICATION OF MENTAL DIRECT PERCEIVERS
TO DHARMA PRACTICE

If we are to gain authentic Dharma realizations that have the power actually to remove suffering we need to develop mental direct perceivers induced by meditation. In *King of Concentration Sutra* Buddha says:

> Just as we cannot quench our thirst by listening to the sound of water and watching it flow past, so we cannot overcome our suffering simply by listening to teachings on emptiness and understanding them intellectually, without meditating on them.

The main point of this quotation is that once we have developed some understanding of Dharma through sincere study, we then need to familiarize our mind with this understanding by meditating on it repeatedly. Only then will we be able to gain deep realizations that will enable us to pacify our suffering and overcome our problems.

YOGIC DIRECT PERCEIVERS

DEFINITION OF YOGIC DIRECT PERCEIVER

The definition of yogic direct perceiver is a direct perceiver that realizes the true nature of phenomena directly, in dependence upon its uncommon dominant condition, a concentration that is a union of tranquil abiding and superior seeing.

Someone who has the realization of a yogic direct perceiver is called a 'Yogi', or Superior being. Because we do not realize the true nature of phenomena we remain an ordinary being who abides in the deep ocean of samsara, experiencing suffering continuously without end. However, with the wisdom of a yogic direct perceiver we will become a Superior being, a Yogi, who abides in the blissful ocean of tranquil abiding and superior seeing absorbed in emptiness, and we will be free from samsara's problems permanently. Understanding this we should make the determination to train in yogic direct perceivers. The object of training in yogic direct perceivers is the emptiness of all phenomena, the mere absence of all phenomena that we normally see or perceive. How to train in yogic direct perceivers will be explained below in the chapter on meditation.

DIVISIONS OF YOGIC DIRECT PERCEIVER

All yogic direct perceivers are included within two types:

1 Yogic direct perceivers in the continuum of Hinayanists
2 Yogic direct perceivers in the continuum of Mahayanists

There is also a threefold division of yogic direct perceiver:

1 Yogic direct perceivers that are paths of seeing
2 Yogic direct perceivers that are paths of meditation
3 Yogic direct perceivers that are Paths of No More Learning

GENERATION OF YOGIC DIRECT PERCEIVERS

Although yogic direct perceivers are non-conceptual minds, the way that they are generated is quite unlike the way that other non-conceptual minds, such as sense awarenesses, are generated. For example, a yogic direct perceiver is generated as follows. First we listen to teachings on emptiness and develop a correct belief that all phenomena we normally see or perceive do not exist. Then, through contemplating conclusive reasons, we develop a subsequent cognizer realizing emptiness, the mere absence of all phenomena that we normally see. This is our first valid cognizer realizing emptiness, and the first mental abiding.

By placing our mind single-pointedly on this emptiness we then gradually progress through the other mental abidings until we attain tranquil abiding. At this point we have a very vivid and powerful experience of emptiness, but we have still not realized it directly. Our mind is still a conceptual mind that apprehends its object through a generic image. Before we can realize emptiness directly without a generic image we first need to attain superior seeing observing emptiness. Thus, we continue meditating on emptiness with a concentration of tranquil abiding until we attain the special wisdom of superior seeing observing emptiness. At this stage our mind is still conceptual, and emptiness still appears to our mind mixed with a generic image. If we continue to meditate on emptiness with a union of the concentration of tranquil abiding and the wisdom of superior seeing, the generic image will gradually fade until it disappears altogether and emptiness appears directly to our mind.

This mind directly realizing emptiness that is generated in dependence upon the union of tranquil abiding and superior seeing is a yogic direct perceiver. All the previous concentrations from the second mental abiding up to just before attaining the yogic direct perceiver are re-cognizers.

APPLICATION OF YOGIC DIRECT PERCEIVERS TO DHARMA PRACTICE

Yogic direct perceivers are essential for our spiritual development because without them we cannot realize emptiness directly and thereby attain liberation. However, since we cannot attain yogic direct perceivers until we become Superior beings, or Yogis, we may wonder how we can apply them to our present Dharma practice. The way to do this is to meditate on facsimiles of yogic direct perceivers. We do this whenever we engage in correct conceptual meditation on emptiness with the motivation of attaining yogic direct perceivers. Even though to begin with we may attain only a very rough generic image of the object, if we do the meditation repeatedly with a strong motivation to attain a yogic direct perceiver we will sow the seeds for the object to appear more and more clearly, and create the cause to attain an actual yogic direct perceiver in the future.

Subsequent Cognizers

A subsequent cognizer means a mind that realizes its object after listening to or contemplating conclusive reasons.

DEFINITION OF SUBSEQUENT COGNIZER

The definition of subsequent cognizer is a completely reliable cognizer whose object is realized in direct dependence upon a conclusive reason.

There are three types of object: manifest objects, slightly hidden objects and deeply hidden objects. In general, manifest objects are phenomena such as visual forms and sounds that can be perceived directly by ordinary beings; slightly hidden objects are phenomena such as impermanence and emptiness that can be known initially only by depending upon a conclusive reason; and deeply hidden objects are phenomena such as the specific workings of the laws of karma that can be perceived directly only by Buddhas. However, these three types of object are relative. Thus hell beings, for example, are deeply hidden phenomena from the human viewpoint, but manifest objects from the viewpoint of hell beings themselves. Manifest objects can be realized initially by direct cognizers, but both types of hidden object can be realized initially only by subsequent cognizers. Some books use the words 'inferential cognizer' instead of 'subsequent cognizer', but the meaning is the same.

Subsequent cognizers are very common, and we normally have many during each day. For example, if we see a person go into a room that has only one entrance, and not leave by that entrance, we know with certainty that he is still in the room even though we cannot see him. Similarly, if we see smoke billowing from the chimney of a house, we know for certain that there is a fire in the house even though we cannot see the fire directly. These are both examples of subsequent cognizers that realize their object in dependence upon conclusive reasons. Most scientific and historical knowledge is based on subsequent cognizers. For example, if an archaeologist finds a few bones, broken pots and stone tools, he or she can infer many things about the life of the people to whom they originally belonged and, provided that he does not go beyond the evidence, his knowledge will be reliable.

There is one philosophical school, known as the Charavakas, that denies the existence of hidden objects and asserts that everything that exists can be realized directly by ordinary sense awarenesses. Thus, they do not accept subsequent cognizers, and they deny that we can have reliable knowledge of anything that does not appear directly to one of our five sense awarenesses. This view is obviously incorrect because it is refuted by our everyday experiences. For example, if we stir sugar into tea we can know that the tea will be sweet without having to taste it to find out. Similarly, if we see a car we can know with certainty that there must have been a person or group of persons who manufactured it even though we may never have seen them ourself. We know these facts because we realize them with subsequent cognizers.

Subsequent cognizers are very important for our spiritual practice. Most of the essential topics explained in Dharma are hidden objects that can be realized initially only through subsequent cognizers. Once we have realized these objects with a subsequent cognizer, if we continue to meditate on them we will eventually realize them directly, and then they will become manifest objects for us. There are some objects that are not presently manifest for us but that would become manifest for us if we were simply to move to a different position or just wait for something to happen. For example, we can establish that there is a fire inside a house simply by entering the house to have a look, or we can discover that a candle will eventually burn down simply by waiting for it to do so; but we cannot establish the existence of subtle objects such as emptiness in this way. The only way we can gain incontrovertible knowledge of these objects is by generating subsequent cognizers in dependence upon conclusive reasons.

Whenever we realize something by means of a conclusive reason we use a special form of logical reasoning known as a 'syllogism'. An example of such syllogistic reasoning is, 'There is a fire in the house because there is smoke.' Like all syllogisms this has three parts – a subject, a predicate and a reason. The subject is 'in the house', the predicate is 'there is a fire', and the reason is 'because there is smoke.' The combination of the subject and the predicate is known as the 'probandum'. In this case the probandum is 'There is a fire in the house', and it is this that we realize in dependence upon the reason.

A conclusive reason is a reason that is able to establish a probandum incontrovertibly. A conclusive reason must have a definite relationship with the predicate. Generally there are two types of relationship – natural relationships and causal relationships. A natural relationship obtains between objects that have the same entity, or nature. For example, there is a natural relationship between dog and animal because a dog is an animal. Similarly there is a natural relationship between re-cognizer and valid cognizer because whatever is a re-cognizer is necessarily a valid cognizer. A causal relationship obtains between objects when one is the cause of the other. Thus, causal relationships exist between acorn and oak tree, fire and smoke, and eye sense power and eye aware-ness. Because there are two types of relationship there are also two types of reason – those based on a natural relation-ship (which are known as 'nature reasons'), and those based on a causal relationship (which are known as 'effect reasons'). Examples of the first are the reason in the statement 'This white dog is an animal because it is a dog', and the reason in the statement 'The second moment of a subsequent cognizer is a valid cognizer because it is a re-cognizer.' Examples of the second are the reason in the statement 'There is a fire in the house because there is smoke' and the reason in the statement 'A newborn baby's mind must have arisen from its previous continuum of awareness because it is a mind.'

The definition of conclusive reason is a reason that is qualified by the three modes. The three modes are: the property of the subject, the forward pervasion, and the reverse pervasion; and any conclusive reason will be qualified by all three. We can understand these three modes by considering the syllogism stated above, 'There is a fire in the house because there is smoke.'

The first mode is called the 'property of the subject' because for a reason to be conclusive it must apply to, or be a property of, the subject. In this case, the reason is a property of the subject because there is smoke (reason) in the house (subject). The second mode is called the 'forward pervasion' because for a reason to be a conclusive reason it must be per-vaded by the predicate. In this case, the reason is qualified by the second mode because wherever there is smoke (reason), there is fire (predicate). The third mode is called the 'reverse pervasion' because if the predicate does not apply the reason must also not apply. In this case, the reason is qualified by the third mode because if there is no fire there is no smoke.

If a reason lacks any of the three modes it is not a con-clusive reason. Thus, if we were to say 'There is a fire in the house because there is a chimney', the reason would not be a conclusive reason because it would not be qualified by the second and third modes. Similarly the statement 'There is a fire in the house because fire is hot' also does not have a conclusive reason.

By considering examples like the one used here we can learn to identify the different components of a syllogism and to understand the three modes of a conclusive reason. Then once we understand these we can apply them to our Dharma practice. For example, to realize the emptiness of our body we must first generate subsequent cognizers of it. Thus, to realize that our body is empty of inherent existence we can begin by contemplating the syllogism, 'My body is empty of inherent existence because, when I search for it with wisdom, it disappears like a mirage.' This reasoning is correct because the reason used is a conclusive reason. It is qualified by the first mode because our body disappears when we search for it with wisdom; it is qualified by the second mode because whatever disappears when we search for it with wisdom is necessarily empty of inherent existence; and it is qualified by the third mode because if something were not empty of inherent existence it would necessarily not disappear when we search for it with wisdom.

DIVISIONS OF SUBSEQUENT COGNIZER

There are three types of subsequent cognizer from the point of view of the type of reason upon which they depend:

1 Subsequent cognizers through the power of fact
2 Subsequent cognizers through belief
3 Subsequent cognizers through renown

Subsequent cognizers through the power of fact realize slightly hidden objects. Examples are a subsequent cognizer realizing that there is a fire in a house because there is smoke, and a subsequent cognizer realizing that the body is impermanent because it disintegrates. Most of our subsequent cognizers are of this type. We gain initial realizations of impermanence, emptiness, pervasive suffering, and so forth through such subsequent cognizers.

Subsequent cognizers through belief realize deeply hidden objects such as the specific law of karma that from giving comes wealth and from discipline comes happiness. Sentient beings cannot prove the existence of such deeply hidden objects through their own direct experience or through subsequent cognizers through the power of fact. The only way we can know such objects incontrovertibly is by relying upon Buddha's scriptures, having already ascertained that Buddha is a thoroughly non-deceptive person.

For example, to realize that the scripture revealing 'From giving comes wealth, from discipline comes happiness' is a completely reliable scripture we need to use the following reasoning: 'This scripture is completely reliable because it is free from contradiction by direct perception, free from contradiction by subsequent cognizers through the power of fact, and free from contradiction by subsequent cognizers through belief.' In dependence upon this reasoning we can generate a subsequent cognizer realizing that this scripture is completely reliable. Then we can generate a subsequent cognizer that realizes that from giving comes wealth and from discipline comes happiness because the scripture that reveals this is completely reliable. This subsequent cognizer is a subsequent cognizer through belief.

Subsequent cognizers through renown realize the suitability of terms on the basis of renown, or convention. In principle any object is suitable to be called by any name because the suitability of a particular name arises not from characteristics in the object but simply from convention. Thus the white orb we see in the night sky is suitable to be called 'the moon' because that is how it is commonly known, but it could just as easily be known by any other name. Similarly the term 'moon' could be used to designate any other object. Thus, for example, if we had grown used to referring to the white orb in the night sky as 'the sun' and the yellow orb in the day sky as 'the moon', these terms would be entirely suitable because they would have been established by convention.

Subsequent cognizers through renown realize a terminological suitability – that an object is suitable to be called anything because it exists among objects of conception. There is no natural relationship between objects and sounds. Thus, we can call a person 'Patience' even though a person cannot be patience because patience is a state of mind, not a person. Even so, it is suitable to call a person 'Patience' simply because that name is established by common usage. Moreover, since countless different languages exist, any object of a conceptual mind can be an object of any language, and so any object is suitable to be called anything.

In *Commentary to Valid Cognition* Dharmakirti says:

> An expressive sound is dependent upon the wish of whoever expresses it.

One person may say 'John is good' because that is his experience of John, but someone else, with a different experience of John, may say 'John is bad.' Thus, our speech has no freedom because what we say depends upon our mind. In the same text Dharmakirti says 'Sound is everywhere', which means that we can express a sound for anything.

There is also a twofold division of subsequent cognizer from the point of view of how they are generated:

1 Subsequent cognizers arisen from listening or reading
2 Subsequent cognizers arisen from contemplation

An example of the first is a subsequent cognizer realizing that the body is empty of inherent existence simply in dependence upon listening to or reading the statement 'The body is empty of inherent existence because when we search for it with wisdom it will disappear.' If we generate a subsequent cognizer realizing the emptiness of the body principally through the force of our contemplating the meaning of such a statement, this is an example of a subsequent cognizer arisen from contemplation.

When we first realize subtle objects such as emptiness in dependence upon subsequent cognizers, we attain an intellectual understanding of them, but we should not be satisfied with this. We need to deepen our experience of the object through meditation.

GENERATION OF SUBSEQUENT COGNIZERS

As mentioned before, we can generate a subsequent cognizer either in dependence upon listening or reading, or in dependence upon contemplation, but either way it is necessary for us to realize fully the three modes. When it is said that a conclusive reason is qualified by the three modes, this means that for a reason to be conclusive for us we must realize all three modes. For example, if we simply think 'My body is impermanent because it will finally die', without realizing each of the three modes, this reason will not be a conclusive reason, and our understanding will not be a subsequent cognizer. The reason will become conclusive and lead to a subsequent cognizer only if we fully realize the three modes – that our body will finally die, that whatever finally dies is impermanent, and that whatever is not impermanent will not finally die.

APPLICATION OF SUBSEQUENT COGNIZERS TO DHARMA PRACTICE

Most objects of meditation mentioned in the Sutras and Tantras are either slightly hidden objects or deeply hidden objects, and so we must realize them initially by generating subsequent cognizers. This initial knowledge obtained through subsequent cognizers is like a sprout that will later grow into an abundant crop of Dharma realizations. By repeatedly meditating on the continuum of these subsequent cognizers, eventually we will gain deep realizations of Sutra and Tantra, like a crop ripening into a rich harvest. Knowing this we should make a strong determination to generate these precious subsequent cognizers in the way explained here, and then put this determination into practice.

Enjoy the purity of your mind and actions

Re-cognizers

DEFINITION OF RE-COGNIZER

The definition of re-cognizer is a cognizer that realizes what has already been realized through the force of a previous valid cognizer.

The function of a re-cognizer is to maintain the continuum of an understanding initially gained by a valid cognizer. The first moment of an eye awareness apprehending a tree, for example, realizes its object freshly, through its own power. Subsequent moments of that eye awareness do not realize the tree through their own power but through the power of the first moment; hence they are re-cognizers. In a similar way, the first moment of a subsequent cognizer realizing emptiness is generated directly in dependence upon a conclusive reason and realizes its object through its own power. Subsequent moments of the same subsequent cognizer realize emptiness through the power of the first moment. Whereas the first moment of a subsequent cognizer brings the mind from the state of correct belief to a state of incontrovertible realization, later moments merely prolong this initial realization. 'Moment' in this context means the shortest time it takes to notice or realize an object.

Although the second and third moments of omniscient mind realize what has already been realized by the first moment, they do so through their own power and are not mere continuations of the first moment. Every moment of Buddha's mind realizes all phenomena freshly through the force of having eliminated the two obstructions, and not simply through remembering the understanding gained by the first moment. Therefore, Buddhas have no re-cognizers. The second moment of a Buddha's eye awareness, for example, is just as fresh as the first moment. By contrast, the second moment of our eye awareness realizing a particular object lacks the quality of freshness that is possessed by the first moment. It does not understand the object in a new way but merely maintains the original understanding.

Re-cognizers are necessarily valid cognizers. According to the Sautrantikas, however, this is not the case because they assert that all valid cognizers necessarily realize their objects freshly.

DIVISIONS OF RE-COGNIZER

Because there are two types of valid cognizer, there are two types of re-cognizer:

1 Non-conceptual re-cognizers
2 Conceptual re-cognizers

There are three types of non-conceptual re-cognizer:

1 Re-cognizers that are sense direct perceivers
2 Re-cognizers that are mental direct perceivers
3 Re-cognizers that are yogic direct perceivers

An example of the first is the second moment of an eye awareness realizing form, an example of the second is the second moment of clairvoyance, and an example of the third is the second moment of a direct realization of emptiness.

When we look at an object, the first moment of that eye awareness apprehends the object through its own power, and later moments are re-cognizers that are sense direct perceivers. However, if we look away from the object and then look at it again, the first moment of the new eye awareness must engage the object freshly through its own power; it cannot rely upon the previous eye awareness because the continuum has been broken. The first moment of that new eye awareness is therefore not a re-cognizer even though it realizes an object that has already been realized. Similarly, during a meditation session all the moments of a Superior being's meditative equipoise on emptiness after the first moment are re-cognizers, but when he or she begins a new session the first moment is not a re-cognizer.

There are two types of conceptual re-cognizer: those induced by direct perceivers and those induced by subsequent cognizers. The former can further be divided into those induced by sense direct perceivers, those induced by mental direct perceivers, and those induced by yogic direct perceivers. An example of the first is a conceptual mind that thinks 'This is a flower' that occurs when we look at a flower. An example of the second is remembering dream things that were previously seen with dream eye awareness in dreams. An example of the third is a Superior being's illusion-like subsequent attainment induced by his or her direct realization of emptiness. Examples of conceptual re-cognizers induced by subsequent cognizers are the second moment of a subsequent cognizer and the second mental abiding.

GENERATION OF RE-COGNIZERS

We should maintain continually, without forgetting, any perfect knowledge of Dharma subjects that we gain through sincere study by generating and maintaining re-cognizers, and the way to do this is to maintain mindfulness. The object of mindfulness is an object that has already been realized, the nature of mindfulness is not to forget its object, and the function of mindfulness is to prevent distraction. Maintaining mindfulness is the best method for improving our Dharma knowledge and experience, and it is the root of all meditation practices.

APPLICATION OF RE-COGNIZERS TO DHARMA PRACTICE

Those who wish to be liberated from suffering must understand the ultimate truth of phenomena. In Tibetan, ultimate truth is called 'don dam denpa', in which 'don' means 'object', 'dam' means 'holy', and 'denpa' means truth. Thus, ultimate truth is the supreme object of knowledge. All phenomena lack true existence, and this lack of true existence is ultimate truth. In *King of Concentration Sutra* Buddha says:

A magician creates various things
Such as horses, elephants and so forth.
His creations do not actually exist;
You should know all things in the same way.

If we contemplate sincerely the conclusive reasons given in authentic scriptures such as *Modern Buddhism*, *The New Heart of Wisdom* and *Ocean of Nectar* we will generate a subsequent cognizer realizing ultimate truth. This is the first step towards the attainment of tranquil abiding and superior seeing observing emptiness. We should then meditate on the continuum of this subsequent cognizer, which is the nature of a re-cognizer, until we attain the union of tranquil abiding and superior seeing observing emptiness.

With respect to virtuous objects, the practice of re-cognizers is of paramount importance because it is through this practice that we maintain and increase all our spiritual experiences.

*Listen to the precious sound of the conch of Dharma
and contemplate and meditate on its meaning*

Correct Beliefs

DEFINITION OF CORRECT BELIEF

The definition of correct belief is a non-valid cognizer that realizes its conceived object.

In general, conceptual minds apprehending chair, table, tree, and so on are correct beliefs; except that those that are induced by sense direct perceivers are not correct beliefs but re-cognizers. A mind that believes that future lives do not exist is not a correct belief but an incorrect belief because it is a wrong conceptual mind.

In the Sutras, Buddha explains a special meditation practice for abandoning attachment to samsaric environments in which we meditate on the whole earth covered with bone, marrow, pus and blood. This meditation is a concentration that realizes its conceived object, which is an imaginary earth covered with imaginary bone, marrow, pus and blood. This concentration can be a correct belief or a valid cognizer. The meditations on generation stage mentioned in the Tantric teachings can also be understood in the same way.

DIVISIONS OF CORRECT BELIEF

There are two types of correct belief:

1 Correct beliefs that do not depend upon a reason
2 Correct beliefs that depend upon a reason

An example of the first is a correct belief in impermanence that develops from just listening to instructions on it. An example of the second is a correct belief that develops from contemplating either a correct or an incorrect reason. Some people, who believe the same as the Vaibhashikas, think that the body is impermanent because it is first produced, then it remains, and finally it disintegrates. Contemplating these reasons they develop a conceptual mind conceiving the body to be impermanent. This conceptual mind is a correct belief developed from an incorrect reason.

Some people might think that the Vaibhashika's view that functioning things are first produced, then remain, and finally disintegrate is correct. This indicates that they do not understand subtle impermanence. In reality, the production and disintegration of functioning things occur simultaneously. Since no functioning thing remains for one moment without changing, the reason mentioned above is incorrect. On the other hand, if we contemplate 'My body is impermanent because it will finally die', we can develop a rough understanding that our body is impermanent. This knowledge is a correct belief developed from contemplating a correct reason. This correct belief can later transform into a subsequent cognizer that perfectly realizes the impermanence of the body.

GENERATION OF CORRECT BELIEFS

In general, a mind that simply believes something that exists is a correct belief. These are easy to generate because they can develop either from just listening or from contemplating. The most meaningful correct beliefs are those that cause living beings to be liberated from suffering, such as beliefs in karma, reincarnation, the six realms, the Three Jewels and the four noble truths. These correct beliefs can be generated by developing strong faith in Buddha and his teachings. Believing that all living beings are our mothers is a very beneficial correct belief because it helps us to develop bodhichitta. The methods for generating such correct beliefs are explained in the Lamrim teachings.

The Tantric teachings explain a special practice of correct imagination, such as regarding oneself as a Deity and everything as completely pure. These kinds of correct imagination are special correct beliefs that we can generate once we have received an empowerment.

APPLICATION OF CORRECT BELIEFS TO DHARMA PRACTICE

In general, all objects of knowledge are objects of correct belief. Among these, the most meaningful are the objects of knowledge that are presented in the Lamrim and Tantric teachings. Through listening to and contemplating these teachings we will first gain a rough understanding of their meaning. This understanding will have the nature of a correct belief. This is like a painter of a Buddha image initially drawing a rough outline of the image. Once we have gained a rough understanding of the Lamrim and Tantric teachings, if we continue to study and practise them sincerely we will gain a deep knowledge and experience of the entire Lamrim and Tantra, and eventually we will attain full enlightenment. This is like the painter completing the painting of the Buddha image. Contemplating this, we should make a strong determination thinking 'I must accomplish both the initial knowledge and the final attainment', and then put this determination into practice.

Apply great effort to attaining enlightenment

Non-ascertaining Perceivers

DEFINITION OF NON-ASCERTAINING PERCEIVER

The definition of non-ascertaining perceiver is a cognizer to which a phenomenon that is its engaged object appears clearly without being ascertained.

An example is an eye awareness of a new-born baby that apprehends its father's face. Also, when we are in a big city we see many people, but we do not know who they are. Our minds that see these people are non-ascertaining perceivers because they clearly see something but do not realize it.

Non-ascertaining perceivers are always manifest within our mind, even during single-pointed meditation. All living beings have these minds – only Buddhas are completely free from them. Most sense awarenesses of new-born babies are non-ascertaining perceivers.

DIVISIONS OF NON-ASCERTAINING PERCEIVER

There are two types of non-ascertaining perceiver:

1 Non-ascertaining sense awarenesses
2 Non-ascertaining mental awarenesses

An example of the first is an ear awareness that occurs while we are engrossed in looking at an attractive form. Even though sounds appear to such an awareness they are not recognized or understood because most of our attention is directed towards the visual form. We might also develop a non-ascertaining ear awareness while we are listening to teachings given in a foreign language. The sounds appear to our ear awareness but since we do not understand the language we do not ascertain their meaning.

Examples of the second are dream awarenesses apprehending dream colour blue.

GENERATION OF NON-ASCERTAINING PERCEIVERS

In general, a non-ascertaining perceiver develops when the conditions for a phenomenon to appear are assembled but the conditions for its nature to be realized are not. When looked at from the point of view of their causes we can distinguish five main types of non-ascertaining perceiver. These will now be explained.

The first type occurs when the mind is unable to ascertain the nature of its object due to external conditions. For example, an eye awareness may not be able to recognize what it sees because the light is too dim; because the object is too far away, too small, or moving too fast; or because it closely resembles another object. Similarly, an ear awareness might be unable to ascertain its object because the sound is too faint or because it is unclear. These conditions may also lead to doubts or wrong awarenesses. For example, we might not be able to tell whether a particular sound is the sound of a car or the sound of the wind. If we simply listen to the sound without being able to identify it, this is a non-ascertaining perceiver. If we then begin to wonder 'Is that a car or is it the wind?' this is doubt. If we incorrectly decide that it is the sound of a car when in fact it is the sound of the wind, this is a wrong awareness. Non-ascertaining perceivers often lead to doubts or wrong awarenesses.

The second type of non-ascertaining perceiver is dependent upon the mental power. Sometimes non-ascertaining perceivers develop because the gross consciousnesses are gathering inwards, as they do during the death process or when we fall asleep. As death advances, other minds such as valid direct perceivers, subsequent cognizers, re-cognizers and correct beliefs gradually cease, and non-ascertaining perceivers increase. Even before their eye sense powers have ceased to operate, dying people lose the ability to recognize the people gathered around them because their discrimination has become unclear. At present all our subtle minds are non-ascertaining perceivers because although subtle appearances such as white appearance or clear light appear to our subtle minds, we do not recognize them.

Alcohol and other drugs can also make our discrimination unclear and, while they might not cause us to hallucinate, they do often prevent us from recognizing what appears to us. Over-tiredness has a similar effect. Another example is a newborn baby seeing its mother. Although all the conditions for the eye awareness apprehending the mother have been met, the conditions for ascertaining or understanding the mother have not been assembled. Because the object, the eye sense power, and the eye awareness have come together, the baby apprehends its mother, but because the baby's discrimination is unclear it cannot understand what it perceives. As the baby grows, however, it will learn to recognize its mother as its mother.

The third type of non-ascertaining perceiver can develop because we have decided, or learned, to ignore a particular stimulus. People who live close to busy roads, for example, learn to ignore the noise of the traffic. This type of non-ascertaining perceiver can be very useful because it enables us to pay full attention to more meaningful objects. Thus, a mother living in a house near a busy road may be able to ignore the noise of the traffic while she reads a book, yet still be able to hear and ascertain the much fainter sound of her baby starting to cry. Her non-ascertaining perceiver with respect to the sound of the traffic arises through the power of her decision not to pay attention to it, and so even when that sound appears to her ear awareness it does not attract the attention of her mental awareness.

The fourth type is similar to the third in that a stimulus is shut out, but here it is because we have been distracted by an object of delusion. For example, when we are engrossed in an object of attachment or when we are very angry we become oblivious to many things that occur around us, even to our own physical pain. Car accidents often happen because the driver has been distracted by objects of attachment such as an attractive person on the pavement.

The fifth type of non-ascertaining perceiver occurs when we do not understand some part of the nature of an object. An example of this might occur when we are shopping in a foreign country. We see many strange fruits and vegetables but do not know what they are, whether they are tasty, or how to prepare them. Our eye awareness clearly perceives the items but it does not ascertain those aspects that are relevant to us. This type of non-ascertaining perceiver develops because we have not previously learnt to recognize that aspect of the object that we now wish to recognize. In general, whenever we clearly perceive an object but do not know what it is or what it is for we have developed this type of non-ascertaining perceiver.

APPLICATION OF NON-ASCERTAINING PERCEIVERS
TO DHARMA PRACTICE

At the moment, when we meet an attractive object we usually pay considerable attention to it and try to gain as vivid a perception of it as possible. Similarly, when we meet an unattractive object we dwell on its bad qualities until anger develops. Instead of paying so much attention to objects of delusion it would be wiser to develop non-ascertaining perceivers with respect to them. Training in non-ascertaining perceivers with respect to objects of delusion is the practice of restraining the doors of the sense powers.

In *Guide to the Bodhisattva's Way of Life* Shantideva advises us to remain like a block of wood whenever we encounter an object that stimulates strong delusions. His meaning is that we should practise non-ascertaining perceivers towards these objects. When our attachment or anger towards these objects becomes less intense we can begin to practise other methods to overcome our delusions. If we are successful in overcoming our anger towards someone, then when we see them again they will no longer be an object of anger for us but an object of patience. Eventually they may even become an object of pure love or compassion!

For those who wish to attain tranquil abiding it is very important to restrain the doors of the sense powers by practising non-ascertaining perceivers towards distracting objects. During the meditation session it is necessary to practise non-ascertaining perceivers towards all the objects of the senses so that we can pay full attention to the internal object on which we are meditating.

To prevent too many unnecessary conceptual thoughts or distractions from arising it is better not to pay much attention to things that are not relevant to our spiritual practice, such as mundane business activities, the quality of our food, or the quality of our accommodation.

The five minds explained so far – direct perceivers, subsequent cognizers, re-cognizers, correct beliefs and non-ascertaining perceivers – are all correct minds. A correct mind is a mind that is not mistaken with respect to its engaged object. However, this does not mean that all correct minds are unmistaken awarenesses. Within the minds of sentient beings, only the exalted awareness of meditative equipoise of Superior beings observing emptiness is an unmistaken awareness. All other minds of sentient beings are mistaken awarenesses because their objects appear to be truly existent; and this appearance is a mistaken appearance that is by nature an obstruction to omniscience. Only Buddhas have abandoned this obstruction. These explanations are very different from those of the lower Buddhist schools such as the Sautrantikas.

Non-deluded Doubts

DEFINITION OF NON-DELUDED DOUBT

The definition of non-deluded doubt is a doubt that does not disturb our peace of mind and gives rise to positive results.

When, for example, we think, 'Maybe I need to practise Dharma purely', 'maybe' implies that this thought is doubt, but it is a beneficial doubt. Initially we need to develop this doubt, and then it will transform into the intention, 'I will practise Dharma purely', which is very precious.

DIVISIONS OF NON-DELUDED DOUBT

There are two types of non-deluded doubt:

1 Non-deluded doubts with respect to ultimate truth
2 Non-deluded doubts with respect to conventional truths

An example of the first is the thought, 'Maybe the things that I normally see do not exist.' An example of the second is the thought, 'Maybe things exist as mere name.' These non-deluded doubts gradually lead us to a correct belief, subsequent cognizer, re-cognizer and finally to a yogic direct perceiver with respect to ultimate truth and subtle conventional truth. In this way, we will become a Yogi, a Superior being.

Be victorious over the enemy of your delusions

Wrong Awarenesses

DEFINITION OF WRONG AWARENESS

The definition of wrong awareness is a cognizer that is mistaken with respect to its engaged object.

An example of a wrong awareness is a mind that apprehends a toy snake as being a real snake. Since a toy snake is not a real snake, any mind that apprehends it as such is mistaken with respect to its engaged object. Whereas a mistaken awareness is mistaken with respect to its appearing object, a wrong awareness is mistaken with respect to its engaged object or its conceived object. If a mind is a wrong awareness it is necessarily a mistaken awareness, but if it is a mistaken awareness it is not necessarily a wrong awareness. As mentioned above, apart from the exalted awareness of meditative equipoise of a Superior being, all minds of sentient beings are mistaken awarenesses because their objects appear to them to be truly existent when in fact they are not. However, this does not mean that all these minds are also wrong awarenesses. A mind is a wrong awareness only if it is mistaken with respect to its engaged object or its conceived object.

There are two types of wrong awareness: non-conceptual wrong awarenesses and conceptual wrong awarenesses, and of these the latter are the more harmful. All delusions are conceptual wrong awarenesses. Whereas non-conceptual wrong awarenesses can cause temporary problems, leading to embarrassment, accidents, and sometimes even death, they are by no means as harmful as conceptual wrong awarenesses because they are not the main cause of engaging in negative actions. Conceptual wrong awarenesses, on the other hand, cause us to commit negative actions and so lead us into lower rebirths in future lives. Because the harmful results of these minds extend beyond this life they are far more damaging than non-conceptual wrong awarenesses. Moreover, by obscuring the ultimate nature of phenomena, conceptual wrong awarenesses prevent us from attaining liberation and so cause us to remain trapped within samsara. We normally blame other people or external circumstances for our problems but in reality all our problems are caused by these wrong awarenesses.

All wrong awarenesses are objects to be abandoned. The entire spiritual path consists of eliminating wrong awarenesses and developing the correct awarenesses that are their opposites. When we have completely removed wrong awarenesses and their imprints from our mental continuum we will be a Buddha. The only difference between a sentient being and a Buddha is that a sentient being has wrong awarenesses or their imprints and a Buddha does not.

DIVISIONS OF WRONG AWARENESS

As mentioned above, there are two types of wrong awareness:

1 Non-conceptual wrong awarenesses
2 Conceptual wrong awarenesses

Non-conceptual wrong awarenesses can be divided into wrong sense awarenesses and wrong non-conceptual mental awarenesses. A wrong sense awareness can be mistaken with respect to its object in any of seven different ways: being mistaken with respect to its object's shape, colour, activity, number, time, measurement or entity.

A sense awareness can be mistaken with respect to shape when the shape of the object resembles the shape of another object. Examples are an eye awareness seeing a toy snake as a real snake, an eye awareness seeing artificial flowers as real flowers, and an eye awareness seeing the reflection of a face in the mirror as a real face.

Examples of sense awarenesses that are mistaken with respect to colour are an eye awareness seeing a white conch shell as yellow as a result of jaundice, or an eye awareness seeing a distant snow mountain as blue due to hazy atmospheric conditions.

An example of a sense awareness mistaken with respect to activity can occur when we are in a stationary train and a train next to us begins to move. Because at that time our eye awareness is deceived with respect to the activity of the other train, it seems as if it is our train that is moving. Another example of this type of wrong sense awareness is an eye awareness seeing trees moving past when we are travelling by train or car.

An example of a sense awareness mistaken with respect to number is an eye awareness seeing two moons in the sky when we are squinting at the moon.

An example of a sense awareness mistaken with respect to time is when we wake from an afternoon sleep and our eye awareness sees the light of morning, making us feel that it is morning.

Examples of sense awarenesses that are mistaken with respect to measurement are an eye awareness seeing a large object in the distance as smaller than a nearby small object, an eye awareness misjudging the distance of the car in front of us when we are driving, an eye awareness mistaking the position of a fish in the water because of refraction, and an eye awareness seeing a rainbow as having a fixed location.

All the above types of wrong sense awareness are mistaken with respect to an aspect of the object and therefore do not identify the object correctly, but they are not mistaken with respect to all aspects of the object. A person who sees two moons, for example, is mistaken with respect to number, but is not mistaken with respect to the shape of the object, nor with respect to its being the moon. On the other hand, a sense awareness that is mistaken with respect to the entity of the object is mistaken with respect to the whole object. Examples are an eye awareness seeing hairs floating in front of us when our eyes are tired or sore, an eye awareness seeing a mirage as actual water, or an ear awareness hearing an echo of a voice as the actual sound of a voice.

Examples of wrong non-conceptual mental awarenesses are a dream eye awareness apprehending a dream mountain as a real mountain, dream money as real money, and so on.

There are two types of conceptual wrong awareness: intellectually-formed wrong awarenesses and innate wrong awarenesses. Intellectually-formed wrong awarenesses are those that develop from incorrect philosophical views or incorrect reasons, and innate wrong awarenesses are those that develop naturally from imprints carried over from previous lives. Examples of the first are the twenty intellectually-formed views of the transitory collection, listed on pages 137–139, and the sixteen wrong awarenesses, listed in the Sutras, that contradict the sixteen characteristics of the four noble truths. We can also develop intellectually-formed anger and attachment. Although most of our anger and attachment arise spontaneously, without our having to contemplate reasons, sometimes we develop anger as a result of strong adherence to particular views, attachment to a certain lifestyle, and so on. These are also intellectually-formed wrong awarenesses. All intellectually-formed wrong awarenesses are abandoned on the path of seeing. Examples of innate wrong awareness are innate self-grasping and all the other innate delusions.

It is important to note that not all wrong awarenesses are delusions. An eye awareness seeing an artificial flower as a real flower, for example, is a wrong awareness that arises from ignorance or the imprints of ignorance, but it is not a delusion.

GENERATION OF WRONG AWARENESSES

There are two causes of wrong awareness: ultimate causes and temporary causes. The ultimate cause of all wrong awarenesses is ignorance. As long as ignorance exists in our mind we will develop many kinds of wrong awareness. Even after we have eliminated ignorance from our mind we will still have the imprints of ignorance, and these can cause us to develop non-deluded wrong awarenesses. However, these are not so harmful. Only a Buddha is completely free from wrong awarenesses.

As for the temporary causes of wrong awareness, there are temporary causes of wrong sense awareness and temporary causes of wrong mental awareness. There are four temporary causes of wrong sense awareness:

1 A deceptive quality of the object
2 A deceptive situation
3 A defective sense power
4 A fault in the preceding awareness

The first two are external causes of error and the second two are internal causes of error. As for the first, objects can act as causes of wrong awareness when they closely resemble other objects. For example, artificial flowers can be mistaken for real flowers, or a toy snake for a real snake. Other ways that objects can deceive us are if they are small, camouflaged or transparent. Sometimes railway lines seem to converge in the distance, which causes an eye awareness mistaken with respect to shape.

As for the second cause, certain situations make it difficult to identify objects clearly and so they often lead to mistakes. For example, when it is too dark to see properly, or too noisy or windy to hear properly, or when we are moving quickly, we can easily develop wrong awarenesses. Mirages and rainbows are both appearances arising from an interaction between special conditions – the light, moisture and the position of the observer – but they seem to be real with a definite location and therefore often cause mistaken minds. When we look through a microscope tiny objects appear very large, and looking through binoculars makes distant objects appear close. A straight stick half submerged in water appears bent, and a white object seen through brown sunglasses looks brown. These are all examples of how a situation can lead to wrong awareness.

As for the third cause, certain diseases impair the sense powers and cause us to apprehend objects incorrectly. Jaundice, for example, can impair the eye sense power and make white objects appear yellow, tiredness of the eyes can give rise to the appearance of hairs floating in front of us, and a fever can impair the tactile sense power and cause a warm room to feel cold. When the inner winds mounted by the sense awarenesses begin to gather inwards during the death process, many wrong sense awarenesses occur. Alcohol and drugs can also affect our sense powers. Swallowing the drug datura, for example, can cause us to see the ground as golden in colour.

As for the fourth cause, when our mind is in a very disturbed or preoccupied state we often develop wrong sense awarenesses. It is said that sometimes violent anger makes everything appear red. Someone who is 'on edge' is much more likely than someone in a calm state of mind to make mistakes, such as seeing a piece of rope as a snake. We also tend to make mistakes when our attention is strongly directed towards another object. For example, if we are engrossed in a book and a stranger walks by, we may mistake him for someone we know. Sometimes when we are strongly expecting to see something we will 'see' it, even if it is not there.

External causes of error do not always lead to the development of wrong awarenesses. For example, when we look into a mirror the reflection of our face looks like our face but we do not mistake it for our face, and so our eye awareness seeing the reflection is not a wrong awareness. The reason we are sometimes deceived by external causes of error is that we still have the ultimate cause of mistaken minds, ignorance. Buddhas have abandoned ignorance completely and so even when they meet a deceptive external condition they do not develop wrong awarenesses.

There are many temporary causes of wrong mental awareness. Usually a wrong sense awareness will induce a wrong conceptual mind. Seeing a rope as a snake for example will probably lead to a conceptual mind thinking 'This is a snake.' However, if we understand the object well a wrong sense awareness will not lead to a wrong conceptual mind. Although a rainbow appears to our eye awareness to have a definite location, if we understand the nature of rainbows we will know that this appearance is deceptive and we will not think that the rainbow exists where it appears to.

Another cause of wrong mental awareness is our winds gathering inwards during sleep or death. When the winds gather, the mind becomes more subtle, and as a result our mindfulness deteriorates and we are not able to use our mind in a reliable way. When we dream, we rarely realize that we are dreaming, so we regard the pleasant or frightening appearances of the dream as real, and consequently develop attachment or fear towards them. When advanced Bodhisattvas sleep, however, the power of their mindfulness does not decrease and so they do not develop wrong awarenesses. They are able to transform sleep and dreaming into the spiritual path.

As mentioned earlier, there are two types of conceptual wrong awareness – innate and intellectually-formed. Innate wrong awarenesses arise through the force of imprints of delusions. These delusions arise naturally because we have been familiar with delusions since beginningless time. Intellectually-formed wrong awarenesses arise either through being influenced by misleading teachings or through our own incorrect reasoning. Even if we have not formally studied mistaken philosophies we can acquire wrong views through the influence of our parents, friends, and so forth. For example, we may have been brought up to think that although it is wrong to kill human beings there is no fault in killing animals, or that the only purpose of a human life is to enjoy ourself as much as possible. To practise Dharma purely and wholeheartedly we must discard any such wrong views that we may have adopted.

We can also develop wrong awareness through our own illogical reasoning. For example, if we do not seem to be making much progress in our Dharma practice we may think that Dharma has little power, or that Buddhas and Bodhisattvas either do not exist or are not interested in helping us. False reasoning such as this arises very easily and can destroy our practice, so we must always be on our guard against it and counter it as soon as it occurs. If we are disappointed with our progress we should examine our mind to see what it is that is hindering us. In general, our greatest obstacle is that we do not have complete confidence in the practice we are doing, or in our Teacher, and this prevents us from committing ourself wholeheartedly to the practice. Instead of blaming Dharma for our slow progress we should blame our lack of faith.

APPLICATION OF OUR UNDERSTANDING OF WRONG AWARENESSES TO DHARMA PRACTICE

There are two main purposes of Dharma practice – to eliminate wrong awarenesses and to cultivate correct awarenesses. Wrong awareness is the source of suffering, and correct awareness is the source of happiness. By clearly distinguishing these two we should strive to abandon wrong awarenesses in general, and self-grasping in particular.

To abandon minds such as anger and attachment we need to understand that their conceived objects do not exist but are merely fabrications of ignorance. The observed object of attachment, for example, is a contaminated phenomenon, but the mind of attachment views it as a source of true happiness. In reality there is no such thing as a contaminated phenomenon that is a source of true happiness because all contaminated phenomena are true sufferings. When through contemplating in this way we realize that the conceived object of attachment, or of any other delusion, is non-existent, we will find it easy to abandon that delusion.

The root cause of all our suffering is the wrong awareness, self-grasping; but because it is so deeply ingrained in our mind it is difficult for us to understand that it is a wrong awareness. The objects of self-grasping – the truly existent I and so forth – appear so vividly to our mind that we find it difficult to believe that they do not actually exist. How can something appear so clearly if it does not exist? The main reason we study all the different types of non-conceptual wrong awareness listed above is to help us to overcome such doubts. By considering these examples, which are part of our everyday experience, we can see that just because something appears in a certain way to our mind it does not follow that it actually exists in that way. For example, when we press our eyeball and look at the moon, two moons appear vividly to our eye awareness. Though two moons appear, we know that two moons do not exist. Similarly, just because a truly existent I appears vividly to our mind it does not mean that a truly existent I actually exists.

Every spiritual realization has a wrong awareness that is its opposite and that must be removed by that particular realization. To eliminate these wrong thoughts we must first identify them, understand how they arise, and recognize their faults. In the preparatory practices of the stages of the path we offer a mandala to the Buddhas and Bodhisattvas and request the attainment of the three great purposes. The first purpose is to overcome wrong awarenesses quickly, the second is to develop correct awarenesses quickly, and the third is to be free from external and internal obstacles. Internal obstacles are our delusions. Specifically, we pray to be able to overcome the sixteen wrong thoughts and attitudes and replace them with the sixteen correct thoughts and attitudes. These were listed previously (see pages 177–179). We should memorize this list so that we can identify the wrong thoughts and attitudes as soon as they arise. If we can do this we can immediately apply the appropriate opponent, and then that wrong awareness will not harm us greatly; but if we fail to recognize them they will grow stronger and may even destroy our spiritual practice. Each of these wrong thoughts can be overcome temporarily by refuting its object and then familiarizing our mind with the opposite correct awareness. To eliminate them completely, however, we must eradicate the root of all wrong awarenesses, self-grasping ignorance, by attaining a yogic direct perceiver realizing emptiness.

Benefit others by turning the Wheel of Dharma

Valid and Non-valid Cognizers

In general 'valid' means 'non-deceptive' or 'completely reliable'. There are three ways in which the term can be applied:

1 Valid Teachers
2 Valid teachings
3 Valid cognizers

If we rely upon valid Teachers, valid teachings and valid cognizers they will never lead us astray because they will not cause us to develop non-virtuous states of mind or to commit non-virtuous actions. Instead they will lead us in the direction of purity and happiness. To attain liberation we need to develop valid cognizers with respect to the two truths, and to do this we need to rely upon valid teachings given by valid Teachers.

In the second chapter of *Commentary to Valid Cognition* Dharmakirti defines a valid Teacher as a Teacher who knows fully and without error what objects are to be abandoned and what objects are to be practised, and who, out of compassion, reveals this knowledge to others.

A valid Teacher, therefore, must have five qualities:

(1) Unmistaken knowledge of all objects to be abandoned
(2) Complete knowledge of the methods for abandoning them

(3) Unmistaken knowledge of all objects to be practised

(4) Complete knowledge of the methods for practising them

(5) Revealing all this to others with the motivation of compassion

If we meet a Teacher who has these five qualities we can place our complete and unreserved trust in him or her. The supreme example of a valid Teacher is Buddha. His mind perfectly accords with the way things are, he is free from the two obstructions, and he sees clearly what binds sentient beings to samsara and how to release them. Since he has completely fulfilled his own purpose he has nothing to gain from deceiving sentient beings – his only motivation for teaching is great compassion. Just as a valid mind can never lead us into error because its nature is non-deceptive, so Buddha can never deceive us or disappoint us because his nature is non-deceptive. Merely by looking at Buddha or his image we receive immense benefits, and because he is such a pure and powerful being any virtuous action that we do with respect to him is a cause of attaining enlightenment.

The definition of valid teaching is an instruction that principally explains without error the objects to be abandoned and how to abandon them, and the objects to be practised and how to practise them. All the eighty-four thousand teachings of Buddha are included within these two types of instruction.

Buddha Shakyamuni skilfully included all spiritual practices within the practice of the four noble truths. All objects to be abandoned are included within true sufferings and true origins, and all objects to be practised are included within true cessations and true paths. From this we can see that even though they seem to be very concise, the four noble truths have a very extensive meaning. The four noble truths can be practised according to any of the four schools, but the most profound way of practising them is according to the Madhyamika-Prasangika school. The sixteen characteristics of the four noble truths can be understood at a gross, subtle, and very subtle level; and someone who is skilled at presenting these various levels of explanation is indeed a valid Teacher. As Dharmakirti says in *Commentary to Valid Cognition*, if we wish to attain liberation we do not need a Teacher who has clairvoyance and miracle powers; we need only a Teacher who has a clear understanding of the four noble truths and the ability to explain them well.

In essence, Dharma practice consists of gaining valid cognizers of all the objects of the stages of the path, and in this way eradicating all our wrong awarenesses. Every valid cognizer has a wrong awareness to which it is the opponent. The valid cognizer realizing the faults of samsara, for example, is the opponent of the wrong awareness that views samsara as pleasant, and the wisdom realizing emptiness is the opponent of self-grasping.

We need valid cognizers realizing both the objects to be abandoned and the objects to be practised. Without realizing these with valid cognizers our experience of Dharma will not be stable, and may even degenerate. Therefore, it is most important to know the defining characteristics of valid cognizers so that we can distinguish them from less reliable states of mind. It was principally to explain these characteristics that Dignaga wrote *Compendium of Valid Cognition* and Dharmakirti composed a commentary to it entitled *Commentary to Valid Cognition*. These two texts are quite technical and difficult to understand, and in the past many scholars have thought that they were of no practical value. Je Tsongkhapa, however, saw the great importance of these texts and showed how they are an indispensable prerequisite for a deep understanding of Sutra and Tantra. By explaining valid cognizers, these texts show exactly what types of mind we need to cultivate if we wish to attain true and lasting experience of Dharma.

Dignaga developed the wish to compose *Compendium of Valid Cognition* while he was in retreat in a forest cave. He composed the first stanza, praising Buddha Shakyamuni as a valid Teacher, wrote it on a slate, and left it in a high place inside his cave while he went out to collect some food. When he returned he noticed that the verse had been erased, and so he rewrote it. The next day he left the cave again to collect food and, once again when he returned, the verse had been erased. Determined to find out who was interfering with his work Dignaga wrote a message on the slate, 'I wish to compose this text for the benefit of all living beings, but you are obstructing me. If you have some objection you should remain here until I return and discuss it with me.' The following day he went out as usual and, when he returned, a non-Buddhist teacher called Tubgyal Nagpo was waiting there. 'Is it you who have been interfering with my composition?' he asked. 'Yes', replied Tubgyal Nagpo. 'Then we must debate the issue', Dignaga continued, 'and the view of whoever wins the debate will prevail.' Tubgyal Nagpo agreed, and they proceeded to debate the merits of composing such a special text. Dignaga won the debate outright, but Tubgyal Nagpo refused to abide by the terms of the debate and tried to destroy Dignaga. Using his mundane miracle powers he blew fire at Dignaga from his mouth, but he was unable to harm him. Dignaga was so upset by the evil and treachery of Tubgyal Nagpo that he despaired of his work ever benefiting living beings. Seizing the slate, he threw it into the air saying 'As soon as this slate lands on the ground I will stop working on this text', but to his amazement the slate did not come down again! When he looked up to see what had happened, Dignaga beheld the Wisdom Buddha Manjushri above him. 'Do not be discouraged, my Son', Manjushri said, 'This work will benefit many living beings in the future; it will be like their eyes guiding them in the darkness of their ignorance and leading them to liberation. You must complete this text.' Inspired by this, Dignaga immediately set about completing his composition, and as a result many living beings have subsequently benefited from *Compendium of Valid Cognition*.

Later, many Tibetan Geshes came to believe that Dignaga's slate finally landed in central Tibet, in a small town called Jang, near Lhasa. They believed that if Dignaga's text was studied in that town their understanding would develop very quickly, and so every year many monks from Sera, Drepung, and Ganden monasteries would go to Jang for three months at a time to study Dharmakirti's commentary to *Compendium of Valid Cognition*. They felt that three months' study in that town was equal to three years' study in other places. It was believed that the slate moved about, so at night, when their classes had finished, the monks would make many prostrations in different places hoping to place their head on the slate!

If we do not understand with valid cognizers the objects to be practised and the objects to be abandoned our Dharma practice will be inconsistent. For example, some people are inspired by their first Dharma teachings and then apply themselves with great enthusiasm to meditation for a few months, but when they find that they have not made much progress they become discouraged and give up their practice. This kind of thing happens because we do not realize the meaning of the teachings with valid cognizers, and so our understanding remains unstable and vulnerable to doubts and wrong awarenesses. If we realize a Dharma subject with a valid cognizer, however, we will never be disturbed by doubts or wrong awarenesses, and we will never feel that we want to abandon our efforts to attain liberation.

Correct beliefs are useful but they are not completely reliable. If we meet a famous Teacher from another tradition, or if we meet with unfavourable circumstances, our correct beliefs may easily turn into doubts and eventually be lost altogether. Therefore, we should not be satisfied with correct beliefs alone, but strive continuously to transform them into valid cognizers.

The supreme valid cognizer is omniscient wisdom. Because Buddhas validly understand all objects of knowledge simultaneously, they are able to help all living beings. Although we have only a few valid cognizers of Dharma subjects, these are extremely important because they are the seeds of omniscient wisdom.

Valid cognizers will now be explained under three headings:

1 Definition of valid cognizer
2 Function of valid cognizers
3 Divisions of valid cognizer

DEFINITION OF VALID COGNIZER

The definition of valid cognizer is a cognizer that is non-deceptive with respect to its engaged object.

Correct beliefs, non-ascertaining perceivers, doubts and wrong awarenesses are all deceptive cognizers. It is not difficult to understand why wrong awarenesses are deceptive. For example, the wrong awareness that sees worldly pleasures as true happiness and regards them as the essence of human life deceives us by preventing us from seeking release from samsara; the wrong awareness of a moth seeing a flame as an attractive abode encourages the moth to fly into the flame and die; and the wrong awareness of our self-grasping mind conceiving our I to be truly existent encourages us to commit heavy non-virtuous actions that cause us to be reborn in the hell realms and experience unbearable pain for a long time. Wrong awarenesses cloud our judgement and make us see the impure as pure, the pure as impure, the existent as non-existent, and the non-existent as existent. When we are under the influence of wrong awareness the causes of hell can seem reliable and the causes of enlightenment meaningless!

It is also not difficult to see why doubts and non-ascertaining perceivers are deceptive or unreliable states of mind. Doubts are unreliable because they prevent certainty about correct objects, and non-ascertaining perceivers are unreliable because they do not realize their object.

It is a little more difficult to understand why correct beliefs are deceptive. After all, for as long as we have a correct belief in an object we do not have doubts or wrong awarenesses about that object. However, correct beliefs do not penetrate their object in sufficient depth to eliminate all misconceptions about the object, and therefore they leave us vulnerable to doubts and wrong awarenesses. This is why they are deceptive. At present, most of our Dharma understanding consists of correct beliefs. Unless we have learned to distinguish correct beliefs from valid cognizers, we may mistake these correct beliefs for firm realizations, and this may lead to complacency. After listening to an inspiring teaching on renunciation, for example, we may develop a correct belief and feel that samsara has no good qualities, but this alone will not change our mind. On the other hand, if we realize this with a valid cognizer our mind will definitely change.

FUNCTION OF VALID COGNIZERS

The special function of valid cognizers is to act as the opponent to wrong awarenesses. Each valid cognizer counteracts a specific wrong awareness. The valid cognizer realizing that the body is impermanent, for example, counteracts the wrong awareness believing the body to be permanent, and the valid cognizer realizing the faults of samsara counteracts the wrong awareness that sees good qualities in samsara. Even a valid cognizer realizing a book counteracts the wrong awareness thinking that it is not a book. Whenever a valid cognizer manifests it is impossible for the particular wrong awareness that it opposes to manifest. For example, for as long as we have a manifest valid cognizer realizing selflessness of persons, self-grasping will not be able to function in our mind. Je Tsongkhapa said that to check whether or not we have developed a valid cognizer realizing emptiness we should watch our mind of self-grasping. If as a result of our meditation our self-grasping is reduced, this indicates that we have a valid cognizer realizing emptiness and that we are meditating correctly; but if our self-grasping is not reduced, this indicates that we have not yet attained a valid cognizer realizing emptiness. A valid cognizer realizing emptiness is the direct antidote not only to self-grasping but also to all the other delusions.

All our suffering is caused by our negative actions of body, speech and mind, which in turn are caused by our wrong awarenesses. We can see, therefore, the importance of opposing wrong awarenesses with valid cognizers. First we need to weaken specific delusions by developing valid cognizers realizing their faults and by familiarizing our mind with the opposing virtue. Then we need to attack the root of all delusions by meditating on emptiness. Through continued meditation we will attain the exalted awareness of meditative equipoise of a Superior being, and by improving this wisdom we will eventually attain the ultimate valid cognizer, omniscient wisdom.

DIVISIONS OF VALID COGNIZER

There are two types of valid cognizer:

1 A valid cognizer that is non-deceptive with respect to its manifest object
2 A valid cognizer that is non-deceptive with respect to its hidden object

Some texts list four types, adding valid cognizers through belief and valid cognizers through analogy, but these are not separate divisions because they are included within valid cognizers that are non-deceptive with respect to their hidden objects. The twofold division is definite in number because more than two types of valid cognizer would be superfluous and fewer than two would be insufficient. This is because there are definitely two types of object of knowledge – manifest objects and hidden objects – and so there are definitely two types of valid cognizer, which are mentioned above.

The definition of manifest object is an object whose initial realization by a valid cognizer does not depend upon logical reasons. In general, any object that can be realized by an ordinary being by means of a direct valid cognizer, without their first gaining a subsequent cognizer of that object, is a manifest object. From this point of view all sense objects are manifest objects. However, from the point of view of particular persons an object can be a manifest object for one person and a hidden object for another. For example, a fire in a house is a manifest object for the people sitting by the fireplace but a hidden object for people outside the house. Similarly, hell is a manifest object for hell beings but a hidden object for humans, and vice versa.

The definition of hidden object is an object whose initial realization by a valid cognizer depends upon correct logical reasons. In general, there are certain objects that it is impossible for anyone to realize directly without their first realizing them with a subsequent cognizer. These include subtle impermanence, emptiness and the laws of karma. The only way that these objects can become manifest objects is if we first realize them with a subsequent cognizer and then go on to generate a re-cognizer and eventually a direct perceiver of them. There are other objects, however, that are hidden to some beings but manifest to others who live in different places or at different times, or who have different karma. These objects can become manifest simply through a change in external circumstances – they do not necessarily have to be realized first by a subsequent cognizer.

The definition of direct valid cognizer is a non-deceptive cognizer that realizes its object directly. There are three types of direct valid cognizer: valid sense direct cognizers, valid mental direct cognizers and valid yogic direct cognizers. These have already been explained in the section on direct perceivers.

The definition of subsequent valid cognizer is a non-deceptive cognizer that realizes its hidden object by depending upon a conclusive reason. There are three types of subsequent valid cognizer: subsequent valid cognizers through the power of fact, subsequent valid cognizers through belief, and subsequent valid cognizers through renown. These have already been explained.

NON-VALID COGNIZERS

The definition of non-valid cognizer is a cognizer that is deceptive with respect to its engaged object.

There are two types of non-valid cognizer: non-conceptual non-valid cognizers and conceptual non-valid cognizers. All wrong sense awarenesses and non-ascertaining sense direct perceivers are examples of the first, and all wrong mental awarenesses, such as delusions, and all correct beliefs and doubts, are examples of the second. Non-valid cognizers are called 'deceptive' because they are not perfect knowledge and so are unreliable.

Meditation

DEFINITION OF MEDITATION

The definition of meditation is a mind that is single-pointedly focused on a virtuous object and whose function is to make the mind peaceful and calm.

We want to be happy all the time, even during sleep. How can we do this? We can do this through training in meditation because meditation makes our mind peaceful, and when our mind is peaceful we are happy all the time, even if our external conditions are poor. On the other hand, when our mind is not peaceful we are not happy, even if our external conditions are excellent. We can understand this through our own experience. Since the actual method to make our mind peaceful is training in meditation, we should apply effort to training in meditation. Whenever we meditate, we are performing an action or karma that causes us to experience peace of mind in the future. From this we can understand the importance of meditation practice.

The difference between concentration and meditation is that concentration is necessarily a mental factor but meditation can be either a mental factor or a primary mind. The object of concentration can be anything, but the object of meditation is necessarily a virtuous object. Whether an object is virtuous or non-virtuous depends on our position. For example, when our enemy harms us and we practise patience, our enemy is our virtuous object, the object of our patience, but if instead we get angry with him he is our non-virtuous object, the object of our anger. So it is our choice whether someone or something is our virtuous object or non-virtuous object. We should learn to use all living beings as our virtuous objects, the object of our compassion and patience, and all phenomena as the objects of our training in emptiness. There is no greater Dharma practice than this.

THE DIVISIONS OF MEDITATION

There is a threefold division of meditation:

1 Meditation of a person of initial scope
2 Meditation of a person of middling scope
3 Meditation of a person of great scope

MEDITATION OF A PERSON OF INITIAL SCOPE

There are five meditations of a person of initial scope:

1 Meditation on the preciousness of our human life
2 Meditation on death
3 Meditation on the dangers of lower rebirth
4 Meditation on going for refuge
5 Meditation on karma

MEDITATION ON THE PRECIOUSNESS OF OUR HUMAN LIFE

THE PURPOSE OF THIS MEDITATION

The purpose of this meditation is to encourage ourself to take the real meaning of our human life and not to waste it in meaningless activities. Our human life is very precious, but only if we use it to attain permanent liberation and the supreme happiness of enlightenment through practising Dharma purely and sincerely. We should encourage ourself to accomplish the real meaning of our human life. What is the real meaning of human life?

Many people believe that material development is the real meaning of human life, but we can see that no matter how much material development there is in the world it never reduces human suffering and problems. Instead, it often causes suffering and problems to increase; therefore it is not the real meaning of human life. We should know that at present we have reached the human world for just a brief moment from our former lives, and we have the opportunity to attain the supreme happiness of enlightenment through practising Dharma. This is our extraordinary good fortune. When we attain enlightenment we will have fulfilled our own wishes, and we can fulfil the wishes of all other living beings; we will have liberated ourself permanently from the sufferings of this life and countless future lives, and we can directly benefit each and every living being every day. The attainment of enlightenment is therefore the real meaning of human life.

Enlightenment is the inner light of wisdom that is permanently free from all mistaken appearance, and whose function is to bestow mental peace upon each and every living being every day. Right now we have obtained a human rebirth and have the opportunity to attain enlightenment through

Dharma practice, so if we waste this precious opportunity in meaningless activities there is no greater loss and no greater foolishness. This is because in future such a precious opportunity will be extremely hard to find. In one Sutra Buddha illustrates this by giving the following analogy. He asks his disciples, 'Suppose there existed a vast and deep ocean the size of this world, and on its surface there floated a golden yoke, and at the bottom of the ocean there lived a blind turtle who surfaced only once in every one hundred thousand years. How often would that turtle raise its head through the middle of the yoke?' His disciple, Ananda, answers that, indeed, it would be extremely rare.

In this context, the vast and deep ocean refers to samsara – the cycle of impure life that we have experienced since beginningless time, continually in life after life without end – the golden yoke refers to Buddhadharma, and the blind turtle refers to us. Although we are not physically a turtle, mentally we are not much different; and although our physical eyes may not be blind, our wisdom eyes are. For most of our countless previous lives we have remained at the bottom of the ocean of samsara, in the three lower realms – the animal, hungry ghost and hell realms – surfacing only once in every one hundred thousand years or so as a human being. Even when we briefly reach the upper realm of samsara's ocean as a human being, it is extremely rare to meet the golden yoke of Buddhadharma: the ocean of samsara is extremely vast, the golden yoke of Buddhadharma does not remain in one place but moves from place to place, and our wisdom eyes are always blind. For these reasons, Buddha says that in the future, even if we obtain a human rebirth, it will be extremely rare to meet Buddhadharma again; meeting Kadam Dharma is even more rare than this. We can see that the great majority of human beings in the world, even though they have briefly reached the upper realm of samsara as human beings, have not met Buddhadharma. This is because their wisdom eyes have not opened.

What does 'meeting Buddhadharma' mean? It means entering into Buddhism by sincerely seeking refuge in Buddha, Dharma and Sangha, and thus having the opportunity to enter and make progress on the path to enlightenment. If we do not meet Buddhadharma we have no opportunity to do this, and therefore we have no opportunity to accomplish the pure and everlasting happiness of enlightenment, the real meaning of human life.

THE OBJECT OF THIS MEDITATION

The object of this meditation, or the object on which we focus single-pointedly, is our determination to practise Dharma purely and sincerely. We should learn to develop this determination through contemplating the above explanation of the purpose of this meditation. When through this contemplation a firm determination to practise Dharma purely and sincerely develops in our heart, we have found the object of this meditation.

THE ACTUAL MEDITATION

We should think:

At present I have briefly reached the human world and have the opportunity to attain permanent liberation from suffering and the supreme happiness of enlightenment through putting Dharma into practice. If I waste this precious opportunity in meaningless activities there is no greater loss and no greater foolishness.

Thinking in this way we make the strong determination to practise the Dharma of Buddha's teachings on renunciation, universal compassion and the profound view of emptiness now, while we have the opportunity. We hold this determination without forgetting it and remain on it single-pointedly for as long as possible. Through learning this meditation continually we should maintain this determination day and night throughout our life and put it into practice.

MEDITATION ON DEATH

THE PURPOSE OF THIS MEDITATION

The purpose of this meditation is to prevent the laziness of attachment, the main obstacle to Dharma practice. Because our desire for worldly enjoyment is so strong, we have little or no interest in Dharma practice. From a spiritual point of view, this lack of interest in Dharma practice is a type of laziness called the 'laziness of attachment'. For as long as we have this laziness, the door to liberation will be closed to us, and consequently we will continue to experience misery and suffering in this life and in countless future lives. The way to overcome this laziness, the main obstacle to our Dharma practice, is to meditate on death.

We need to contemplate and meditate on our death again and again until we gain a deep realization of death. Although on an intellectual level we all know that eventually we are going to die, our awareness of death remains superficial. Since our intellectual knowledge of death does not touch our hearts, each and every day we continue to think 'I will not die today, I will not die today.' Even on the day of our death, we are still thinking about what we will do tomorrow or next week. This mind that thinks every day 'I will not die today' is deceptive – it leads us in the wrong direction and causes our human life to become empty. On the other hand, through meditating on death we will gradually replace the deceptive thought 'I will not die today' with the non-deceptive thought 'I may die today.' The mind that spontaneously thinks each and every day 'I may die today' is the realization of death. It is this realization that directly eliminates our laziness of attachment and opens the door to the spiritual path.

In general, we may die today or we may not die today – we do not know. However, if we think each day 'I may not die today', this thought will deceive us because it comes from our ignorance; whereas if instead we think each day 'I may die today', this thought will not deceive us because it comes from our wisdom. This beneficial thought will prevent our laziness of attachment, and will encourage us to prepare for the welfare of our countless future lives or to put great effort into entering the path to liberation and enlightenment. In this way, we will make our present human life meaningful. Until now we have wasted our countless former lives without any meaning; we have brought nothing with us from our former lives except delusions and suffering.

WHAT DOES OUR DEATH MEAN?

Our death is the permanent separation of our body and mind. We may experience many temporary separations of our body and mind, but these are not our death. For example, when those who have completed their training in the practice known as 'transference of consciousness' engage in meditation, their mind separates from their body. Their body remains where they are meditating, and their mind goes to a Pure Land and then returns to their body. At night, during dreams, our body remains in bed but our mind goes to various places of the dream world and then returns to our body.

These separations of our body and mind are not our death because they are only temporary.

At death our mind separates from our body permanently. Our body remains at the place of this life but our mind goes to various places of our future lives, like a bird leaving one nest and flying to another. This clearly shows the existence of our countless future lives, and that the nature and function of our body and mind are very different. Our body is a visual form that possesses colour and shape, but our mind is a formless continuum that always lacks colour and shape. As explained in Part One, the nature of our mind is empty like space, and its function is to perceive or understand objects. Through this we can understand that our brain is not our mind. The brain is simply a part of our body that, for example, can be photographed, whereas our mind cannot.

We may not be happy to hear about our death, but contemplating and meditating on death is very important for the effectiveness of our Dharma practice. This is because it prevents the main obstacle to our Dharma practice – the laziness of attachment to the things of this life – and it encourages us to practise pure Dharma right now. If we do this we will accomplish the real meaning of human life before our death.

THE OBJECT OF THIS MEDITATION

The object of this meditation is our thought 'I may die today, I may die today.' We should learn to develop this thought through contemplating the above explanation of the purpose of this meditation. When through this contemplation the thought 'I may die today, I may die today' develops in our heart, we have found the object of this meditation.

THE ACTUAL MEDITATION

We contemplate and think:

I will definitely die. There is no way to prevent my body from finally decaying. Day by day, moment by moment, my life is slipping away. I have no idea when I will die; the time of death is completely uncertain. Many young people die before their parents, some die the moment they are born – there is no certainty in this world. Furthermore, there are so many causes of untimely death. The lives of many strong and healthy people are destroyed by accidents. There is no guarantee that I will not die today.

Having repeatedly contemplated these points, we mentally repeat over and over again 'I may die today, I may die today', and concentrate on the feeling it evokes. We transform our mind into this feeling 'I may die today' and remain on it single-pointedly for as long as possible. We should practise this meditation repeatedly until we spontaneously believe each and every day 'I may die today.' Eventually we will come to a conclusion: 'Since I will soon have to depart from this world, there is no sense in my becoming attached to the things of this life. Instead, from now on I will devote my whole life to practising Dharma purely and sincerely.' We then maintain this determination day and night.

During the meditation break, without laziness we should apply effort to our Dharma practice. Realizing that worldly pleasures are deceptive, and that they distract us from using our life in a meaningful way, we should abandon attachment to them. In this way, we can eliminate the main obstacle to pure Dharma practice.

MEDITATION ON THE DANGER OF LOWER REBIRTH

THE PURPOSE OF THIS MEDITATION

The purpose of this meditation is to encourage us to prepare protection from the dangers of lower rebirth. If we do not do this now, while we have a human life with its freedoms and endowments and we have the opportunity to do so, it will be too late once we have taken any of the three lower rebirths; and it will be extremely difficult to obtain such a precious human life again. A precious human life means a human rebirth in which we have the opportunity to attain permanent liberation from all suffering, known as 'nirvana'. It is said to be easier for human beings to attain enlightenment than it is for beings such as animals to attain a precious human rebirth. Understanding this will encourage us to abandon non-virtue, or negative actions; to practise virtue, or positive actions, and to seek refuge in Buddha, Dharma and Sangha (the supreme spiritual friends); this is our actual protection.

Performing non-virtuous actions is the main cause of taking lower rebirth, whereas practising virtue and seeking refuge in Buddha, Dharma and Sangha are the main causes of taking a precious human rebirth. Heavy non-virtuous actions are the main cause of rebirth as a hell being, middling non-virtuous actions are the main cause of rebirth as a hungry ghost, and lesser non-virtuous actions are the main cause of rebirth as an animal. There are many examples given in Buddhist scriptures of how non-virtuous actions lead to rebirth in the three lower realms.

There was once a hunter whose wife came from a family of animal farmers. After he died he took rebirth as a cow belonging to his wife's family. A butcher then bought this cow, slaughtered it and sold the meat. The hunter was reborn seven times as a cow belonging to the same family, and in this way became food for other people.

In Tibet there is a lake called Yamdroktso, where many people from the nearby town used to spend their whole lives fishing. At one time a great Yogi with clairvoyance visited the town and said, 'I see the people of this town and the fish in this lake are continually switching their positions.' What he meant was that the people of the town who enjoyed fishing were reborn as the fish, the food of other people, and the fish in the lake were reborn as the people who enjoyed fishing. In this way, changing their physical aspect, they were continually killing and eating each other. This cycle of misery continued from generation to generation.

THE OBJECT OF THIS MEDITATION

The object of this meditation is our feeling of fear of taking rebirth in the lower realms as an animal, a hungry ghost or a hell being. We should learn to develop this feeling of fear through contemplating the above explanation of the purpose of this meditation. When through this contemplation a feeling of fear of taking such a rebirth develops in our heart, we have found the object of this meditation.

In general fear is meaningless, but the fear generated here has great meaning. It arises from our wisdom and directly leads us to prepare the actual protection from taking lower rebirth, which is sincerely seeking refuge in Buddha, Dharma and Sangha, or in Guru Sumati Buddha Heruka. As the result of this, our next rebirth will be a precious human rebirth, which will give us the opportunity to continually make progress in our practice of Dharma, both Sutra and Tantra. Or our next rebirth will be in Keajra Pure Land through being led by Guru Sumati Buddha Heruka. If we do not generate this fear now we will never prepare these protections.

THE ACTUAL MEDITATION

We contemplate as follows:

When the oil of an oil lamp is exhausted, the flame goes out because the flame is produced from the oil; but when our body dies our consciousness is not extinguished, because consciousness is not produced from the body. When we die our mind has to leave this present body, which is just a temporary abode, and find another body, rather like a bird leaving one nest to fly to another. Our mind has no freedom to remain and no choice about where to go. We are blown to the place of our next rebirth by the winds of our actions or karma (our good fortune or misfortune). If the karma that ripens at our death time is negative, we will definitely take a lower rebirth. Heavy negative karma causes rebirth in hell, middling negative karma causes rebirth as a hungry ghost, and lesser negative karma causes rebirth as an animal.

It is very easy to commit heavy negative karma. For example, simply by swatting a mosquito out of anger we create the cause to be reborn in hell. Throughout this and all our countless previous lives we have committed many heavy negative actions. Unless we have already purified these actions by practising sincere confession, their potentialities remain in our mental continuum, and any one of these negative potentialities could ripen when we die. Bearing this in mind, we should ask ourself, 'If I die today, where will I be tomorrow? It is quite possible that I will find myself in the animal realm, among the hungry ghosts, or in hell. If someone were to call me a stupid cow today, I would find it difficult to bear, but what will I do if I actually become a cow, a pig, or a fish – the food of human beings?'

Having repeatedly contemplated these points and understood how beings in the lower realms, such as animals, experience suffering, we generate a strong fear of taking rebirth in the lower realms. We then hold this without forgetting it; our mind should remain on this feeling of fear single-pointedly for as long as possible. If we lose the object of our meditation we renew the feeling of fear by immediately remembering it or by repeating the contemplation.

During the meditation break we try never to forget our feeling of fear of taking rebirth in the lower realms.

MEDITATION ON GOING FOR REFUGE

THE PURPOSE OF THIS MEDITATION

The purpose of this meditation is to protect ourself permanently from taking lower rebirth. In this context, 'going for refuge' means seeking refuge in Buddha, Dharma and Sangha. At present, because we are human, we are free from rebirth as an animal, hungry ghost or hell being, but this is only temporary. We are like a prisoner who gets permission to stay at home for a week, but then has to return to prison. We need permanent liberation from the sufferings of this life and countless future lives. This depends upon entering, making progress on and completing the Buddhist path to liberation, which in turn depends upon entering Buddhism.

We enter Buddhism through the practice of going for refuge. For our practice of refuge to be qualified, while visualizing Buddha in front of us we should verbally or mentally make the promise to seek refuge in Buddha, Dharma and Sangha throughout our life. This promise is our refuge vow, and is the gateway through which we enter Buddhism. For as long as we keep this promise we are inside Buddhism, but if we break this promise we are outside. By entering and remaining inside Buddhism we have the opportunity to begin, make progress on and complete the Buddhist path to liberation and enlightenment.

We should never give up our promise to seek refuge in Buddha, Dharma and Sangha throughout our life. Going for refuge to Buddha, Dharma and Sangha means that we apply effort to receiving Buddha's blessings, to putting Dharma into practice and to receiving help from Sangha. These are the three principal commitments of the refuge vow. Through maintaining and sincerely practising these three principal commitments of refuge we can fulfil our final goal.

The main reason why we need to make the determination and promise to seek refuge in Buddha, Dharma and Sangha throughout our life is that we need to attain permanent liberation from suffering. At present we may be free from physical suffering and mental pain, but as mentioned earlier this freedom is only temporary. Later in this life and in our countless future lives we will have to experience unbearable physical suffering and mental pain continually, in life after life without end.

When our life is in danger or we are threatened by someone, we usually seek refuge in the police. Of course, sometimes the police can protect us from a particular danger, but they cannot give us permanent liberation from death. When we are seriously ill we seek refuge in doctors. Sometimes doctors can cure a particular illness, but no doctor can give us permanent liberation from sickness. What we really need is permanent liberation from all sufferings, and as human beings we can achieve this by seeking refuge in Buddha, Dharma and Sangha.

Buddhas are 'awakened', which means that they have awakened from the sleep of ignorance and are free from the dreams of samsara, the cycle of impure life. They are completely pure beings who are permanently free from all delusions and mistaken appearance. Buddha's function is to bestow mental peace on each and every living being every day by giving blessings. We know that we are happy when our mind is peaceful, and unhappy when it is not. It is therefore clear that our happiness depends upon our having a peaceful mind and not on good external conditions. Even if our external conditions are poor, if we maintain a peaceful mind all the time we will always be happy. Through continually receiving Buddha's blessings we can maintain a peaceful mind all the time. Buddha is therefore the source of our happiness. Dharma is the actual protection through which we are permanently released from the sufferings of sickness, ageing, death and rebirth; and Sangha are the supreme spiritual friends who guide us to correct spiritual paths. Through these three precious wishfulfilling jewels, Buddha, Dharma and Sangha – known as the 'Three Jewels' – we can fulfil our own wishes as well as the wishes of all living beings.

Every day from the depths of our heart we should recite requesting prayers to the enlightened Buddhas, while maintaining deep faith in them. This is a simple method for us to receive the Buddhas' blessings continually. We should also join group prayers, known as 'pujas', organized at Buddhist Temples or Prayer Halls, which are powerful methods to receive the Buddhas' blessings and protection.

THE OBJECT OF THIS MEDITATION

The object of this meditation is our determination and promise to seek refuge sincerely in Buddha, Dharma and Sangha throughout our life. We should learn to develop this determination and promise through contemplating the above explanation of the purpose of this meditation. When through this contemplation a firm determination to seek refuge in Buddha, Dharma and Sangha develops in our heart, we have found the object of this meditation.

THE ACTUAL MEDITATION

We should think:

> *I want to protect and liberate myself permanently from the sufferings of this life and countless future lives. I can accomplish this only by receiving Buddha's blessings, putting Dharma into practice and receiving help from Sangha – the supreme spiritual friends.*

Thinking deeply in this way, we first make the strong determination and then the mental promise to seek refuge sincerely in Buddha, Dharma and Sangha throughout our life. We hold this determination and promise without forgetting, and we remain on this determination and promise single-pointedly for as long as possible. We should practise this meditation continually.

As the commitments of our refuge vow we should always apply effort to receiving Buddha's blessings, to putting Dharma into practice and to receiving help from Sangha, our pure spiritual friends including our Spiritual Teacher. This is how we go for refuge to Buddha, Dharma and Sangha. Through this we will accomplish our aim – permanent liberation from all the sufferings of this life and countless future lives, the real meaning of our human life.

To maintain our promise to go for refuge to Buddha, Dharma and Sangha throughout our life, and so that we and all living beings may receive Buddha's blessings and protection, we recite the following refuge prayer every day with strong faith:

> *I and all sentient beings, until we achieve enlightenment,*
> *Go for refuge to Buddha, Dharma and Sangha.*

MEDITATION ON KARMA

THE PURPOSE OF THIS MEDITATION

The purpose of this meditation is to prevent future suffering and to build the basic foundation for the path to liberation and enlightenment. Generally, karma means 'action'. From non-virtuous actions comes suffering and from virtuous actions comes happiness: if we believe this, we believe in karma. Buddha gave extensive teachings that prove the truth of this statement, and many different examples that show the special connection between the actions of our former lives and our experiences of this life, some of which are explained in *Joyful Path of Good Fortune*.

Non-virtuous actions mean actions that are the opposite of virtue. Speaking generally, virtue means good fortune, which brings good results; and non-virtue means misfortune, which brings bad results. In our previous lives we performed various kinds of non-virtuous actions that caused others suffering. As a result of these non-virtuous actions, various kinds of miserable conditions and situations arise and we experience endless human suffering and problems. This is the same for all other living beings.

We should judge whether or not we believe that the main cause of suffering is our non-virtuous actions and the main cause of happiness is our virtuous actions. If we do not believe this we will never apply effort to accumulating virtuous actions, or merit, and we will never purify our non-virtuous actions, and because of this we will experience suffering and difficulties continually, in life after life without end.

Every action we perform leaves an imprint on our very subtle mind, and each imprint eventually gives rise to its own effect. Our mind is like a field, and performing actions

271

is like sowing seeds in that field. Virtuous actions sow seeds of future happiness and non-virtuous actions sow seeds of future suffering. These seeds remain dormant in our mind until the conditions for them to ripen occur, and then they produce their effect. In some cases, this can happen many lifetimes after the original action was performed.

The seeds that ripen when we die are very important because they determine what kind of rebirth we will take in our next life. Which particular seed ripens at death depends upon the state of mind in which we die. If we die with a peaceful mind, this will stimulate a virtuous seed and we will experience a fortunate rebirth. However, if we die with an unpeaceful mind, such as in a state of anger, this will stimulate a non-virtuous seed and we will experience an unfortunate rebirth. This is similar to the way in which nightmares are triggered by our being in an agitated state of mind just before falling asleep.

All inappropriate actions, including killing, stealing, sexual misconduct, lying, divisive speech, hurtful speech, idle chatter, covetousness, malice and holding wrong views, are non-virtuous actions. When we abandon non-virtuous actions and apply effort to purifying our previous non-virtuous actions we are practising moral discipline. This will prevent us from experiencing future suffering and from taking a lower rebirth. Examples of virtuous actions are training in all the meditations and other spiritual practices presented in this book. Meditation is a virtuous mental action that is the main cause for experiencing mental peace in the future. Whenever we practise meditation, whether or not our meditation is clear, we are performing a virtuous mental action that is a cause of our future happiness and peace of mind. We are normally concerned mainly about bodily and verbal actions, but in reality mental actions are more important. Our bodily and verbal actions depend upon our mental action – upon our mentally making a decision.

Whenever we perform virtuous actions such as meditation or other spiritual practices we should have the following mental determination:

While riding the horse of virtuous actions
I will guide it into the path of liberation with the reins
of renunciation;
And through urging this horse onward with the whip
of effort,
I will quickly reach the Pure Land of liberation and
enlightenment.

THE OBJECT OF THIS MEDITATION

The object of this meditation is our determination to abandon and to purify our non-virtuous actions, and to accumulate virtuous actions or merit. We should learn to develop this determination through contemplating the above explanation of the purpose of this meditation. When through this contemplation a firm determination to abandon non-virtuous actions and to accumulate virtuous actions develops in our heart, we have found the object of this meditation.

THE ACTUAL MEDITATION

We contemplate and think:

Since I myself never wish to suffer and always want to be happy, I must abandon and purify my non-virtuous actions and sincerely perform virtuous actions.

We hold this determination firmly and remain on it single-pointedly for as long as possible. We should practise this meditation every day and put our determination into practice.

MEDITATION OF A PERSON OF MIDDLING SCOPE

There are four meditations of a person of middling scope. These are:

1 Meditation on renunciation
2 Meditation on our determination to recognize, reduce and abandon our self-grasping ignorance, the root of samsaric rebirth
3 Meditation on our determination to enter and make progress on the path to liberation
4 Meditation on the ultimate truth of cessation

MEDITATION ON RENUNCIATION

THE PURPOSE OF THIS MEDITATION

The purpose of this meditation is to enter, make progress on and complete the path to liberation. To achieve this aim we need to consider what we should know, what we should abandon, what we should practise and what we should attain.

In *Sutra of the Four Noble Truths* Buddha says, 'You should know sufferings.' In saying this Buddha is advising us that we should know about the unbearable sufferings that we will experience in our countless future lives, and therefore develop renunciation, the determination to liberate ourself permanently from these sufferings.

In general, everyone who has physical or mental pain, even animals, understands their own suffering; but when

Buddha says 'You should know sufferings' he means that we should know the sufferings of our future lives. Through knowing these, we will develop a strong wish to liberate ourself from them. This practical advice is important for everybody because, if we have the wish to liberate ourself from the sufferings of future lives, we will definitely use our present human life for the freedom and happiness of our countless future lives. There is no greater meaning than this.

If we do not have this wish, we will waste our precious human life only for the freedom and happiness of this one short life. This would be foolish because our intention and actions would be no different from the intention and actions of animals who are only concerned with this life alone. The great Yogi Milarepa once said to a hunter called Gonpo Dorje:

> Your body is human but your mind is that of an
> animal.
> You, a human being, who possess an animal's mind,
> please listen to my song.

Normally we believe that solving the suffering and problems of our present life is most important, and we dedicate our whole life for this purpose. In reality, the duration of the suffering and problems of this life is very short; if we die tomorrow, they will end tomorrow. However, since the duration of the suffering and problems of future lives is endless, the freedom and happiness of our future lives is vastly more important than the freedom and happiness of this one short life. With the words 'You should know sufferings' Buddha encourages us to use our present human life to prepare for the freedom and happiness of our countless future lives. Those who do this are truly wise.

In future lives, when we are born as an animal, such as a cow or a fish, we will become the food of other living beings, and we will have to experience many other kinds of animal suffering. Animals have no freedom, and are used by human beings for food, work and enjoyment. They have no opportunity to improve themselves; even if they hear precious Dharma words it is as meaningless to them as hearing the wind blowing. When we are born as a hungry ghost we will not have even a tiny drop of water to drink; our only water will be our tears. We will have to experience the unbearable sufferings of thirst and hunger for many hundreds of years. When we are born as a hell being in the hot hells our body will become inseparable from fire, and others will be able to distinguish between our body and fire only by hearing our suffering cries. We will have to experience the unbearable torment of our body being burned for millions of years. Like all other phenomena, the hell realms do not exist inherently but exist as mere appearances to mind, like dreams.

When we are born as a desire realm god we experience great conflict and dissatisfaction. Even if we experience some superficial enjoyment, still our desires grow stronger, and we have even more mental suffering than human beings. When we are born as a demi-god we are always jealous of the gods' glory and because of this we have great mental suffering. Our jealousy is like a thorn piercing our mind, causing us to experience both mental and physical suffering for long periods of time. When we are born as a human being we will have to experience various kinds of human suffering, including the sufferings of birth, sickness, ageing and death.

BIRTH

When our consciousness first enters the union of our father's sperm and our mother's ovum, our body is a very hot, watery substance like white yoghurt tinted red. In the first moments after conception we have no gross feelings, but as soon as these develop we begin to experience pain. Our body gradually becomes harder and harder, and as our limbs grow it feels as if our body is being stretched out on a rack. Inside our mother's womb it is hot and dark. Our home for nine months is this small, tightly compressed space full of unclean substances. It is like being squashed inside a small water tank full of filthy liquid with the lid tightly shut so that no air or light can come through.

While we are in our mother's womb we experience much pain and fear all on our own. We are extremely sensitive to everything our mother does. When she walks quickly it feels as if we are falling from a high mountain and we are terrified. If she has sexual intercourse it feels as if we are being crushed and suffocated between two huge weights and we panic. If our mother makes just a small jump it feels as if we are being dashed against the ground from a great height. If she drinks anything hot it feels like boiling water scalding our skin, and if she drinks anything cold it feels like an ice-cold shower in midwinter.

When we are emerging from our mother's womb it feels as if we are being forced through a narrow crevice between two hard rocks, and when we are newly born our body is so delicate that any kind of contact is painful. Even if someone holds us very tenderly, his or her hands feel like thorn bushes piercing our flesh, and the most delicate fabrics feel rough and abrasive. By comparison with the softness and smoothness of our mother's womb, every tactile sensation is harsh and painful. If someone picks us up it feels as if we are being swung over a huge precipice, and we feel frightened and insecure. We have forgotten all that we knew in our previous life; we bring only pain and confusion from our mother's womb. Whatever we hear is as meaningless as the sound of wind, and we cannot comprehend anything we perceive. In the first few weeks we are like someone who is blind, deaf and dumb, and suffering from profound amnesia. When we are hungry we cannot say 'I need food', and when we are in pain we cannot say 'This is hurting me.' The only signs we can make are hot tears and furious gestures. Our mother often has no idea what pains and discomforts we are experiencing. We are completely helpless and have to be taught everything – how to eat, how to sit, how to walk, how to talk.

Although we are most vulnerable in the first few weeks of our life, our pains do not cease as we grow up. We continue to experience various kinds of suffering throughout our life. Just as when we light a fire in a large house, the heat from the fire pervades the whole house and all the heat in the house comes from the fire, so when we are born in samsara, suffering pervades our whole life, and all the miseries we experience arise because we took a contaminated rebirth.

Our human rebirth, contaminated by the poisonous delusion of self-grasping, is the basis of our human suffering; without this basis, there are no human problems. The pains of birth gradually turn into the pains of sickness, ageing and death – they are one continuum.

SICKNESS

Our birth also gives rise to the suffering of sickness. Just as the wind and snow of winter take away the glory of green meadows, trees, forests and flowers, so sickness takes away the youthful splendour of our body, destroying its strength and the power of our senses. If we are usually fit and well, when we become sick we are suddenly unable to engage in all our normal physical activities. Even a champion boxer who is usually able to knock out all his opponents becomes completely helpless when sickness strikes. Sickness makes all our experiences of daily enjoyments disappear and causes us to experience unpleasant feelings day and night.

When we fall ill, we are like a bird that has been soaring in the sky and is suddenly shot down. When a bird is shot, it falls straight to the ground like a lump of lead, and all its glory and power are immediately destroyed. In a similar way, when we become ill we are suddenly incapacitated. If we are seriously ill we may become completely dependent upon others and lose even the ability to control our bodily functions. This transformation is hard to bear, especially for those who pride themselves on their independence and physical well-being.

When we are ill, we feel frustrated as we cannot do our usual work or complete all the tasks we have set ourself. We easily become impatient with our illness and depressed about all the things we cannot do. We cannot enjoy the things that usually give us pleasure, such as sport, dancing, drinking, eating rich foods, or the company of our friends. All these limitations make us feel even more miserable; and, to add to our unhappiness, we have to endure all the physical pains the illness brings.

When we are sick, not only do we have to experience all the unwanted pains of the illness itself, but we also have to experience all sorts of other unwished for things. For example, we have to take whatever cure is prescribed, whether it be a foul-tasting medicine, a series of injections, a major operation, or abstinence from something we like very much. If we are to have an operation, we have to go to hospital and accept all the conditions there. We may have to eat food we do not like and stay in bed all day long with nothing to do, and we may feel anxiety about the operation. Our doctor may not explain to us exactly what the problem is and whether or not he or she expects us to survive.

If we learn that our sickness is incurable, and we have no spiritual experience, we will suffer anxiety, fear and regret.

We may become depressed and give up hope, or we may become angry with our illness, feeling that it is an enemy that has maliciously deprived us of all joy.

AGEING

Our birth also gives rise to the pains of ageing. Ageing steals our beauty, our health, our good figure, our fine complexion, our vitality and our comfort. Ageing turns us into objects of contempt. It brings many unwanted pains and takes us swiftly to our death.

As we grow old we lose all the beauty of our youth, and our strong, healthy body becomes weak and burdened with illness. Our once firm and well-proportioned figure becomes bent and disfigured, and our muscles and flesh shrink so that our limbs become like thin sticks and our bones poke out. Our hair loses its colour and shine, and our complexion loses its lustre. Our face becomes wrinkled and our features grow distorted. Milarepa said:

How do old people get up? They get up as if they were heaving a stake out of the ground. How do old people walk about? Once they are on their feet they have to walk gingerly, like bird-catchers. How do old people sit down? They crash down like heavy luggage whose harness has snapped.

We can contemplate the following poem on the sufferings of growing old, written by the scholar Gungtang:

When we are old, our hair becomes white,
But not because we have washed it clean;
It is a sign we will soon encounter the Lord of Death.

We have wrinkles on our forehead,
But not because we have too much flesh;
It is a warning from the Lord of Death: 'You are about
    to die.'

Our teeth fall out,
But not to make room for new ones;
It is a sign we will soon lose the ability to eat human food.

Our faces are ugly and unpleasant,
But not because we are wearing masks;
It is a sign we have lost the mask of youth.

Our heads shake to and fro,
But not because we are in disagreement;
It is the Lord of Death striking our head with the stick
    he holds in his right hand.

We walk bent and gazing at the ground,
But not because we are searching for lost needles;
It is a sign we are searching for our lost beauty and
    memories.

We get up from the ground using all four limbs,
But not because we are imitating animals;
It is a sign our legs are too weak to support our body.

We sit down as if we had suddenly fallen,
But not because we are angry;
It is a sign our body has lost its strength.

Our body sways as we walk,
But not because we think we are important;
It is a sign our legs cannot carry our body.

Our hands shake,
But not because they are itching to steal;
It is a sign the Lord of Death's itchy fingers are stealing
    our possessions.

We eat very little,
But not because we are miserly;
It is a sign we cannot digest our food.

We wheeze frequently,
But not because we are whispering mantras to the sick;
It is a sign our breathing will soon disappear.

When we are young we can travel around the whole world,
but when we are old we can hardly make it to our own front
gate. We become too weak to engage in many worldly activities, and our spiritual activities are often curtailed. For
example, we have little physical strength to perform virtuous
actions, and little mental energy to memorize, contemplate
and meditate. We cannot attend teachings that are given in
places that are hard to reach or uncomfortable to inhabit. We
cannot help others in ways that require physical strength
and good health. Deprivations such as these often make old
people very sad.

When we grow old, we become like someone who is blind
and deaf. We cannot see clearly, and we need stronger and
stronger glasses until we can no longer read. We cannot hear
clearly, and so it becomes more and more difficult to listen
to music or to the television, or to hear what others are saying. Our memory fades. All activities, worldly and spiritual,
become more difficult. If we practise meditation it becomes
harder for us to gain realizations because our memory and
concentration are too weak. We cannot apply ourself to study.
Thus, if we have not learnt and trained in spiritual practices

when we were younger, the only thing to do when we grow old is to develop regret and wait for the Lord of Death to come.

When we are old we cannot derive the same enjoyment from the things we used to enjoy, such as food, drink and sex. We are too weak to play games and we are often too exhausted even for entertainments. As our lifespan runs out we cannot join young people in their activities. When they travel about we have to stay behind. No one wants to take us with them when we are old, and no one wants to visit us. Even our own grandchildren do not want to stay with us for very long. Old people often think to themselves, 'How wonderful it would be if young people would stay with me. We could go out for walks and I could show them things'; but young people do not want to be included in their plans. As their life draws to an end, old people experience the sorrow of abandonment and loneliness. They have many special sorrows.

DEATH

Our birth also gives rise to the sufferings of death. If during our life we have worked hard to acquire possessions, and if we have become very attached to them, we will experience great suffering at the time of death, thinking 'Now I have to leave all my precious possessions behind.' Even now we find it difficult to lend one of our most treasured possessions to someone else, let alone to give it away. No wonder we become so miserable when we realize that in the hands of death we must abandon everything.

When we die we have to part from even our closest friends. We have to leave our partner, even though we may have been together for years and never spent a day apart. If we are very attached to our friends we will experience great misery at the time of death, but all we will be able to do is hold their hands. We will not be able to halt the process of death, even if they plead with us not to die. Usually when we are very attached to someone we feel jealous if he or she leaves us on our own and spends time with someone else, but when we die we will have to leave our friends with others forever. We will have to leave everyone, including our family and all the people who have helped us in this life.

When we die, this body that we have cherished and cared for in so many ways will have to be left behind. It will become mindless like a stone, and will be buried in the ground or cremated. If we do not have the inner protection of spiritual experience, at the time of death we will experience fear and distress, as well as physical pain.

When our consciousness departs from our body at death, all the potentialities we have accumulated in our mind by performing virtuous and non-virtuous actions will go with it. Other than these we cannot take anything out of this world. All other things deceive us. Death ends all our activities – our conversation, our eating, our meeting with friends, our sleep. Everything draws to a close on the day of our death and we must leave all things behind, even the rings on our fingers. In Tibet beggars carry a stick to defend themselves against dogs. To understand the complete deprivation of death we should remember that at the time of death beggars have to leave even this old stick, the most meagre of human possessions. All over the world we can see that names carved on stone are the only possessions of the dead.

OTHER TYPES OF SUFFERING

We also have to experience the sufferings of separation, having to encounter what we do not like and not fulfilling our wishes – which include the sufferings of poverty, and of being harmed by humans and non-humans and by water, fire, wind and earth. Before the final separation at the time of death we often have to experience temporary separation from the people and things we like, which causes us mental pain. We may have to leave our country where all our friends and relatives live, or we may have to leave the job we like. We may lose our reputation. Many times in this life we have to experience the misery of departing from the people we like, or forsaking and losing the things we find pleasant and attractive; but when we die we have to part forever from all our companions and enjoyments, and from all the outer and inner conditions for our Dharma practice, of this life.

We often have to meet and live with people whom we do not like, or encounter situations that we find unpleasant. Sometimes we may find ourself in a very dangerous situation such as in a fire or a flood, or where there is violence such as in a riot or a battle. Our lives are full of less extreme situations that we find annoying. Sometimes we are prevented from doing the things we want to do. On a sunny day we may set off for the beach but find ourself stuck in a traffic jam. We continually experience interference from our inner demon of delusions, which disturbs our mind and our spiritual practices. There are countless conditions that frustrate our plans and prevent us from doing what we want. It is as if we are naked and living in a thorn bush – whenever we try to move, we are wounded by circumstances. People and things are like thorns piercing our flesh and no situation ever feels entirely comfortable. The more desires and plans we have, the more frustrations we experience. The more we want certain situations, the more we find ourself stuck in situations we do not want. Every desire seems to invite its own obstacle. Undesired situations befall us without our looking for them. In fact, the only things that come effortlessly are the things we do not want. No one wants to die, but death comes effortlessly. No one wants to be sick, but sickness comes effortlessly. Because we have taken rebirth without freedom or control, we have an impure body and inhabit an impure environment, and so undesirable things pour in upon us. In samsara, this kind of experience is entirely natural.

We have countless desires, but no matter how much effort we make we never feel that we have satisfied them. Even when we get what we want, we do not get it in the way we want. We possess the object but we do not derive satisfaction from possessing it. For example, we may dream of becoming wealthy, but if we actually become wealthy our life is not the way we imagined it would be, and we do not feel that we have fulfilled our desire. This is because our desires do not decrease as our wealth increases. The more wealth we have, the more we desire. The wealth we seek is unfindable because we seek an amount that will satiate our desires, and no amount of wealth can do that. To make things worse, in obtaining the object of our desire we create new occasions for discontent. With every object we desire come other objects we do not want. For example, with wealth come taxes, insecurity and complicated financial affairs. These unwished for side-effects prevent us from ever feeling fully satisfied. Similarly, we may dream of having a holiday in the South Seas, and we may actually go there on holiday, but the experience is never quite what we expect, and with our holiday come other things such as sunburn and great expense.

If we examine our desires we will see that they are excessive. We want all the best things in samsara – the best job, the best partner, the best reputation, the best house, the best car, the best holiday. Anything that is not the best leaves us with a feeling of disappointment – still searching for but not finding what we want. No worldly enjoyment, however, can give us the complete and perfect satisfaction we desire. Better things are always being produced. Everywhere, new advertisements announce that the very best thing has just arrived on the market, but a few days later another best thing arrives that is better than the best thing of a few days ago. There is no end of new things to captivate our desires.

Children at school can never satisfy their own or their parents' ambitions. Even if they come top of their class they feel they cannot be content unless they do the same the following year. If they go on to be successful in their jobs, their ambitions will be as strong as ever. There is no point at which they can rest, feeling that they are completely satisfied with what they have done.

We may think that at least people who lead a simple life in the country must be content, but if we look at their situation we will find that even farmers search for but do not find what they want. Their lives are full of problems and anxieties, and they do not enjoy real peace and satisfaction. Their livelihoods depend upon many uncertain factors beyond their control, such as the weather. Farmers have no more freedom from discontent than businessmen who live and work in the city. Businessmen look smart and efficient as they set off to work each morning carrying their briefcases but, although they look so smooth on the outside, in their hearts they carry many dissatisfactions. They are still searching for but not finding what they want.

If we reflect on this situation we may decide that we can find what we are searching for by abandoning all our possessions. We can see, however, that even poor people are looking for but not finding what they seek, and many poor people have difficulty in finding even the most basic necessities of life; millions of people in the world experience the sufferings of extreme poverty.

We cannot avoid the suffering of dissatisfaction by frequently changing our situation. We may think that if we keep getting a new partner or a new job, or keep travelling about, we will eventually find what we want; but even if we were to travel to every place on the globe, and have a new lover in every town, we would still be seeking another place and another lover. In samsara there is no real fulfilment of our desires.

Whenever we see anyone in a high or low position, male or female, they differ only in appearance, dress, behaviour and status. In essence they are all equal – they all experience problems in their lives. Whenever we have a problem, it is easy to think that it is caused by our particular circumstances, and that if we were to change our circumstances our problem would disappear. We blame other people, our friends, our food, our government, our times, the weather, society, history and so forth. However, external circumstances such as these are not the main causes of our problems. We need to recognize that all the physical suffering and mental pain we experience are the consequences of our taking a rebirth that is contaminated by the inner poison of delusions. Human beings have to experience various kinds of human suffering because they have taken a contaminated human rebirth; animals have to experience animal suffering because they have taken a contaminated animal rebirth; and hungry ghosts and hell beings have to experience their own sufferings because they have taken contaminated rebirth as hungry ghosts and hell beings. Even gods are not free from suffering because they too have taken a contaminated rebirth. Just as a person trapped inside a raging fire develops intense fear, so we should develop intense fear of the unbearable sufferings of the endless cycle of impure life. This fear is real renunciation and arises from our wisdom.

THE OBJECT OF THIS MEDITATION

The object of this meditation is our determination to liberate ourself permanently from the sufferings of this life and of countless future lives. This determination is renunciation. We should learn to develop this determination through contemplating the above explanation of the purpose of this meditation. When through this contemplation a firm determination to liberate ourself permanently from the sufferings of this life and of countless future lives develops in our heart, we have found the object of this meditation.

THE ACTUAL MEDITATION

From our heart we should think:

> *There is no benefit in denying the sufferings of future lives; when they actually descend upon me it will be too late to protect myself from them. Therefore I definitely need to prepare protection now, while I have this human life that gives me the opportunity to liberate myself permanently from the sufferings of my countless future lives. If I do not apply effort to accomplish this, but allow my human life to become empty of meaning, there is no greater deception and no greater foolishness. I must put effort now into liberating myself permanently from the sufferings of my countless future lives.*

We hold this determination firmly and we remain on it single-pointedly for as long as possible. We should practise this meditation continually until we develop the spontaneous wish to liberate ourself permanently from the sufferings of countless future lives. This is the actual realization of renunciation. The moment we develop this realization we enter the path to liberation. In this context, liberation refers to the supreme permanent peace of mind known as 'nirvana', which gives us pure and everlasting happiness.

MEDITATION ON OUR DETERMINATION TO RECOGNIZE, REDUCE AND ABANDON OUR SELF-GRASPING IGNORANCE, THE ROOT OF SAMSARIC REBIRTH

THE PURPOSE OF THIS MEDITATION

The purpose of this meditation is to fulfil the aim of our renunciation. In *Sutra of the Four Noble Truths* Buddha says, 'You should abandon origins.' In saying this Buddha is advising us that if we wish to liberate ourself permanently from the sufferings of our countless future lives we should abandon origins. 'Origins' means our delusions, principally our delusion of self-grasping. Self-grasping is called an 'origin' because it is the source of all our suffering and problems, and is also known as the 'inner demon'. Delusions are wrong awarenesses whose function is to destroy mental peace, the source of happiness; they have no function other than to harm us. Delusions such as self-grasping abide at our heart and continually harm us day and night without rest by destroying our peace of mind. In samsara, the cycle of impure life, no one has the opportunity to experience real happiness because their mental peace, the source of happiness, is continually being destroyed by the inner demon of self-grasping.

Our self-grasping ignorance is a mind that mistakenly believes that our self, our body and all the other things that we normally see actually exist. Because of this ignorance we develop attachment to the things we like and anger at the things we do not like. We then perform various kinds of non-virtuous action, and as a result of these actions we experience various kinds of suffering and problems in this life and in life after life.

Self-grasping ignorance is an inner poison that causes far greater harm than any outer poison. Because of being polluted by this inner poison, our mind sees everything in a mistaken way, and as a result we experience hallucination-like sufferings and problems. In reality, our self, our body and all the other things that we normally see do not exist. Self-grasping can be likened to a poisonous tree, all other delusions to its branches, and all our suffering and problems to its fruit; it is the fundamental source of all our other delusions and of all our suffering and problems. Through this we can understand that if we abandon our self-grasping permanently, all our suffering and problems of this life and of countless future lives will cease permanently. The great Yogi Saraha said: 'If your mind is released permanently from self-grasping, there is no doubt that you will be released permanently from suffering.'

THE OBJECT OF THIS MEDITATION

The object of this meditation is our determination to abandon our self-grasping ignorance. We should learn to develop this determination through contemplating the above explanation of the purpose of this meditation. When through this contemplation a firm determination to abandon our ignorance of self-grasping develops in our heart, we have found the object of this meditation.

THE ACTUAL MEDITATION

From our heart we should think:

> *Since I want to liberate myself permanently from all the sufferings of this life and countless future lives, I must apply great effort to recognizing, reducing and finally abandoning my ignorance of self-grasping completely.*

We hold this determination firmly and we remain on it single-pointedly for as long as possible. We should practise this meditation continually and put our determination into practise.

MEDITATION ON OUR DETERMINATION TO ENTER AND MAKE PROGRESS ON THE PATH TO LIBERATION

THE PURPOSE OF THIS MEDITATION

The purpose of this meditation is to encourage ourself to engage in the actual path to liberation, the three higher trainings. In *Sutra of the Four Noble Truths* Buddha says, 'You should practise the path.' In this context, 'path' does not mean an external path that leads from one place to another, but an inner path, a spiritual realization that leads us to the pure happiness of liberation and enlightenment.

The practice of the stages of the path to liberation can be condensed into the three higher trainings: training in higher moral discipline, training in higher concentration and training in higher wisdom. These trainings are called 'higher' because they are motivated by renunciation. They are therefore the actual path to liberation that we need to practise.

The nature of moral discipline is a virtuous determination to abandon inappropriate actions. When we practise moral discipline we abandon inappropriate actions, maintain pure behaviour and perform every action correctly with a virtuous motivation. Moral discipline is most important for everybody in order to prevent future problems for ourself and for others. It makes us pure because it makes our actions pure. We need to be clean and pure ourself; just having a clean body is not enough, since our body is not our self. Moral discipline is like a great earth that supports and nurtures the crops of spiritual realizations. Without practising moral discipline, it is very difficult to make progress in spiritual training. Training in higher moral discipline is learning to be deeply familiar with the practice of moral discipline, motivated by renunciation.

The second higher training is training in higher concentration. In this practice, the nature of concentration is a single-pointed virtuous mind. For as long as we remain with this mind we will experience mental peace, and thus we will be happy. When we practise concentration we prevent distractions and concentrate on virtuous objects. It is very important to train in concentration, as with distractions we cannot accomplish anything. Training in higher concentration is learning to be deeply familiar with the ability to stop distractions and concentrate on virtuous objects, with a motivation of renunciation. With regard to any Dharma practice, if our concentration is clear and strong it is very easy to make progress. Normally, distraction is the main obstacle to our Dharma practice. The practice of moral discipline prevents gross distractions, and concentration prevents subtle distractions; together they give rise to quick results in our Dharma practice.

The third higher training is training in higher wisdom. The nature of wisdom is a virtuous intelligent mind that functions to understand meaningful objects such as the existence of past and future lives, karma and emptiness. This chapter presents many different meditation practices. The objects of all these meditations are meaningful objects. Understanding these objects gives us great meaning in this life and in countless future lives. Many people are very intelligent in destroying their enemies, caring for their families, finding what they want and so forth, but this is not wisdom. Even animals have such intelligence. Worldly intelligence is deceptive, whereas wisdom will never deceive us. It is our inner Spiritual Guide who leads us to correct paths, and it is the divine eye through which we can see past and future lives, and the special connection between our actions in past lives and our experiences in this life, known as 'karma'. The subject of karma is very extensive and subtle, and we can understand it only through wisdom. Training in higher wisdom is learning to develop and increase our wisdom realizing emptiness through contemplating and meditating on emptiness, with a motivation of renunciation. This wisdom is extremely profound. Its object, emptiness, is not nothingness but is the real nature of all phenomena. A detailed explanation of emptiness is given in *Modern Buddhism*, in the chapter on *Training in Ultimate Bodhichitta*.

The three higher trainings are the actual method to attain permanent liberation from the suffering of this life and countless future lives. This can be understood by the following analogy. When we cut down a tree using a saw, the saw alone cannot cut the tree without the use of our hands, which in turn depend upon our body. Training in higher moral discipline is like our body, training in higher concentration is like our hands, and training in higher wisdom is like the saw. By using these three together, we can cut down the poisonous tree of our self-grasping ignorance, and automatically all other delusions – its branches – and all our suffering and problems – its fruits – will cease completely. Then we will have attained the permanent cessation of the suffering of this life and future lives – the supreme permanent peace of mind known as 'nirvana', or liberation. We will have solved all our human problems and accomplished the real meaning of our life.

THE OBJECT OF THIS MEDITATION

The object of this meditation is our determination to practise the three higher trainings. We should learn to develop this determination through contemplating the above explanation of the purpose of this meditation. When through this contemplation a firm determination to practise the three higher trainings develops in our heart, we have found the object of this meditation.

THE ACTUAL MEDITATION

From our heart we should think:

> *Since the three higher trainings are the actual method to attain permanent liberation from the suffering of this life and countless future lives, I must put great effort into practising them.*

We hold this determination firmly and we remain on it single-pointedly for as long as possible. We should practise this meditation continually and put our determination into practice.

MEDITATION ON THE ULTIMATE TRUTH OF CESSATION

THE PURPOSE OF THIS MEDITATION

The purpose of this meditation is to prevent us from being satisfied with a merely temporary cessation of particular sufferings, which is deceptive. In *Sutra of the Four Noble Truths* Buddha says, 'You should attain cessations.' In this context, 'cessation' means the permanent cessation of suffering and its root, self-grasping ignorance. In saying this, Buddha is advising us not to be satisfied with a temporary liberation from particular sufferings, but that we should have the intention to accomplish the ultimate goal of human life, the supreme permanent peace of mind (nirvana), and the pure and everlasting happiness of enlightenment.

Every living being without exception has to experience the cycle of the sufferings of sickness, ageing, death and rebirth, in life after life, endlessly. Following Buddha's example, we should develop strong renunciation for this endless cycle. When he was living in the palace with his family, Buddha saw how his people were constantly experiencing these sufferings and he made the strong determination to attain enlightenment, great liberation, and to lead every living being to this state.

Buddha did not encourage us to abandon daily activities that provide necessary conditions for living, or that prevent poverty, environmental problems, particular diseases and so forth. However, no matter how successful we are in these activities, we will never achieve permanent cessation of such problems. We will still have to experience them in our countless future lives and, even in this life, although we work very hard to prevent these problems, the sufferings of poverty, environmental pollution and disease are increasing throughout the world. Furthermore, because of the power of modern technology there are now many great dangers developing in the world that have never been experienced before. Therefore, we should not be satisfied with merely temporary freedom from particular sufferings, but apply great effort to attaining permanent freedom while we have this opportunity.

We should remember the preciousness of our human life. Because of their previous deluded views denying the value of spiritual practice, those who have taken rebirth as animals, for example, have no opportunity to engage in spiritual practice, which alone gives rise to a meaningful life. Since it is impossible for them to listen to, understand, contemplate and meditate on spiritual instructions, their present animal rebirth itself is an obstacle. As mentioned earlier, only human beings are free from such obstacles and have all the necessary conditions for engaging in spiritual paths, which alone lead to everlasting peace and happiness. This combination of freedom and the possession of necessary conditions is the special characteristic that makes our human life so precious.

THE OBJECT OF THIS MEDITATION

The object of this meditation is our determination to realize the ultimate truth of cessation, the supreme inner peace of nirvana, through our own experience. We should learn to develop this determination through contemplating the above explanation of the purpose of this meditation. When through this contemplation a firm determination to realize the ultimate truth of cessation, the supreme inner peace of nirvana, through our own experience develops in our heart, we have found the object of this meditation.

THE ACTUAL MEDITATION

From our heart we should think:

I should not be satisfied with a merely temporary cessation of particular sufferings, which even animals can experience. I must realize the ultimate truth of cessation, the supreme inner peace of nirvana, through my own experience.

We should hold this determination firmly and remain on it single-pointedly for as long as possible. We should practise this meditation continually and put our determination into practice.

MEDITATION OF A PERSON OF GREAT SCOPE

There are five meditations of a person of great scope, which are:

1 Meditation on cherishing all living beings
2 Meditation on universal compassion
3 Meditation on the supreme good heart, bodhichitta
4 Meditation on our determination and promise to sincerely practise the six perfections
5 Meditation on training in yogic direct perceivers

MEDITATION ON CHERISHING ALL LIVING BEINGS

THE PURPOSE OF THIS MEDITATION

The purpose of this meditation is to develop universal compassion – compassion for all living beings. We should know that learning to cherish others is the best solution to our daily problems, and is the source of all our future happiness and good fortune. We believe that our self that we normally see is so important and its happiness and freedom are most important, and we neglect the happiness and freedom of others. This belief is ignorance, because our self that we normally see does not actually exist. If we search for ourself that we normally see with wisdom, it will disappear. This proves that it does not exist at all. Therefore, our normal view believing that our self is important but others are not is ignorance of self-cherishing. Because of this ignorance we have wasted countless former lives without any meaning. We brought nothing from our former lives only suffering and ignorance. This will be the same in our future lives. In truth, the happiness and freedom of others are more important than our own because we are only one person but others are countless. We must believe that the happiness and freedom of all other living beings are more important than our own.

THE OBJECT OF THIS MEDITATION

The object of this meditation is the belief that the happiness and freedom of all other living beings are more important than our own. We should learn to develop this belief through contemplating the above explanation of the purpose of this meditation. When through this contemplation a strong belief that the happiness and freedom of all other living beings are more important than our own develops in our heart, we have found the object of this meditation.

THE ACTUAL MEDITATION

From the heart we should think:

> *Just as all the Buddhas of the ten directions changed the object of their cherishing from themselves to all living beings and as the result attained the supreme happiness of enlightenment, so must I do the same. Thinking in this way I generate the belief that the happiness and freedom of all other living beings are more important than my own.*

We hold this view firmly and remain on it single-pointedly for as long as possible. We should practise this meditation continually until we develop a spontaneous belief that the happiness and freedom of all other living beings are more important that our own. This is the actual realization of cherishing all living beings.

MEDITATION ON UNIVERSAL COMPASSION

THE PURPOSE OF THIS MEDITATION

The purpose of this meditation is to develop bodhichitta – wanting to become an enlightened being to liberate all living beings. All the previous Buddhas were born from the mother of universal compassion. We should follow their example and apply effort to generate compassion for all living beings without exception. The more our compassion for all living beings increases, the closer and closer we become to attaining enlightenment. This is because our compassion for all living beings makes our mind and our actions become more and more pure, and when through this our mind and our actions become completely pure we become an enlightened being.

Universal compassion is a mind that sincerely wishes to liberate all living beings from suffering permanently. If, on the basis of cherishing all living beings, we contemplate the fact that they experience the cycle of physical suffering and mental pain in life after life without end, their inability to liberate themselves from suffering, their lack of freedom and how, by engaging in negative actions, they create the causes of future suffering, we will develop deep compassion for them. We need to empathize with them and feel their pain as keenly as we feel our own.

No one wants to suffer, yet out of ignorance living beings create suffering by performing non-virtuous actions. We should therefore feel equal compassion for all living beings without exception; there is no single living being who is not a suitable object of our compassion.

All living beings suffer because they take contaminated rebirths. Human beings have no choice but to experience immense human sufferings because they have taken human rebirth, which is contaminated by the inner poison of delusions. Similarly, animals have to experience animal suffering, and hungry ghosts and hell beings have to experience all the sufferings of their respective realms. If living beings were to experience all this suffering for just one single life, it would not be so bad, but the cycle of suffering continues life after life, endlessly.

To develop renunciation, we previously contemplated how in our countless future lives we will have to experience the unbearable sufferings of animals, hungry ghosts, hell beings, humans, demi-gods and gods. Now, at this point, to develop compassion for all living beings who are our mothers, we contemplate how in their countless future lives they will have to experience the unbearable sufferings of animals, hungry ghosts, hell beings, humans, demi-gods and gods.

THE OBJECT OF THIS MEDITATION

The object of this meditation is our determination to liberate all living beings from suffering permanently. We should learn to develop this determination through contemplating the above explanation of the purpose of this meditation. When through this contemplation a firm determination to liberate all living beings from suffering permanently develops in our heart, we have found the object of this meditation.

THE ACTUAL MEDITATION

From the heart we should think:

I cannot bear the suffering of these countless mother beings. Drowning in the vast and deep ocean of samsara,

the cycle of contaminated rebirth, they have to experience
unbearable physical suffering and mental pain in this life
and in countless future lives. I must permanently liberate
all these living beings from their suffering.

We hold this determination firmly and remain on it single-pointedly for as long as possible. We should practise this meditation continually until we maintain this determination in our heart day and night, without ever forgetting it. This is the realization of universal compassion.

MEDITATION ON THE SUPREME GOOD HEART, BODHICHITTA

THE PURPOSE OF THIS MEDITATION

The purpose of this meditation is to engage in the Bodhisattva's path – the actual path to enlightenment. Bodhichitta is an inner vehicle that possesses six wheels, the six perfections. 'Bodhi' means enlightenment, and 'chitta' means mind. Bodhichitta is a mind that spontaneously wishes to attain enlightenment to benefit each and every living being every day. The moment we develop bodhichitta we become a Bodhisattva, a person who spontaneously wishes to attain enlightenment for the benefit of all living beings. Initially we will be a Bodhisattva on the path of accumulation. Then, by following the path to enlightenment with the vehicle of bodhichitta, we can progress from being a Bodhisattva on the path of accumulation to being a Bodhisattva on the path of preparation, a Bodhisattva on the path of seeing, and then a Bodhisattva on the path of meditation. From there we will reach the Path of No More Learning, which is the actual state of enlightenment. As already mentioned, enlightenment is the inner light of wisdom that is permanently free from all mistaken appearance, and whose function is to bestow mental peace upon each and every living being every day. When we attain a Buddha's enlightenment we will be able to benefit each and every living being directly through bestowing blessings and through our countless emanations.

In Sutra teachings, Buddha says:

In this impure life of samsara
No one experiences real happiness;
The actions they perform
Will always be the causes of suffering.

The happiness that we normally experience through having good conditions, such as a good reputation, a good position, a good job, good relationships, seeing attractive forms, hearing good news or beautiful music, eating, drinking and sex is not real happiness, but changing suffering – a reduction in our previous suffering. Out of ignorance, however, we believe that only these things bring happiness, and because of this we never wish to attain real happiness, the pure and everlasting happiness of liberation and enlightenment, even for our own benefit. We are always searching for happiness in this impure life of samsara, like the thief who searched for gold in Milarepa's empty cave and found nothing. The great Yogi Milarepa heard a thief rummaging around his cave one night and called out to him, 'How do you expect to find anything valuable here at night, when I cannot find anything valuable here during the day?'

When, through training, we develop the precious mind of enlightenment, bodhichitta, we spontaneously think:

How wonderful it would be if I and all living beings attained real happiness, the pure and everlasting happiness of enlightenment! May we attain this happiness. I myself will work for this aim.

We need to have this precious mind of bodhichitta in our heart. It is our inner Spiritual Guide, who leads us directly to the state of supreme happiness of enlightenment; and it is the real wishfulfilling jewel through which we can fulfil our own and others' wishes. There is no greater beneficial intention than this precious mind.

THE OBJECT OF THIS MEDITATION

The object of this meditation is our determination to attain enlightenment to benefit each and every living being every day. We should learn to develop this determination through contemplating the above explanation of the purpose of this meditation. When through this contemplation a firm determination to attain enlightenment to benefit each and every living being every day develops in our heart, we have found the object of this meditation.

THE ACTUAL MEDITATION

From the depths of our heart we should think:

I am one single person but other living beings are countless, and they are all my kind mothers. These countless mother beings have to experience unbearable physical suffering and mental pain in this life and in their countless future lives. Compared with the suffering of these countless living beings, my own suffering is insignificant. I must liberate all living beings from suffering permanently, and for this purpose I must attain a Buddha's enlightenment.

We hold this determination firmly and remain on it single-pointedly for as long as possible. We should practise this meditation continually until we develop the spontaneous wish to attain enlightenment to benefit each and every living being every day, which is the actual realization of bodhichitta.

MEDITATION ON OUR DETERMINATION AND PROMISE TO SINCERELY PRACTISE THE SIX PERFECTIONS

THE PURPOSE OF THIS MEDITATION

The purpose of this meditation is to reach directly the state of enlightenment. The six perfections are the actual path to enlightenment, and they are also the path of bodhichitta and the Bodhisattva's path. Through following this path with the vehicle of bodhichitta we will definitely reach the state of enlightenment. Our bodhichitta wish is to attain enlightenment to benefit each and every living being directly. To fulfil this wish, in front of our Spiritual Guide or an image of Buddha regarded as the living Buddha, we should promise to engage in the Bodhisattva's path or training while reciting the following ritual prayer three times. This promise is the Bodhisattva's vow.

Just as all the previous Sugatas, the Buddhas,
Generated the mind of enlightenment, bodhichitta,
And accomplished all the stages
Of the Bodhisattva's training,

So will I too, for the sake of all beings,
Generate the mind of enlightenment
And accomplish all the stages
Of the Bodhisattva's training.

When we take the Bodhisattva's vow we are taking the commitment to engage in the path to enlightenment, the

Bodhisattva's training, which is the practice of the six perfections. Normally, when we start a job, we commit ourself to fulfilling our employer's wishes; otherwise we will quickly lose our job. In the same way, having generated bodhichitta – the determination to attain enlightenment to benefit each and every living being directly – we need to commit ourself to engaging in the practice of the six perfections. If we do not make this commitment by taking the Bodhisattva's vow, we will lose our opportunity to attain enlightenment. Through contemplating this we should encourage ourself to take the Bodhisattva's vow and sincerely practise the six perfections.

The six perfections are the practices of giving, moral discipline, patience, effort, concentration and wisdom, motivated by bodhichitta. We should recognize that the six perfections are our daily practice.

In the practice of giving we should practise: (1) giving material help to those in poverty, including giving food to animals; (2) giving practical help to those sick or physically weak; (3) giving protection by always trying to save others' lives, including those of insects; (4) giving love – learning to cherish all living beings by always believing that their happiness and freedom are important; and (5) giving Dharma, helping others to solve their problems of anger, attachment and ignorance by giving Dharma teachings or meaningful advice.

In the practice of moral discipline we should abandon any inappropriate actions including those that cause others suffering. We should especially abandon breaking our commitments of the Bodhisattva's vow. This is the basic foundation upon which we can make progress on the Bodhisattva's path. By doing this our actions of body, speech and mind will be pure, so that we become a pure being.

In the practice of patience we should never allow ourself to become angry or discouraged, by temporarily accepting any difficulties or harm from others. When we practise patience we are wearing the supreme inner armour that directly protects us from physical sufferings, mental pain and other problems. Anger destroys our merit, or good fortune, so that we will continually experience many obstacles, and because of lacking good fortune it will be difficult to fulfil our wishes, especially our spiritual aims. There is no greater evil than anger. With the practice of patience we can accomplish any spiritual aim; there is no greater virtue than patience.

In the practice of effort we should rely upon irreversible effort to accumulate the great collections of merit and wisdom, which are the main causes of attaining Buddha's Form Body (Rupakaya), and Truth Body (Dharmakaya); and especially we should emphasize contemplation and meditation on emptiness, the way things really are. By doing this we can easily make progress on the path to enlightenment. With effort we can accomplish our aim, whereas with laziness we cannot achieve anything.

In the practice of concentration, at this stage we should emphasize accomplishing the concentration of tranquil abiding observing emptiness. An explanation of this can be found in *Modern Buddhism* in the section *A Simple Training in Ultimate Bodhichitta*. When, through the power of this concentration, we experience a special wisdom called 'superior seeing' that realizes the emptiness of all phenomena very clearly, we will have progressed from being a Bodhisattva on the path of accumulation to being a Bodhisattva on the path of preparation.

In the practice of wisdom, at this stage we need to emphasize increasing the power of our wisdom of superior seeing by continually meditating on the emptiness of all phenomena with bodhichitta motivation. Through this, when our superior seeing transforms into the path of seeing, which is the direct realization of the emptiness of all phenomena, we will have progressed from being a Bodhisattva on the path of preparation to being a Bodhisattva on the path of seeing. The moment we attain the path of seeing we are a Superior Bodhisattva and no longer experience samsara's sufferings. Even if someone cuts our body piece by piece with a knife we have no pain because we have the direct realization of the way things really are.

Having completed the path of seeing, to make further progress we need to engage continually in the meditation on the emptiness of all phenomena with bodhichitta motivation. This meditation is called the 'path of meditation'. When we reach this stage we will have progressed from being a Bodhisattva on the path of seeing to being a Bodhisattva on the path of meditation.

Having completed the path of meditation, when our wisdom of the path of meditation transforms into an omniscient wisdom that is permanently free from all mistaken appearances, this omniscient wisdom is called the 'Path of No More Learning', which is actual enlightenment. When we reach this stage we will have progressed from being a Bodhisattva on the path of meditation to being an enlightened being, a Buddha. We will have completed the ultimate goal of living beings.

The Bodhisattva's initial training in accumulating merit or wisdom is the Bodhisattva's path of accumulation; the Bodhisattva's training in accumulating merit or wisdom that is a preparation for attaining the path of seeing is the Bodhisattva's path of preparation; the Bodhisattva's training that is the initial direct realization of emptiness is the Bodhisattva's path of seeing; after completing the path of seeing, the Bodhisattva's training that meditates continually on emptiness is the Bodhisattva's path of meditation; and Buddha's omniscient wisdom that is attained through completing all the trainings of Sutra and Tantra is the Path of No More Learning, the state of enlightenment.

THE OBJECT OF THIS MEDITATION

The object in this meditation is our determination and promise to sincerely practise the six perfections. We should learn to develop this determination and promise through contemplating the above explanation of the purpose of this meditation. When through this contemplation a firm determination and promise to sincerely practise the six perfections develops in our heart, we have found the object of this meditation.

THE ACTUAL MEDITATION

From our heart we should think:

Just as all the previous Buddhas generated the precious mind of bodhichitta and accomplished all the stages of the Bodhisattva's path, so will I too for the sake of all living beings generate the precious mind of bodhichitta and accomplish all the stages of the Bodhisattva's path, the practice of the six perfections.

We hold this determination firmly and remain on it single-pointedly for as long as possible. We should practise this meditation continually until our determination and promise become unchangeable.

MEDITATION ON TRAINING IN YOGIC DIRECT PERCEIVERS

THE PURPOSE OF THIS MEDITATION

The purpose of this meditation is to advance ourself from the state of an ordinary being to that of a great Yogi, a Superior Bodhisattva. The moment we become a Superior Bodhisattva we will be free from receiving any harm from delusions. Our realization of a yogic direct perceiver destroys the power of the delusions. For example, due to their karma peacocks do not receive harm from eating poisonous plants. In the same way, because of their realization of a yogic direct perceiver Superior Bodhisattvas do not receive harm from the inner poison of delusions. Thus, because Superior Bodhisattvas have no gross obstructions to enlightenment they will attain enlightenment easily and joyfully. Whenever we meditate on emptiness with the intention to transform our mind into a yogic direct perceiver we are training in yogic direct perceivers.

However, it is very important that we know the meaning of emptiness correctly. Emptiness is the mere absence of things that we normally see. This is not easy to understand so we need great patience. In truth, due to lacking an understanding of emptiness we are wandering in samsara, the cycle of suffering; and we will never be free from this cycle until we have direct knowledge of emptiness with a yogic direct perceiver. Therefore, there is no doubt that we need to apply effort to understand emptiness correctly. A simple explanation is as follows:

For example, we normally see our body within its parts – the hands, back and so forth – but neither the individual parts nor the collection of the parts are our body because they are the parts of our body and not the body itself. However, there is no 'our body' other than its parts. Through searching with wisdom for our body in this way, we realize that our body is unfindable. This is a valid reason to prove that our body that we normally see does not exist at all.

Also, we normally see our self within our body and mind, but neither our body, nor our mind, nor the collection of our body and mind are our self, because these are our possessions and our self is the possessor; and possessor and possessions cannot be the same. However, there is no 'our self' other than our body and mind. Through searching with wisdom for our self in this way, we realize that our self is unfindable. This is a valid reason to prove that our self that we normally see does not exist at all.

We should apply these reasons to all other phenomena, so that we will understand that all phenomena that we normally see or perceive do not exist. In conclusion, we will understand that the real meaning of emptiness is the mere absence of all phenomena that we normally see or perceive.

Now, the question is: If our body that we normally see does not exist, and there is no body other than this, why do we experience sufferings of the body, such as the sufferings of sickness.

What is your answer? My answer is this: It is true that our body that we normally see does not exist, and there is no body other than this, but we mistakenly believe that our body that we normally see actually exists and, because of this, we experience sufferings of the body such as sickness as a hallucination, as a mistaken appearance, as like a dream. In the Sutras Buddha says, 'You should know all phenomena are like dreams.' Normally, through perceiving either our body or mind, we spontaneously believe and think 'This is me.' This belief is a hallucination because neither our body nor our mind is our self. In the same way, when our body is sick we believe and think 'I am sick', and when our mind is unhappy we believe and think 'I am unhappy.' All these beliefs are hallucinations because neither our body nor our mind is our self. This proves that all our daily experiences of suffering and problems do not truly exist, they are just hallucinations – mistaken appearances. If we realize directly the true nature of our body, the emptiness of our body, these hallucinations will disappear permanently, and then we will no longer have any suffering and problems.

Another question is: If phenomena that we normally see or perceive do not exist then how do phenomena exist?

The answer is: They exist as mere appearance. There are no phenomena other than mere appearance. This appearance and emptiness are non-dual, which means they are one entity. If we realize non-dual appearance and emptiness directly, our mind will be free permanently from dualistic appearance and mistaken appearance, and ultimately we will become an enlightened being. Thus, the attainment of enlightenment is very simple! All we need to do is to apply effort to purify our mind. When our mind becomes completely pure we perceive everything as pure; there are no longer any impure appearance and mistaken appearance.

THE OBJECT OF THIS MEDITATION

The object of this meditation is the emptiness of all phenomena, the mere absence of all phenomena that we normally see or perceive. We should learn to perceive clearly the mere absence of all phenomena that we normally see or perceive through contemplating the above explanation of the purpose of this meditation. When through this contemplation a firm knowledge of the mere absence of all phenomena that we normally see or perceive develops in our heart, we have found the object of this meditation.

THE ACTUAL MEDITATION

When a firm knowledge of the mere absence of all phenomena that we normally see or perceive develops in our heart, while holding this knowledge without forgetting it, we focus on the mere absence of all phenomena that we normally see or perceive and remain on it single-pointedly for as long as possible. We should practise this meditation continually until our mind transforms into a yogic direct perceiver, a direct realization of emptiness. When we attain this realization we will have solved all our samsaric problems and we will have the ability to benefit countless living beings. There is no greater meaning than this.

In summary, we should know that through practising Dharma we can all make ourselves happy all the time. In this context, Dharma means principally Buddha's teaching on selflessness, emptiness. Selflessness means that our self and all other phenomena that we normally see or perceive do not exist. Je Tsongkhapa said that since the son of a childless woman does not exist, its suffering and problems cannot exist. Likewise, since our self that we normally see does not exist, its suffering and problems cannot exist. This instruction teaches us the following profound Dharma practice.

First we develop and maintain a sincere wish to liberate ourself and all living beings permanently from the sufferings of this life and countless future lives, which is both renunciation and compassion. With this motivation we then contemplate the real meaning of Je Tsongkhapa's words. We should understand and think, 'Since my self that I normally see does not exist, its suffering and problems cannot exist. However, due to my ignorance that grasps at my self that I normally see, I experience suffering and problems as hallucinations. Therefore, I must stop grasping at my self that I normally see.' With this determination, and realizing that our self that we normally see does not exist, we should learn to develop on our consciousness the cessation of grasping at our self that we normally see. When this true cessation develops on our consciousness we hold this cessation firmly without forgetting it, and we remain on this cessation single-pointedly for as long as possible.

This meditation is called 'absorption of cessation', which Buddha taught in the *Perfection of Wisdom Sutras*. We should practise this meditation continually until our cessation of grasping at our self and all other phenomena that we normally see or perceive becomes permanent, and is maintained day and night throughout our life. When we attain this permanent cessation, we have attained permanent liberation from all the sufferings of this life and countless future lives, because our self-grasping ignorance, the root of all suffering, has ceased completely. At the same time we will experience the supreme permanent happiness or inner peace called 'nirvana' in Sanskrit. Thus we will be happy all the time in this life and in life after life, and we will have solved all the problems of samsara, the cycle of impure life.

Now, the question is: If we permanently stop grasping at our self and all other phenomena that we normally see or perceive, then how do we communicate with others and engage in daily activities?

Answer: We can do this just through following the mere name of our self and all other phenomena without grasping at them.

In the Sutras Buddha says, 'There are no phenomena other than mere name.' Grasping at any phenomenon other than its mere name is self-grasping ignorance, the root of all suffering. We should learn to recognize our own self-grasping ignorance and apply effort to reduce and finally completely cease this ignorance.

When our understanding of selflessness or emptiness is qualified, it is then important to emphasize practising the meditation on the absorption of cessation as explained above, because this meditation is the special method to reduce and abandon our self-grasping ignorance quickly. If we really want to stop experiencing problems and suffering we must learn how to reduce and abandon our self-grasping ignorance, which is the root of all our problems and suffering. This is special advice from Je Tsongkhapa's heart.

Conclusion

This completes the explanation of *How to Understand the Mind*. It is not enough simply to understand the mind, we also need to put this understanding into practice. The success of our practice depends upon three things: accumulating merit or good fortune, because merit is the main condition for attaining Dharma realizations; purifying negative karma, because negative karma is the main obstacle to attaining Dharma realizations; and receiving the blessings of the Buddhas and Bodhisattvas, because receiving blessings is the principal method for transforming our mind into the stages of the path. We can practise these three in conjunction with the prayers for meditation, which can be found in Appendix II.

Dedication

Through the great collection of virtuous actions that we have accumulated by preparing this book, may pure Buddhadharma flourish extensively throughout the world; and thereby may all living beings become permanently free from every kind of misery and misfortune, and find pure and everlasting happiness.

Appendix I
The Condensed Meaning
of the Text

The Condensed Meaning
of the Text

The explanation of *How to Understand the Mind* begins with an explanation of what is our mind, how the mind is able to move, and the different levels of mind.

The definition of the mind is something whose nature is empty like space, always lacking form, shape and colour, and whose function is to perceive or understand objects.

From the point of view of its different levels, the mind is divided into three:

1 The gross mind
2 The subtle mind
3 The very subtle mind

From the point of view of its function, the mind can be divided into primary minds and mental factors.

The definition of primary mind is a cognizer that principally apprehends the mere entity of an object.

Primary mind, mentality and consciousness are synonyms.

There are six types of primary mind:

1 Eye consciousness
2 Ear consciousness

3 Nose consciousness
4 Tongue consciousness
5 Body consciousness
6 Mental consciousness

The definition of mental factor is a cognizer that principally apprehends a particular attribute of an object.

A primary mind and its mental factors possess five similarities:

1 Basis
2 Object
3 Aspect
4 Time
5 Substance

There are fifty-one mental factors, which are divided into six groups:

1 The five all-accompanying mental factors
2 The five object-ascertaining mental factors
3 The eleven virtuous mental factors
4 The six root delusions
5 The twenty secondary delusions
6 The four changeable mental factors

The five all-accompanying mental factors are:

1 Feeling
2 Discrimination
3 Intention
4 Contact
5 Attention

The definition of feeling is a mental factor that functions to experience pleasant, unpleasant or neutral objects.

There are three types of feeling:

1 Pleasant feelings
2 Unpleasant feelings
3 Neutral feelings

There is also a twofold division of feeling from the point of view of their uncommon dominant condition:

1 Bodily feelings
2 Mental feelings

There is another twofold division of feeling from the point of view of their nature:

1 Contaminated feelings
2 Uncontaminated feelings

The definition of discrimination is a mental factor that functions to apprehend the uncommon sign of an object.

There are six types of discrimination:

1 Discriminations associated with eye consciousness
2 Discriminations associated with ear consciousness
3 Discriminations associated with nose consciousness
4 Discriminations associated with tongue consciousness
5 Discriminations associated with body consciousness
6 Discriminations associated with mental consciousness

There is also a twofold division of discrimination:

1 Mistaken discriminations
2 Non-mistaken discriminations

There is another twofold division of discrimination:

1 Clear discriminations
2 Unclear discriminations

The definition of intention is a mental factor that functions to focus its primary mind on an object.

There are three types of intention:

1 Non-virtuous intentions
2 Virtuous intentions
3 Neutral intentions

There are three types of non-virtuous action:

1 Non-virtuous bodily actions
2 Non-virtuous verbal actions
3 Non-virtuous mental actions

There is another threefold division of intention:

1 Meritorious actions
2 Non-meritorious actions
3 Unfluctuating actions

There is a threefold division of both meritorious and non-meritorious actions: those that are throwing karma, those that are completing karma, and those that are karma whose results are experienced in the same life.

The definition of contact is a mental factor that functions to perceive its object as pleasant, unpleasant or neutral.

There are six types of contact:

1 Contact associated with eye consciousness
2 Contact associated with ear consciousness
3 Contact associated with nose consciousness

    4 Contact associated with tongue consciousness
    5 Contact associated with body consciousness
    6 Contact associated with mental consciousness

The definition of attention is a mental factor that functions to focus the mind on a particular attribute of an object.

There are two types of attention:

    1 Correct attention
    2 Incorrect attention

There is another twofold division of attention:

    1 Appropriate attention
    2 Inappropriate attention

The five object-ascertaining mental factors are:

    1 Aspiration
    2 Firm apprehension
    3 Mindfulness
    4 Concentration
    5 Wisdom

The definition of aspiration is a mental factor that focuses on a desired object and takes an interest in it.

There are four types of aspiration:

    1 Wishing to meet an object
    2 Wishing not to be separated from an object
    3 Wishing to obtain an object
    4 Wishing to be released from an object

Each of these can be virtuous, non-virtuous or neutral, depending upon its motivation.

There is also a twofold division of aspiration:

1 Mistaken aspirations
2 Non-mistaken aspirations

The definition of firm apprehension is a mental factor that makes its primary mind apprehend its object firmly.

There are two types of firm apprehension:

1 Correct firm apprehensions
2 Mistaken firm apprehensions

The definition of mindfulness is a mental factor that functions not to forget the object realized by the primary mind.

There are two types of mindfulness:

1 New mindfulness
2 Old mindfulness

There is another twofold division of mindfulness:

1 Mindfulness with movements of mental sinking and mental excitement
2 Mindfulness without movements of mental sinking and mental excitement

The definition of concentration is a mental factor that makes its primary mind remain on its object single-pointedly.

There are three ways of dividing virtuous concentration: from the point of view of realm, from the point of view of its effect and from the point of view of its object.

There are nine levels of concentration from the point of view of realm:

1 Concentration of the desire realm
2 Concentration of the first form realm
3 Concentration of the second form realm
4 Concentration of the third form realm
5 Concentration of the fourth form realm
6 Concentration of infinite space
7 Concentration of infinite consciousness
8 Concentration of nothingness
9 Concentration of peak of samsara

There are nine levels of desire realm concentration:

1 Placing the mind
2 Continual placement
3 Replacement
4 Close placement
5 Controlling
6 Pacifying
7 Completely pacifying
8 Single-pointedness
9 Placement in equipoise

There are two types of concentration from the point of view of their effect:

1 Mundane concentrations
2 Supramundane concentrations

There is another twofold division of concentration from the point of view of its object:

1 Concentrations observing conventional objects
2 Concentrations observing ultimate objects

The definition of wisdom is a virtuous, intelligent mind that makes its primary mind realize a meaningful object.

There are three types of wisdom:

1 Wisdom arisen from listening or reading
2 Wisdom arisen from contemplation
3 Wisdom arisen from meditation

There is also a sevenfold division of wisdom:

1 Great wisdom
2 Clear wisdom
3 Quick wisdom
4 Profound wisdom
5 The wisdom of expounding Dharma
6 The wisdom of spiritual debate
7 The wisdom of composing Dharma books

The eleven virtuous mental factors are:

1 Faith
2 Sense of shame
3 Consideration for others
4 Non-attachment
5 Non-hatred
6 Non-ignorance
7 Effort
8 Mental suppleness
9 Conscientiousness
10 Equanimity
11 Non-harmfulness

The definition of faith is a mental factor that functions principally to eliminate non-faith.

There are three types of faith:

1 Believing faith
2 Admiring faith
3 Wishing faith

The definition of sense of shame is a mental factor that functions to avoid inappropriate actions for reasons that concern ourself.

There are three types of sense of shame:

1 Sense of shame that restrains us from inappropriate bodily actions
2 Sense of shame that restrains us from inappropriate verbal actions
3 Sense of shame that restrains us from inappropriate mental actions

There is also a twofold division of sense of shame:

1 Sense of shame that restrains us from inappropriate actions out of concern simply for ourself
2 Sense of shame that restrains us from inappropriate actions out of concern for the specific undesirable results for ourself

The definition of consideration for others is a mental factor that functions to avoid inappropriate actions for reasons that concern others.

There are three types of consideration for others:

1 Consideration for others that restrains us from inappropriate bodily actions
2 Consideration for others that restrains us from inappropriate verbal actions
3 Consideration for others that restrains us from inappropriate mental actions

There is also a twofold division of consideration for others:

1 Consideration for others that restrains us from inappropriate actions out of concern simply for others

2 Consideration for others that restrains us from inappropriate actions out of concern for the specific undesirable results for others

The definition of non-attachment is a mental factor that functions as the direct opponent of attachment.

There are three types of non-attachment:

1 Non-attachment to samsaric places
2 Non-attachment to samsaric enjoyments
3 Non-attachment to samsaric bodies

There is another threefold division of non-attachment:

1 Non-attachment to this life
2 Non-attachment to samsara
3 Non-attachment to solitary peace

The definition of non-hatred is a mental factor that functions as the direct opponent of hatred.

There are three types of non-hatred:

1 Non-hatred towards those who harm us
2 Non-hatred towards inanimate objects that cause us suffering
3 Non-hatred towards resultant suffering

The definition of non-ignorance is a mental factor that functions as the direct opponent of ignorance.

There are four types of non-ignorance:

1 Non-ignorance arisen from listening or reading
2 Non-ignorance arisen from contemplation
3 Non-ignorance arisen from meditation
4 Non-ignorance arisen from imprints

The definition of effort is a mental factor that makes its primary mind delight in virtue.

There are four types of effort:

1 Armour-like effort
2 Effort of non-discouragement
3 Effort of application
4 Effort of non-satisfaction

There is also a fivefold division of effort:

1 Armour-like effort
2 Effort of non-discouragement
3 Effort of application
4 Effort of non-satisfaction
5 Effort of irreversibility

There is also a threefold division of effort:

1 Armour-like effort
2 Effort of gathering virtuous Dharmas
3 Effort of benefiting others

There are four powers:

1 The power of aspiration
2 The power of steadfastness
3 The power of joy
4 The power of rejection

The definition of mental suppleness is a flexibility of mind induced by virtuous concentration.

There are two types of mental suppleness:

1 Subtle mental suppleness
2 Gross mental suppleness

The definition of conscientiousness is a mental factor that, in dependence upon effort, cherishes what is virtuous and guards the mind from delusion and non-virtue.

There are two types of conscientiousness:

1 Conscientiousness that is a virtuous root of mundane paths
2 Conscientiousness that is a virtuous root of supra-mundane paths

The definition of equanimity is a mental factor that functions to keep the primary mind free from mental sinking and mental excitement.

There are three types of equanimity:

1 Equanimity that requires gross effort
2 Equanimity that requires subtle effort
3 Equanimity that requires no effort

The definition of non-harmfulness is a mental factor that wishes sentient beings not to suffer.

There are two types of non-harmfulness, or compassion:

1 Compassion wishing sentient beings to be free from suffering
2 Compassion wishing sentient beings to be free from the causes of suffering

There is another twofold division of compassion:

1 Mere compassion
2 Superior compassion

The definition of virtue is a phenomenon that functions as a main cause of happiness.

There are five types of virtue:

1 Natural virtue
2 Virtue by association
3 Virtue by motivation
4 Virtue by subsequent relation
5 Ultimate virtue

The definition of non-virtue is a phenomenon that functions as a main cause of suffering.

There are five types of non-virtue:

1 Natural non-virtue
2 Non-virtue by association
3 Non-virtue by motivation
4 Non-virtue by subsequent relation
5 Ultimate non-virtue

The definition of delusion is a mental factor that arises from inappropriate attention and that functions to make the mind unpeaceful and uncontrolled.

There are six causes of delusion:

1 The seed
2 The object
3 Inappropriate attention
4 Familiarity
5 Distraction and being influenced by others
6 Bad habits

There are three types of delusion from the point of view of realm:

1 Delusions of the desire realm
2 Delusions of the form realm
3 Delusions of the formless realm

There are nine levels, from big-big to small-small, of each of the delusions of the desire realm, and of each of the delusions of each level of the form and formless realms, making eighty-one levels of delusion in all.

There is also a twofold division of delusion from the point of view of their cause:

1 Innate delusions
2 Intellectually-formed delusions

There is another twofold division of delusion from the point of view of entity:

1 Root delusions
2 Secondary delusions

The six root delusions are:

1 Desirous attachment
2 Anger
3 Deluded pride
4 Ignorance
5 Deluded doubt
6 Deluded view

The definition of desirous attachment is a deluded mental factor that observes its contaminated object, regards it as a cause of happiness, and wishes for it.

There are three types of desirous attachment from the point of view of time:

1 Desirous attachment to past objects
2 Desirous attachment to present objects
3 Desirous attachment to future objects

From the point of view of entity, desirous attachment can be divided into three – big, middling and small – or into eighty-one – the nine levels of desirous attachment of each of the nine realms. These are all included within three:

1 Desire realm desirous attachment
2 Form realm desirous attachment
3 Formless realm desirous attachment

There is another threefold division of desirous attachment from the point of view of its object:

1 Desirous attachment to samsaric places
2 Desirous attachment to samsaric enjoyments
3 Desirous attachment to samsaric bodies

The definition of anger is a deluded mental factor that observes its contaminated object, exaggerates its bad qualities, considers it to be undesirable, and wishes to harm it.

There are nine types of anger from the point of view of entity, from big-big to small-small.

There is another ninefold division of anger from the point of view of how it is generated:

1 Anger towards someone or something that harmed us in the past
2 Anger towards someone or something that is harming us now
3 Anger towards someone or something that might harm us in the future
4 Anger towards someone or something that harmed our friends or relatives in the past
5 Anger towards someone or something that is harming our friends or relatives now

6 Anger towards someone or something that might harm our friends or relatives in the future
7 Anger towards someone or something that helped our enemy in the past
8 Anger towards someone or something that is helping our enemy now
9 Anger towards someone or something that might help our enemy in the future

The definition of deluded pride is a deluded mental factor that, through considering and exaggerating one's own good qualities or possessions, feels arrogant.

There are seven types of deluded pride:

1 Pride over inferiors
2 Pride over equals
3 Pride over superiors
4 Pride in identity
5 Pretentious pride
6 Emulating pride
7 Wrong pride

The definition of ignorance is a mental factor that is confused about the nature of an object and that functions to induce wrong awareness, doubt and other delusions.

There are two types of ignorance:

1 Ignorance of conventional truths
2 Ignorance of ultimate truths

There is another twofold division of ignorance:

1 Ignorance of actions and their effects, or karma
2 Ignorance of emptiness

The definition of deluded doubt is a two-pointedness of mind that interferes with the attainment of liberation or enlightenment.

There are three types of doubt in general:

1 Doubts tending towards the truth
2 Doubts tending away from the truth
3 Balanced doubts

The definition of deluded view is a view that functions to obstruct the attainment of liberation.

There are five types of deluded view:

1 View of the transitory collection
2 Extreme view
3 Holding false views as supreme
4 Holding wrong moral disciplines and conduct as supreme
5 Wrong view

The definition of view of the transitory collection is a type of self-grasping of persons that grasps our own I as being an inherently existent I.

There are two types of view of the transitory collection:

1 View of the transitory collection conceiving I
2 View of the transitory collection conceiving mine

There is another twofold division of view of the transitory collection:

1 Innate view of the transitory collection
2 Intellectually-formed view of the transitory collection

There are twenty intellectually-formed views of the transitory collection, four in relation to each of the five aggregates.

The definition of extreme view is an exaggerated incorrect view.

There are two types of extreme view: the extreme view of existence, and the extreme view of non-existence.

The definition of holding false views as supreme is a deluded view that believes our own or others' incorrect views are supreme views.

The definition of holding wrong moral disciplines and conduct as supreme is a deluded view that holds any wrong moral discipline or conduct to be correct and considers it to be superior to other forms of moral discipline or conduct.

The definition of wrong view is an intellectually-formed wrong awareness that denies the existence of an object that it is necessary to understand to attain liberation or enlightenment.

The twenty secondary delusions are:

1 Aggression
2 Resentment
3 Spite
4 Jealousy
5 Miserliness
6 Concealment
7 Pretension
8 Denial
9 Self-satisfaction
10 Harmfulness

11 Shamelessness
12 Inconsideration
13 Dullness
14 Distraction
15 Mental excitement
16 Non-faith
17 Laziness
18 Non-conscientiousness
19 Deluded forgetfulness
20 Non-alertness

The definition of aggression is a deluded mental factor that is an increase of the root delusion anger that wishes to hurt or harm others physically or verbally.

The definition of resentment is a deluded mental factor that maintains the continuum of anger without forgetting it, and wishes to retaliate.

The definition of spite is a deluded mental factor that, motivated by resentment or aggression, wishes to speak harshly.

The definition of jealousy is a deluded mental factor that feels displeasure when observing others' enjoyments, good qualities or good fortune.

The definition of miserliness is a deluded mental factor that, motivated by desirous attachment, holds on to things tightly and does not want to part with them.

The definition of concealment is a deluded mental factor that, motivated by attachment to wealth or reputation, wishes to conceal our faults from others.

The definition of pretension is a deluded mental factor that, motivated by attachment to wealth or reputation, wishes to pretend that we possess qualities that we do not possess.

The definition of denial is a deluded mental factor that does not wish to purify non-virtuous actions that we have committed or downfalls that we have incurred.

The definition of self-satisfaction is a deluded mental factor that observes our own physical beauty, wealth or other good qualities, and, being concerned only with these, has no interest in spiritual development.

The definition of harmfulness is a deluded mental factor that wishes other sentient beings to suffer.

The definition of shamelessness is a deluded mental factor that is the opposite of sense of shame.

The definition of inconsideration is a deluded mental factor that is the opposite of consideration for others.

The definition of dullness is a deluded mental factor that functions to make both the body and mind heavy and inflexible.

The definition of distraction is a deluded mental factor that wanders to any object of delusion.

The definition of mental excitement is a deluded mental factor that wanders to any object of attachment.

The definition of non-faith is a deluded mental factor that is the opposite of faith.

The definition of laziness is a deluded mental factor that, motivated by attachment to worldly pleasures or worldly activities, dislikes virtuous activity.

The definition of non-conscientiousness is a deluded mental factor that wishes to engage in non-virtuous actions without restraint.

The definition of deluded forgetfulness is a deluded mental factor that makes us forget a virtuous object.

The definition of non-alertness is a deluded mental factor that, being unable to distinguish faults from non-faults, causes us to develop faults.

The four changeable mental factors are:

1 Sleep
2 Regret
3 Investigation
4 Analysis

The definition of sleep is a mental factor that is developed through dullness or its imprints and that functions to gather the sense awarenesses inwards.

The definition of regret is a mental factor that feels remorse for actions done in the past.

The definition of investigation is a mental factor that examines an object to gain an understanding of its gross nature.

The definition of analysis is a mental factor that examines an object to gain an understanding of its subtle nature.

From the point of view of how they engage their objects, minds can be divided into two:

1 Conceptual minds
2 Non-conceptual minds

The definition of conceptual mind is a thought that apprehends its object through a generic image.

There are five types of object:

1 Appearing object
2 Observed object
3 Engaged object
4 Apprehended object
5 Conceived object

The definition of generic image is the appearing object of a conceptual mind.

There are three types of conceptual mind:

1 Conceptual minds that perceive the generic image of an object mainly through the force of listening or reading
2 Conceptual minds that perceive the generic image of an object mainly through the force of contemplating the meaning of that object
3 Conceptual minds that perceive the generic image of an object mainly through the force of previous imprints

There is also a twofold division of conceptual mind:

1 Correct conceptual minds
2 Wrong conceptual minds

The definition of non-conceptual mind is a cognizer to which its object appears clearly without being mixed with a generic image.

There are two types of non-conceptual mind:

1 Sense awarenesses
2 Non-conceptual mental awarenesses

There are three types of non-conceptual mental awareness:

1 Non-conceptual mental direct perceivers
2 Yogic direct perceivers
3 Non-conceptual mental awarenesses that are neither of these two

There is another twofold division of non-conceptual mind:

1 Correct non-conceptual minds
2 Wrong non-conceptual minds

From the point of view of their uncommon dominant condition, minds can be divided into two:

1 Sense awarenesses
2 Mental awarenesses

The definition of sense awareness is an awareness that is developed in dependence upon its uncommon dominant condition, a sense power possessing form.

There are five types of sense awareness:

1 Eye awareness
2 Ear awareness
3 Nose awareness
4 Tongue awareness
5 Body awareness

The definition of eye awareness is an awareness that is developed in dependence upon its uncommon dominant condition, an eye sense power. This definition can be applied to the other four sense awarenesses by changing the uncommon dominant condition to the ear sense power, the nose sense power, the tongue sense power, or the body sense power.

The definition of dominant condition of sense awareness is that which principally assists in the development of a sense awareness.

There are two types of dominant condition:

    1 Common dominant condition
    2 Uncommon dominant condition

The definition of mental awareness is an awareness that is developed in dependence upon its uncommon dominant condition, a mental power.

The definition of mental power is a mentality that principally functions directly to produce the uncommon aspect of a mental awareness.

There are two types of mental awareness:

    1 Conceptual mental awarenesses
    2 Non-conceptual mental awarenesses

There is also a threefold division of mental awareness:

    1 Non-virtuous mental awarenesses
    2 Virtuous mental awarenesses
    3 Neutral mental awarenesses

From the point of view of enabling us to understand how we can become a Superior being by attaining yogic direct perceivers, minds can be divided into seven:

1 Direct perceivers
2 Subsequent cognizers
3 Re-cognizers
4 Correct beliefs
5 Non-ascertaining perceivers
6 Non-deluded doubt
7 Wrong awarenesses

The definition of direct perceiver is a cognizer that apprehends its object correctly and directly.

There are three types of direct perceiver:

1 Sense direct perceivers
2 Mental direct perceivers
3 Yogic direct perceivers

The definition of sense direct perceiver is a direct perceiver that is generated in dependence upon its uncommon dominant condition, a sense power possessing form.

There are five types of sense direct perceiver:

1 Eye sense direct perceivers
2 Ear sense direct perceivers
3 Nose sense direct perceivers
4 Tongue sense direct perceivers
5 Body sense direct perceivers

There is also a threefold division of sense direct perceiver:

1 Sense direct perceivers that are valid cognizers but not re-cognizers

2 Sense direct perceivers that are both valid cognizers and re-cognizers
3 Sense direct perceivers that are non-ascertaining perceivers

The definition of mental direct perceiver is a direct perceiver that is generated in dependence upon its uncommon dominant condition, a mental power.

There are three types of mental direct perceiver:

1 Mental direct perceivers induced by sense direct perceivers
2 Mental direct perceivers induced by meditation
3 Mental direct perceivers that are induced neither by sense direct perceivers nor by meditation

There are five types of mental direct perceiver induced by sense direct perceivers: these are mental direct perceivers apprehending forms, sounds, smells, tastes and tactile objects.

The definition of yogic direct perceiver is a direct perceiver that realizes the true nature of phenomena directly, in dependence upon its uncommon dominant condition, a concentration that is a union of tranquil abiding and superior seeing.

There are two types of yogic direct perceiver:

1 Yogic direct perceivers in the continuum of Hinayanists
2 Yogic direct perceivers in the continuum of Mahayanists

There is also a threefold division of yogic direct perceiver:

1 Yogic direct perceivers that are paths of seeing

2 Yogic direct perceivers that are paths of meditation
3 Yogic direct perceivers that are Paths of No More Learning

The definition of subsequent cognizer is a completely reliable cognizer whose object is realized in direct dependence upon a conclusive reason.

The definition of conclusive reason is a reason that is qualified by the three modes.

There are three types of subsequent cognizer from the point of view of the type of reason upon which they depend:

1 Subsequent cognizers through the power of fact
2 Subsequent cognizers through belief
3 Subsequent cognizers through renown

There is also a twofold division of subsequent cognizer from the point of view of how they are generated:

1 Subsequent cognizers arisen from listening or reading
2 Subsequent cognizers arisen from contemplation

The definition of re-cognizer is a cognizer that realizes what has already been realized through the force of a previous valid cognizer.

There are two types of re-cognizer:

1 Non-conceptual re-cognizers
2 Conceptual re-cognizers

There are three types of non-conceptual re-cognizer:

1 Re-cognizers that are sense direct perceivers
2 Re-cognizers that are mental direct perceivers
3 Re-cognizers that are yogic direct perceivers

There are two types of conceptual re-cognizer:

1 Conceptual re-cognizers induced by direct perceivers
2 Conceptual re-cognizers induced by subsequent cognizers

There are three types of conceptual re-cognizer induced by direct perceivers:

1 Conceptual re-cognizers induced by sense direct perceivers
2 Conceptual re-cognizers induced by mental direct perceivers
3 Conceptual re-cognizers induced by yogic direct perceivers

The definition of correct belief is a non-valid cognizer that realizes its conceived object.

There are two types of correct belief:

1 Correct beliefs that do not depend upon a reason
2 Correct beliefs that depend upon a reason

The definition of non-ascertaining perceiver is a cognizer to which a phenomenon that is its engaged object appears clearly without being ascertained.

There are two types of non-ascertaining perceiver:

1 Non-ascertaining sense awarenesses
2 Non-ascertaining mental awarenesses

The definition of non-deluded doubt is a doubt that does not disturb our peace of mind and gives rise to positive results.

There are two types of non-deluded doubt:

1 Non-deluded doubts with respect to ultimate truth
2 Non-deluded doubts with respect to conventional truths

The definition of wrong awareness is a cognizer that is mistaken with respect to its engaged object.

There are two types of wrong awareness:

1 Non-conceptual wrong awarenesses
2 Conceptual wrong awarenesses

There are two types of non-conceptual wrong awareness:

1 Wrong sense awarenesses
2 Wrong non-conceptual mental awarenesses

A wrong sense awareness can be mistaken with respect to its object in any of seven different ways: being mistaken with respect to its object's shape, colour, activity, number, time, measurement or entity.

There are two types of conceptual wrong awareness:

1 Intellectually-formed wrong awarenesses
2 Innate wrong awarenesses

There are two causes of wrong awareness:

1 Ultimate causes
2 Temporary causes

There are four temporary causes of wrong sense awareness:

1 A deceptive quality of the object
2 A deceptive situation
3 A defective sense power
4 A fault in the preceding awareness

There are three ways in which the term 'valid' can be applied:

1 Valid Teachers
2 Valid teachings
3 Valid cognizers

The definition of valid Teacher is a Teacher who knows fully and without error what objects are to be abandoned and what objects are to be practised, and who, out of compassion, reveals this knowledge to others.

The definition of valid teaching is an instruction that principally explains without error the objects to be abandoned and how to abandon them, and the objects to be practised and how to practise them.

The definition of valid cognizer is a cognizer that is non-deceptive with respect to its engaged object.

There are two types of valid cognizer:

1 A valid cognizer that is non-deceptive with respect to its manifest object
2 A valid cognizer that is non-deceptive with respect to its hidden object

The definition of manifest object is an object whose initial realization by a valid cognizer does not depend upon logical reasons.

The definition of hidden object is an object whose initial realization by a valid cognizer depends upon correct logical reasons.

The definition of direct valid cognizer is a non-deceptive cognizer that realizes its object directly.

There are three types of direct valid cognizer:

    1 Valid sense direct cognizers
    2 Valid mental direct cognizers
    3 Valid yogic direct cognizers

The definition of subsequent valid cognizer is a non-deceptive cognizer that realizes its hidden object by depending upon a conclusive reason.

There are three types of subsequent valid cognizer:

    1 Subsequent valid cognizers through the power of fact
    2 Subsequent valid cognizers through belief
    3 Subsequent valid cognizers through renown

The definition of non-valid cognizer is a cognizer that is deceptive with respect to its engaged object.

There are two types of non-valid cognizer:

    1 Non-conceptual non-valid cognizers
    2 Conceptual non-valid cognizers

The definition of meditation is a mind that is single-pointedly focused on a virtuous object and whose function is to make the mind peaceful and calm.

There is a threefold division of meditation:

    1 Meditation of a person of initial scope
    2 Meditation of a person of middling scope
    3 Meditation of a person of great scope

There are five meditations of a person of initial scope:

    1 Meditation on the preciousness of our human life
    2 Meditation on death
    3 Meditation on the dangers of lower rebirth

4 Meditation on going for refuge
5 Meditation on karma

There are four meditations of a person of middling scope:

1 Meditation on renunciation
2 Meditation on our determination to recognize, reduce and abandon our self-grasping ignorance, the root of samsaric rebirth
3 Meditation on our determination to enter and make progress on the path to liberation
4 Meditation on the ultimate truth of cessation

There are five meditations of a person of great scope:

1 Meditation on cherishing all living beings
2 Meditation on universal compassion
3 Meditation on the supreme good heart, bodhichitta
4 Meditation on our determination and promise to sincerely practise the six perfections
5 Meditation on training in yogic direct perceivers

Appendix II
Sadhanas

CONTENTS

Liberating Prayer

PRAISE TO BUDDHA SHAKYAMUNI

O Blessed One, Shakyamuni Buddha,
Precious treasury of compassion,
Bestower of supreme inner peace,

You, who love all beings without exception,
Are the source of happiness and goodness;
And you guide us to the liberating path.

Your body is a wishfulfilling jewel,
Your speech is supreme, purifying nectar,
And your mind is refuge for all living beings.

With folded hands I turn to you,
Supreme unchanging friend,
I request from the depths of my heart:

Please give me the light of your wisdom
To dispel the darkness of my mind
And to heal my mental continuum.

Please nourish me with your goodness,
That I in turn may nourish all beings
With an unceasing banquet of delight.

Through your compassionate intention,
Your blessings and virtuous deeds,
And my strong wish to rely upon you,

May all suffering quickly cease
And all happiness and joy be fulfilled;
And may holy Dharma flourish for evermore.

Colophon: This prayer was composed by Venerable Geshe Kelsang Gyatso Rinpoche and is recited at the beginning of teachings, meditations and prayers in Kadampa Buddhist Centres throughout the world.

Essence of Good Fortune

PRAYERS FOR THE SIX PREPARATORY
PRACTICES FOR MEDITATION ON
THE STAGES OF THE PATH TO
ENLIGHTENMENT

Introduction

Developing the realizations of the stages of the path to enlightenment depends upon four things: accumulating merit, purifying negativities, receiving the blessings of the Buddhas, Bodhisattvas and Spiritual Guides, and training the mind in the actual meditation on the stages of the path. The supreme method for accomplishing the first three is the six preparatory practices. These are:

1 Cleaning the meditation room and setting up a shrine with representations of Buddha's body, speech and mind.
2 Arranging suitable offerings.
3 Sitting in the correct meditation posture, going for refuge, generating and enhancing bodhichitta.
4 Visualizing the Field for Accumulating Merit.
5 Accumulating merit and purifying negativity by offering the practice of the seven limbs and the mandala.
6 Requesting the Field for Accumulating Merit in general and the Lamrim lineage Gurus in particular to bestow their blessings.

The essence of these six preparatory practices is contained in the following prayers, which should be recited with each session of meditation.

For more information on the six preparatory practices, see the books *The New Meditation Handbook* or *Joyful Path of Good Fortune*.

Geshe Kelsang Gyatso
1986

Essence of Good Fortune

Mentally purifying the environment

May the whole ground
Become completely pure,
As level as the palm of a hand,
And as smooth as lapis lazuli.

Mentally arranging pure offerings

May all of space be filled
With offerings from gods and men,
Both set out and imagined,
Like offerings of the All Good One.

Visualizing the objects of refuge

In the space in front, on a lion throne, on a cushion of
lotus, sun and moon, sits Buddha Shakyamuni, the
essence of all my kind Teachers, surrounded by the
assembly of direct and indirect Gurus, Yidams, Buddhas,
Bodhisattvas, Hearers, Solitary Conquerors, Heroes,
Dakinis and Dharma Protectors.

Generating the causes of going for refuge

I and all my kind mothers, fearing samsara's torments, turn
to Buddha, Dharma and Sangha, the only sources of refuge.
From now until enlightenment, to the Three Jewels we go
for refuge.

Short prayer of going for refuge

I and all sentient beings, until we achieve enlightenment,
Go for refuge to Buddha, Dharma and Sangha.

(7x, 100x, etc.)

Generating bodhichitta

Through the virtues I collect by giving and other
    perfections,
May I become a Buddha for the benefit of all.

(3x)

Purifying and receiving blessings

From the hearts of all refuge objects, lights and nectars
stream down and dissolve into myself and all living beings,
purifying negative karma and obstructions, increasing our
lives, our virtues and Dharma realizations.

Generating the four immeasurables

May everyone be happy,
May everyone be free from misery,
May no one ever be separated from their happiness,
May everyone have equanimity, free from hatred and
    attachment.

Inviting the Field for Accumulating Merit

You, Protector of all beings,
Great Destroyer of hosts of demons,
Please, O Blessed One, Knower of All,
Come to this place with your retinue.

Prayer of seven limbs

With my body, speech and mind, humbly I prostrate,
And make offerings both set out and imagined.
I confess my wrong deeds from all time,
And rejoice in the virtues of all.
Please stay until samsara ceases,
And turn the Wheel of Dharma for us.
I dedicate all virtues to great enlightenment.

Offering the mandala

The ground sprinkled with perfume and spread with
    flowers,
The Great Mountain, four lands, sun and moon,
Seen as a Buddha Land and offered thus,
May all beings enjoy such Pure Lands.

I offer without any sense of loss
The objects that give rise to my attachment, hatred and
    confusion,
My friends, enemies and strangers, our bodies and
    enjoyments;
Please accept these and bless me to be released directly
    from the three poisons.

IDAM GURU RATNA MANDALAKAM NIRYATAYAMI

Requests to the Field for Accumulating Merit and the Lamrim lineage Gurus

So now my most kind root Guru,
Please sit on the lotus and moon on my crown
And grant me out of your great kindness,
Your body, speech and mind's attainments.

*Visualize that your root Guru comes to the crown of your
head and makes the following requests with you:*

I make requests to you, Buddha Shakyamuni,
Whose body comes from countless virtues,
Whose speech fulfils the hopes of mortals,
Whose mind sees clearly all existence.

I make requests to you, Gurus of the lineage of extensive
 deeds,
Venerable Maitreya, Noble Asanga, Vasubandhu,
And all the other precious Teachers
Who have revealed the path of vastness.

I make requests to you, Gurus of the lineage of profound
 view,
Venerable Manjushri, Nagarjuna, Chandrakirti,
And all the other precious Teachers
Who have revealed the most profound path.

I make requests to you, Gurus of the lineage of Secret
 Mantra,
Conqueror Vajradhara, Tilopa and Naropa,
And all the other precious Teachers
Who have revealed the path of Tantra.

I make requests to you, Gurus of the Old Kadam lineage,
The second Buddha Atisha, Dromtonpa, Geshe Potowa,
And all the other precious Teachers
Who have revealed the union of vast and profound paths.

I make requests to you, Gurus of the New Kadam lineage,
Venerable Tsongkhapa, Jampel Gyatso, Khedrubje,
And all the other precious Teachers
Who have revealed the union of Sutra and Tantra.

I make requests to you, Venerable Kelsang Gyatso,
Protector of a vast ocean of living beings,
Unequalled Teacher of the paths to liberation and
    enlightenment,
Who accomplish and explain everything that was revealed
By the Fourth Deliverer of this Fortunate Aeon.

I make requests to you, my kind precious Teacher,
Who care for those with uncontrolled minds
Untamed by all the previous Buddhas,
As if they were fortunate disciples.

Requesting the three great purposes

Please pour down your inspiring blessings upon myself
and all my mothers so that we may quickly stop all
perverse minds, from disrespect for our kind Teacher to
the most subtle dual appearance.

Please pour down your inspiring blessings so that we
may quickly generate pure minds, from respect for our
kind Teacher to the supreme mind of Union.

Please pour down your inspiring blessings to pacify all
outer and inner obstructions.   (3x)

Receiving blessings and purifying

From the hearts of all the holy beings, streams of light and nectar flow down, granting blessings and purifying.

Prayer of the Stages of the Path

The path begins with strong reliance
On my kind Teacher, source of all good;
O Bless me with this understanding
To follow him with great devotion.

This human life with all its freedoms,
Extremely rare, with so much meaning;
O Bless me with this understanding
All day and night to seize its essence.

My body, like a water bubble,
Decays and dies so very quickly;
After death come results of karma,
Just like the shadow of a body.

With this firm knowledge and remembrance
Bless me to be extremely cautious,
Always avoiding harmful actions
And gathering abundant virtue.

Samsara's pleasures are deceptive,
Give no contentment, only torment;
So please bless me to strive sincerely
To gain the bliss of perfect freedom.

O Bless me so that from this pure thought
Come mindfulness and greatest caution,
To keep as my essential practice
The doctrine's root, the Pratimoksha.

Just like myself all my kind mothers
Are drowning in samsara's ocean;
O So that I may soon release them,
Bless me to train in bodhichitta.

But I cannot become a Buddha
By this alone without three ethics;
So bless me with the strength to practise
The Bodhisattva's ordination.

By pacifying my distractions
And analyzing perfect meanings,
Bless me to quickly gain the union
Of special insight and quiescence.

When I become a pure container
Through common paths, bless me to enter
The essence practice of good fortune,
The supreme vehicle, Vajrayana.

The two attainments both depend on
My sacred vows and my commitments;
Bless me to understand this clearly
And keep them at the cost of my life.

By constant practice in four sessions,
The way explained by holy Teachers,
O Bless me to gain both the stages,
Which are the essence of the Tantras.

May those who guide me on the good path,
And my companions all have long lives;
Bless me to pacify completely
All obstacles, outer and inner.

May I always find perfect Teachers,
And take delight in holy Dharma,
Accomplish all grounds and paths swiftly,
And gain the state of Vajradhara.

You may do your meditation here or at any appropriate point within the Prayer of the Stages of the Path.

Mantra recitation

After our meditation we contemplate that from the heart of Buddha Shakyamuni, the principal Field of Merit in front of us, infinite light rays emanate, reaching all environments and all beings. These dissolve into light and gradually gather into the Field of Merit. This dissolves into the central figure, Buddha Shakyamuni, who then dissolves into our root Guru at the crown of our head, instantly transforming him into the aspect of Guru Buddha Shakyamuni. He then diminishes in size, enters through our crown, and descends to our heart. His mind and our mind become one nature. We recite the mantra:

OM MUNI MUNI MAHA MUNIYE SÖHA   (7x, 100x, etc.)

Dedication prayers

Through the virtues I have collected
By practising the stages of the path,
May all living beings find the opportunity
To practise in the same way.

However many living beings there are
Experiencing mental and physical suffering,
May their suffering cease through the power of my merit,
And may they find everlasting happiness and joy.

May everyone experience
The happiness of humans and gods,
And quickly attain enlightenment,
So that samsara is finally extinguished.

For the benefit of all living beings as extensive as space,
May I attain great wisdom like that of Manjushri,
Great compassion like that of Avalokiteshvara,
Great power like that of Vajrapani.

The Buddhadharma is the supreme medicine
That relieves all mental pain,
So may this precious Dharma Jewel
Pervade all worlds throughout space.

May there arise in the minds of all living beings
Great faith in Buddha, Dharma and Sangha,
And thus may they always receive
The blessings of the Three Precious Gems.

May there never arise in this world
The miseries of incurable disease, famine or war,
Or the dangers of earthquakes, fires,
Floods, storms and so forth.

May all mother beings meet precious Teachers
Who reveal the stages of the path to enlightenment,
And through engaging in this path
May they quickly attain the ultimate peace of full
    enlightenment.

Through the blessings of the Buddhas and Bodhisattvas,
The truth of actions and their effects,
And the power of my pure superior intention,
May all my prayers be fulfilled.

Prayers for the Virtuous Tradition

So that the tradition of Je Tsongkhapa,
The King of the Dharma, may flourish,
May all obstacles be pacified
And may all favourable conditions abound.

Through the two collections of myself and others
Gathered throughout the three times,
May the doctrine of Conqueror Losang Dragpa
Flourish for evermore.

The nine-line *Migtsema* prayer

Tsongkhapa, crown ornament of the scholars of the Land of
the Snows,
You are Buddha Shakyamuni and Vajradhara, the source
of all attainments,
Avalokiteshvara, the treasury of unobservable
compassion,
Manjushri, the supreme stainless wisdom,
And Vajrapani, the destroyer of the hosts of maras.
O Venerable Guru-Buddha, synthesis of all Three Jewels,
With my body, speech and mind, respectfully I make
requests:
Please grant your blessings to ripen and liberate myself
and others,
And bestow the common and supreme attainments.

(3x)

If we are unable to recite all these prayers for the six
preparatory practices in every meditation session,
we should at least always remember Guru Buddha
Shakyamuni at the crown of our head, recalling that his
mind is the synthesis of all Buddha Jewels, his speech the

synthesis of all Dharma Jewels, and his body the synthesis of all Sangha Jewels. Then with strong faith we should go for refuge by reciting the short prayer of going for refuge, generate bodhichitta with the words, 'Through the virtues . . . for the benefit of all', offer the mandala, request the three great purposes, and receive blessings and purify.

If we perform these three practices every time we sit down to meditate – namely, accumulating merit, purifying negative karma, and making requests to receive blessings and inspiration – we shall have accomplished the three purposes of engaging in preparatory practices. At the conclusion of every meditation session, we should dedicate our merit.

Colophon: These prayers were compiled from traditional sources by Venerable Geshe Kelsang Gyatso Rinpoche. The verse of request to Venerable Geshe Kelsang Gyatso Rinpoche was composed by the Dharma Protector Duldzin Dorje Shugden and included in the prayers at the request of Venerable Geshe Kelsang's faithful disciples.

Glossary

Aggregate   In general, all functioning things are aggregates because they are an aggregation of their parts. In particular, a person of the desire realm or form realm has five aggregates: the aggregates of form, feeling, discrimination, compositional factors and consciousness. A being of the formless realm lacks the aggregate of form but has the other four. A person's form aggregate is his or her body. The remaining four aggregates are aspects of his mind. See *The New Heart of Wisdom*.

Asanga   A great Indian Buddhist Yogi and scholar of the fifth century, author of *Compendium of Abhidharma*. See *Living Meaningfully, Dying Joyfully* and *The New Heart of Wisdom*.

Aspiring bodhichitta   A bodhichitta that is a mere wish to attain enlightenment for the benefit of all living beings. See also *Bodhichitta*.

Basis of imputation   All phenomena are imputed upon their parts, therefore any of the individual parts, or the entire collection of the parts, of any phenomenon is its basis of imputation. A phenomenon is imputed by mind in dependence upon its basis of imputation appearing to that mind. See *The New Heart of Wisdom* and *Ocean of Nectar*.

Beginningless time   According to the Buddhist world view, there is no beginning to mind, and so no beginning to time. Therefore, all living beings have taken countless previous rebirths.

Blessing   The transformation of our mind from a negative state to a positive state, from an unhappy state to a happy state, or from a state of weakness to a state of strength, through the inspiration of holy beings such as our Spiritual Guide, Buddhas and Bodhisattvas.

Bodhichitta   Sanskrit term for 'mind of enlightenment'. 'Bodhi' means 'enlightenment', and 'chitta' means 'mind'. There are two types of bodhichitta: conventional bodhichitta and ultimate bodhichitta. Generally speaking, the term 'bodhichitta' refers to conventional bodhichitta, which is a primary mind motivated by great compassion that spontaneously seeks enlightenment to benefit all living beings. There are two types of conventional bodhichitta – aspiring bodhichitta and engaging bodhichitta. Ultimate bodhichitta is a wisdom motivated by conventional bodhichitta that directly realizes emptiness, the ultimate nature of phenomena. See also *Aspiring bodhichitta* and *Engaging bodhichitta*. See *Modern Buddhism, Joyful Path of Good Fortune* and *Meaningful to Behold*.

Bodhisattva A person who has generated spontaneous bodhichitta but who has not yet become a Buddha. See *Modern Buddhism, Joyful Path of Good Fortune* and *Meaningful to Behold*.

Bodies of a Buddha A Buddha has four bodies – the Wisdom Truth Body, the Nature Body, the Enjoyment Body and the Emanation Body. The first is Buddha's omniscient mind. The second is the emptiness, or ultimate nature, of his or her mind. The third is his subtle Form Body. The fourth, of which each Buddha manifests a countless number, are gross Form Bodies that are visible to ordinary beings. The Wisdom Truth Body and the Nature Body are both included within the Truth Body, and the Enjoyment Body and the Emanation Body are both included within the Form Body. See *Joyful Path of Good Fortune, Tantric Grounds and Paths* and *Ocean of Nectar.*

Buddha A being who has completely abandoned all delusions and their imprints. Every living being has the potential to become a Buddha. See also *Buddha Shakyamuni*. See *Modern Buddhism* and *Joyful Path of Good Fortune.*

Buddhadharma See *Dharma.*

Buddha nature The very subtle mind of a sentient being, and its ultimate nature. Buddha seed, Buddha nature, and Buddha lineage are synonyms. All sentient beings have Buddha nature and therefore have the potential to attain Buddhahood. See *Mahamudra Tantra.*

Buddha Shakyamuni The founder of Buddhism in this world age, and the principal object of refuge for all Buddhists. See *Introduction to Buddhism* and *Modern Buddhism.*

Buddhist Anyone who from the depths of his or her heart goes for refuge to the Three Jewels – Buddha Jewel, Dharma Jewel and Sangha Jewel. See *Introduction to Buddhism.*

Central channel The principal channel at the very centre of the body, along which the channel wheels, or chakras, are located. See *Modern Buddhism, Mahamudra Tantra* and *Clear Light of Bliss.*

Chakra Sanskrit term for 'channel wheel'. A focal centre where secondary channels branch out from the central channel. Meditating on these points can cause the inner winds to enter the central channel. See *Modern Buddhism*, *Mahamudra Tantra* and *Clear Light of Bliss*.

Chandrakirti (circa 7th century AD) A great Indian Buddhist scholar and meditation master who composed, among many other books, the well-known *Guide to the Middle Way*, in which he clearly elucidates the view of the Madhyamika-Prasangika school according to Buddha's teachings given in the *Perfection of Wisdom Sutras*. See *Ocean of Nectar*.

Charavaka A non-Buddhist school current in Buddha's day, which denied subsequent cognizers, rebirth, the laws of karma and so forth, and which encouraged a hedonistic attitude to life. See *Ocean of Nectar* and *Meaningful to Behold*.

Chittamatra The lower of the two schools of Mahayana tenets. 'Chittamatra' means 'mind only'. According to this school, all phenomena are the same nature as the mind that apprehends them. They also assert that dependent phenomena are truly existent but do not exist external to the mind. A Chittamatrin is a proponent of Chittamatra tenets. See *Meaningful to Behold* and *Ocean of Nectar*.

Clear light A manifest very subtle mind that perceives an appearance like clear, empty space. See *Modern Buddhism*, *Clear Light of Bliss*, *Mahamudra Tantra* and *Tantric Grounds and Paths*.

Contaminated aggregate Any of the aggregates of form, feeling, discrimination, compositional factors and consciousness of a samsaric being. See also *Aggregate*. See *The New Heart of Wisdom*.

Conventional nature See *Ultimate nature*.

Conventional truth Any phenomenon other than emptiness. Conventional truths are true with respect to the minds of ordinary beings, but in reality they are false. See *Modern Buddhism*, *The New Heart of Wisdom*, *Meaningful to Behold* and *Ocean of Nectar*.

Dakini Land The Pure Land of Heruka and Vajrayogini. In Sanskrit it is called 'Keajra' and in Tibetan 'Dagpa Khacho'. See *The New Guide to Dakini Land*.

Deity 'Yidam' in Tibetan. A Tantric enlightened being.

Dharma Buddha's teachings and the inner realizations that are attained in dependence upon practising them. 'Dharma' means 'protection'. By practising Buddha's teachings we protect ourself from suffering and problems.

Dharmakirti (circa 6th to 7th century AD) A great Indian Buddhist Yogi and scholar who composed *Commentary to Valid Cognition*, a commentary to *Compendium of Valid Cognition*, which was written by his Spiritual Guide, Dignaga.

Dignaga (circa 5th century AD) A great Indian Buddhist Yogi and scholar who composed a number of works on logic and cognition, the most famous being *Compendium of Valid Cognition*.

Empowerment A special potential power to attain any of the four Buddha bodies that is received by a Tantric practitioner from his or her Guru, or from other holy beings, by means of Tantric ritual. It is the gateway to the Vajrayana. See *Tantric Grounds and Paths* and *Mahamudra Tantra*.

Engaging bodhichitta A bodhichitta held by the Bodhisattva vows. See also *Bodhichitta*.

Essence of Good Fortune A sadhana consisting of prayers for the six preparatory practices. See also *Preparatory practices*. For a full commentary, see *Joyful Path of Good Fortune*.

Foe Destroyer 'Arhat' in Sanskrit. A practitioner who has abandoned all delusions and their seeds by training on the spiritual paths, and who will never again be reborn in samsara. In this context, the term 'Foe' refers to the delusions.

Four noble truths True sufferings, true origins, true cessations and true paths. They are called 'noble' truths because they are supreme objects of meditation. Through meditation on these four objects, we can realize ultimate truth directly and thus become a Superior being. Sometimes referred to as the 'four truths of Superiors'. See *How to Solve Our Human Problems*, *Joyful Path of Good Fortune* and *Ocean of Nectar*.

Generation stage A realization of a creative yoga prior to attaining the actual completion stage, which is attained through the practice of bringing the three bodies into the path, in which one mentally generates oneself as a Tantric Deity and one's surroundings as the Deity's mandala. Meditation on generation stage is called a 'creative yoga' because its object is created, or generated, by correct imagination. See *Tantric Grounds and Paths*, *Modern Buddhism* and *Mahamudra Tantra*.

Geshe A title given by Kadampa monasteries to accomplished Buddhist scholars. Contracted form of the Tibetan 'ge wai she nyen', literally meaning 'virtuous friend'.

Ground/Spiritual ground A clear realization that acts as the foundation of many good qualities. A clear realization is a realization held by spontaneous renunciation or bodhichitta. The ten grounds are the realizations of Superior Bodhisattvas: Very Joyful, Stainless, Luminous, Radiant, Difficult to Overcome, Approaching, Gone Afar, Immovable, Good Intelligence, and Cloud of Dharma. See also *Path/Spiritual path*. See *Ocean of Nectar* and *Tantric Grounds and Paths*.

Guide to the Bodhisattva's Way of Life A classic Mahayana Buddhist text composed by the great Indian Buddhist Yogi and scholar Shantideva, which presents all the practices of a Bodhisattva from the initial generation of bodhichitta through to the completion of the practice of the six perfections. For a translation, see *Guide to the Bodhisattva's Way of Life*. For a full commentary, see *Meaningful to Behold*.

Guide to the Middle Way A classic Mahayana Buddhist text composed by the great Indian Buddhist Yogi and scholar Chandrakirti, which provides a comprehensive explanation of the Madhyamika-Prasangika view of emptiness as taught in the *Perfection of Wisdom Sutras*. For a translation and full commentary, see *Ocean of Nectar*.

Guru Sumati Buddha Heruka A special manifestation of Je Tsongkhapa inseparable from our root Guru, Buddha Shakyamuni and Heruka. See *Modern Buddhism* and *Mahamudra Tantra*.

Hashang A Chinese monk of the eighth century who propagated many wrong views in Tibet, including the view that the meaning of Buddha's teachings on emptiness was that we should empty our mind of all conceptions and meditate on nothingness. He was publicly defeated in debate by Kamalashila and banished from Tibet. See *Ocean of Nectar* and *Joyful Path of Good Fortune*.

Hell realm The lowest of the six realms of samsara. See *Joyful Path of Good Fortune*.

Heruka An enlightened Deity of Highest Yoga Tantra who is a manifestation of the compassion of all Buddhas. He has a blue-coloured body, four faces and twelve arms, and embraces his consort Vajravarahi. See *Essence of Vajrayana* and *Modern Buddhism*.

Hinayana Sanskrit term for 'Lesser Vehicle'. The Hinayana goal is to attain merely one's own liberation from suffering by completely abandoning delusions. See *Joyful Path of Good Fortune*.

Impermanent phenomenon   Phenomena are either permanent or impermanent. 'Impermanent' means 'momentary'; thus an impermanent phenomenon is a phenomenon that is produced and disintegrates within a moment. Synonyms of impermanent phenomenon are functioning thing, thing and product. There are two types of impermanence: gross and subtle. Gross impermanence is any impermanence that can be seen by an ordinary sense awareness – for example the ageing and death of a sentient being. Subtle impermanence is the momentary disintegration of a functioning thing. See *The New Heart of Wisdom*.

Imprint   There are two types of imprint: imprints of actions and imprints of delusions. Every action we perform leaves an imprint on the mental consciousness, and these imprints are karmic potentialities to experience certain effects in the future. The imprints left by delusions remain even after the delusions themselves have been abandoned, like the smell of garlic lingers in a container after the garlic has been removed. Imprints of delusions are obstructions to omniscience, and are completely abandoned only by Buddhas.

Imputation, mere   According to the highest school of Buddhist philosophy, the Madhyamika-Prasangika school, all phenomena are merely imputed by conception in dependence upon their basis of imputation. Therefore, they are mere imputations and do not exist from their own side in the least. See *Modern Buddhism, The New Heart of Wisdom* and *Ocean of Nectar*.

Inherent existence   An imagined mode of existence whereby phenomena are held to exist from their own side, independent of other phenomena. In reality, all phenomena lack or are empty of inherent existence because they depend upon other phenomena. See *Modern Buddhism, The New Heart of Wisdom* and *Ocean of Nectar*.

Inner winds   Special subtle winds related to the mind that flow through the channels of our body. Our body and mind cannot function without these winds. See *Modern Buddhism, Mahamudra Tantra, Clear Light of Bliss* and *Tantric Grounds and Paths*.

Je Tsongkhapa   (AD 1357-1419) An emanation of the Wisdom Buddha Manjushri, whose appearance in fourteenth-century Tibet as a monk, and the holder of the lineage of pure view and pure deeds, was prophesied by Buddha. He spread a very pure Buddhadharma throughout Tibet, showing how to combine the practices of Sutra and Tantra, and how to practise pure Dharma during degenerate times. His tradition later became known as the 'Gelug', or 'Ganden Tradition'. See *Heart Jewel* and *Great Treasury of Merit*.

Kadampa A Tibetan term in which 'Ka' means 'word' and refers to all Buddha's teachings, 'dam' refers to Atisha's special Lamrim instructions known as the 'stages of the path to enlightenment', and 'pa' refers to a follower of Kadampa Buddhism who integrates all the teachings of Buddha that they know into their Lamrim practice. See also *Kadampa Buddhism* and *Kadampa Tradition*.

Kadampa Buddhism A Mahayana Buddhist school founded by the great Indian Buddhist Master Atisha (AD 982-1054). See also *Kadampa* and *Kadampa Tradition*.

Kadampa Tradition The pure tradition of Buddhism established by Atisha. Followers of this tradition up to the time of Je Tsongkhapa are known as 'Old Kadampas', and those after the time of Je Tsongkhapa are known as 'New Kadampas'. See also *Kadampa* and *Kadampa Buddhism*.

Khedrubje (AD 1385-1438) One of the principal disciples of Je Tsongkhapa, who did much to promote the tradition of Je Tsongkhapa after he passed away. See *Great Treasury of Merit*.

Liberation Complete freedom from samsara and its cause, the delusions. See *Joyful Path of Good Fortune*.

Madhyamika A Sanskrit term, literally meaning 'Middle Way'. The higher of the two schools of Mahayana tenets. The Madhyamika view was taught by Buddha in the *Perfection of Wisdom Sutras* during the second turning of the Wheel of Dharma and was subsequently elucidated by Nagarjuna and his followers. There are two divisions of this school, Madhyamika-Svatantrika and Madhyamika-Prasangika, of which the latter is Buddha's final view. See *Meaningful to Behold* and *Ocean of Nectar*.

Mahamudra A Sanskrit term, literally meaning 'great seal'. According to Sutra, this refers to the profound view of emptiness. Since emptiness is the nature of all phenomena, it is called a 'seal', and since a direct realization of emptiness enables us to accomplish the great purpose – complete liberation from the sufferings of samsara – it is also called 'great'. According to Tantra, or Vajrayana, Mahamudra is the union of spontaneous great bliss and emptiness. See *Mahamudra Tantra*, *The Oral Instructions of Mahamudra*, *Great Treasury of Merit* and *Clear Light of Bliss*.

Mahayana Sanskrit term for 'Great Vehicle', the spiritual path to great enlightenment. The Mahayana goal is to attain Buddhahood for the benefit of all sentient beings by completely abandoning delusions and their imprints. See *Joyful Path of Good Fortune* and *Meaningful to Behold*.

Mahayana path A clear realization in the mental continuum of a Bodhisattva or a Buddha. There are five Mahayana paths: the Mahayana path of accumulation, the Mahayana path of preparation, the Mahayana path of seeing, the Mahayana path of meditation, and the Mahayana Path of No More Learning. The first four are necessarily in the continuum of a Bodhisattva and the last is necessarily in the continuum of a Buddha. See *Joyful Path of Good Fortune* and *Ocean of Nectar*.

Maitreya The embodiment of the loving kindness of all the Buddhas. At the time of Buddha Shakyamuni he manifested as a Bodhisattva disciple in order to show Buddha's disciples how to be perfect Mahayana disciples. In the future, he will manifest as the fifth founding Buddha.

Manjushri The embodiment of the wisdom of all the Buddhas. At the time of Buddha Shakyamuni he manifested as a Bodhisattva disciple in order to show Buddha's disciples how to be perfect Mahayana disciples. See *Great Treasury of Merit* and *Heart Jewel*.

Mantra A Sanskrit term, literally meaning 'mind protection'. Mantra protects the mind from ordinary appearances and conceptions. There are four types of mantra: mantras that are mind, mantras that are inner wind, mantras that are sound, and mantras that are form. In general, there are three types of mantra recitation: verbal recitation, mental recitation and vajra recitation. See *Tantric Grounds and Paths*.

Merit The good fortune created by virtuous actions. It is the potential power to increase our good qualities and produce happiness.

Method Any spiritual path that functions to ripen our Buddha lineage. Training in renunciation, compassion and bodhichitta are examples of method practices.

Mundane paths Contaminated actions that lead to samsaric rebirth. There are two types: the ten non-virtuous actions that lead to the lower realms, and the ten virtuous actions and contaminated concentrations that lead to the higher realms.

Nagarjuna   A great Indian Buddhist scholar and meditation master who revived the Mahayana in the first century AD by bringing to light the teachings on the *Perfection of Wisdom Sutras.* See *The New Heart of Wisdom* and *Ocean of Nectar.*

Nirvana   Sanskrit term meaning 'state beyond sorrow'. Complete freedom from samsara and its cause, the delusions. See *Joyful Path of Good Fortune.*

Obstructions to liberation   Obstructions that prevent the attainment of liberation. All delusions, such as ignorance, attachment and anger, together with their seeds, are obstructions to liberation. Also called 'delusion-obstructions'.

Obstructions to omniscience   The imprints of delusions, which prevent simultaneous and direct realization of all phenomena. Only Buddhas have overcome these obstructions.

Parinirvana   Sanskrit term literally meaning 'passing away to a state beyond sorrow'. It refers to a Buddha's Emanation Body appearing to die and pass beyond this world.

Path/Spiritual path   An exalted awareness conjoined with non-fabricated, or spontaneous, renunciation. Spiritual path, spiritual ground, spiritual vehicle and exalted awareness are synonyms. See also *Ground/Spiritual ground.* See *Tantric Grounds and Paths* and *Ocean of Nectar.*

Perfection of Wisdom Sutras   Sutras of the second turning of the Wheel of Dharma, in which Buddha revealed his final view of the ultimate nature of all phenomena – emptiness of inherent existence. See *The New Heart of Wisdom* and *Ocean of Nectar.*

Phenomena source   A phenomenon that appears only to mental awareness. It is also the name given to Buddha Vajrayogini's mandala, which is symbolic of the source of all phenomena, emptiness, and shaped like a double tetrahedron. See *The New Guide to Dakini Land.*

Philosophical tenets, schools of Buddhist   Four philosophical views taught by Buddha according to the inclinations and dispositions of disciples. They are the Vaibhashika, Sautrantika, Chittamatra and Madhyamika schools. The first two are Hinayana schools and the second two are Mahayana schools. They are studied in sequence, the lower tenets being the means by which the higher ones are understood. See *Meaningful to Behold* and *Ocean of Nectar.*

Pratimoksha   Sanskrit term for 'personal liberation'. See *The Bodhisattva Vow*.

Preparatory practices   Practices that prepare the mind for successful meditation, such as purifying the mind, accumulating merit and receiving blessings. See also *Essence of Good Fortune*. See *Eight Steps to Happiness*, *Joyful Path of Good Fortune* and *The New Meditation Handbook*.

Produced space   The visible space we can see, for example, inside a room or in the sky. So called because it is produced by causes and conditions and so is impermanent. The characteristic property of produced space is that it does not obstruct objects. See *The New Heart of Wisdom*.

Prostration   An action of showing respect with body, speech or mind. See *Joyful Path of Good Fortune* and *The Bodhisattva Vow*.

Puja   A ceremony in which offerings and other acts of devotion are performed in front of holy beings.

Pure Land   A pure environment in which there are no true sufferings. There are many Pure Lands. For example, Tushita is the Pure Land of Buddha Maitreya, Sukhavati is the Pure Land of Buddha Amitabha, and Dakini Land, or Keajra, is the Pure Land of Buddha Vajrayogini and Buddha Heruka. See *Living Meaningfully, Dying Joyfully*.

Purification   Generally, any practice that leads to the attainment of a pure body, speech or mind. More specifically, a practice for purifying negative karma by means of the four opponent powers. See *Joyful Path of Good Fortune*, *The Bodhisattva Vow*, *Universal Compassion* and *The New Guide to Dakini Land*.

Sadhana   A ritual prayer that is a special method for attaining spiritual realizations, usually associated with a Tantric Deity.

Secret Mantra   Synonymous with Tantra. Secret Mantra teachings are distinguished from Sutra teachings in that they reveal methods for training the mind by bringing the future result, or Buddhahood, into the present path. Secret Mantra is the supreme path to full enlightenment. The term 'Mantra' indicates that it is Buddha's special instruction for protecting our mind from ordinary appearances and conceptions. Practitioners of Secret Mantra overcome ordinary appearances and conceptions by visualizing their body, environment, enjoyments and deeds as those of a Buddha. The term 'Secret' indicates that the practices are to be done in private, and that they can be practised only by those who have received a Tantric empowerment. See *Modern Buddhism*, *Clear Light of Bliss*, *Tantric Grounds and Paths* and *Mahamudra Tantra*.

Seed-letter   The sacred letter from which a Deity is generated. Each Deity has a particular seed-letter. For example, the seed-letter of Manjushri is DHI, of Tara is TAM, of Vajrayogini is BAM, and of Heruka is HUM. To accomplish Tantric realizations, we need to recognize that Deities and their seed-letters are the same nature.

Self-cherishing   A mental attitude that considers oneself to be supremely important and precious. It is regarded as a principal object to be abandoned by Bodhisattvas. See *Modern Buddhism*, *Eight Steps to Happiness* and *Meaningful to Behold*.

Sentient being   Any being who possesses a mind that is contaminated by delusions or their imprints. Both 'sentient being' and 'living being' are terms used to distinguish beings whose minds are contaminated by either of these two obstructions from Buddhas, whose minds are completely free from these obstructions.

Shantideva   (AD 687-763) A great Indian Buddhist scholar and meditation master. He composed *Guide to the Bodhisattva's Way of Life*. See *Meaningful to Behold* and *Guide to Bodhisattva's Way of Life*.

Sixteen characteristics of the four noble truths   Buddha taught that each of the four noble truths has four special characteristics. The four characteristics of true sufferings are: impermanent, suffering, empty and selfless. The four characteristics of true origins are: cause, origin, strong producer and condition. The four characteristics of true cessations are: cessation, peace, supreme attainment and definite abandoner. The four characteristics of true paths are: path, antidote, accomplisher and definite abandoning. See *Ocean of Nectar*.

Superior being   'Arya' in Sanskrit. A being who has a direct realization of emptiness. There are Hinayana Superiors and Mahayana Superiors.

Supramundane path   Any path leading to liberation or enlightenment – for example, the realizations of renunciation, bodhichitta and the correct view of emptiness. Strictly speaking, only Superior beings possess supramundane paths. See *Tantric Grounds and Paths*.

Sutra   The teachings of Buddha that are open to everyone to practise without the need for empowerment. These include Buddha's teachings of the three turnings of the Wheel of Dharma.

Tantra See *Secret Mantra*.

Training the mind 'Lojong' in Tibetan. A special lineage of instructions that came from Buddha Shakyamuni through Manjushri and Shantideva to Atisha and the Kadampa Geshes, which emphasizes the generation of bodhichitta through the practices of equalizing and exchanging self with others combined with taking and giving. See *Universal Compassion* and *Eight Steps to Happiness*.

Tummo Tibetan word for 'inner fire'. An inner heat located at the centre of the navel channel wheel. See *Clear Light of Bliss*.

Ultimate nature All phenomena have two natures – a conventional nature and an ultimate nature. In the case of a table, for example, the table itself, and its shape, colour and so forth are all the conventional nature of the table. The ultimate nature of the table is the table's lack of inherent existence. The conventional nature of a phenomenon is a conventional truth, and its ultimate nature is an ultimate truth. See *The New Heart of Wisdom* and *Ocean of Nectar*.

Ultimate truth The ultimate nature of all phenomena, emptiness. See *Modern Buddhism*, *The New Heart of Wisdom*, *Transform Your Life*, *Meaningful to Behold* and *Ocean of Nectar*.

Vajra recitation A mantra recitation produced from inner winds that is practised in conjunction with Vajrayana practices. See *Tantric Grounds and Paths*.

Vajrayogini A female enlightened Deity of Highest Yoga Tantra who is the manifestation of the wisdom of all Buddhas. She is the same nature as Heruka. See *The New Guide to Dakini Land*.

Vasubandhu A great Indian Buddhist scholar of the fifth century who was converted to the Mahayana by his older brother, Asanga. He wrote *Treasury of Abhidharma* (Skt. *Abhidharmakosha*). See *The New Heart of Wisdom*.

Vinaya Sutras Sutras in which Buddha principally explains the practice of moral discipline, and in particular the Pratimoksha moral discipline.

Wheel of Life A diagram depicting the twelve dependent-related links and the four noble truths. See *Joyful Path of Good Fortune*.

Winds See *Inner winds*.

Yogi/Yogini Sanskrit terms usually referring to a male or a female meditator who has attained the union of tranquil abiding and superior seeing.

Bibliography

Venerable Geshe Kelsang Gyatso Rinpoche is a highly respected meditation master and scholar of the Mahayana Buddhist tradition founded by Je Tsongkhapa. Since arriving in the West in 1977, Venerable Geshe Kelsang has worked tirelessly to establish pure Buddhadharma throughout the world. Over this period he has given extensive teachings on the major scriptures of the Mahayana. These teachings provide a comprehensive presentation of the essential Sutra and Tantra practices of Mahayana Buddhism.

Books

The following books by Venerable Geshe Kelsang Gyatso Rinpoche are all published by Tharpa Publications.

The Bodhisattva Vow A practical guide to helping others. (2nd. edn., 1995)

Clear Light of Bliss A Tantric meditation manual. (3rd. edn., 2014)

Eight Steps to Happiness The Buddhist way of loving kindness. (2nd. edn., 2012)

Essence of Vajrayana The Highest Yoga Tantra practice of Heruka body mandala. (1997)

Great Treasury of Merit How to rely upon a Spiritual Guide. (2nd. edn., 2015)

Guide to the Bodhisattva's Way of Life How to enjoy a life of great meaning and altruism. (A translation of Shantideva's famous verse masterpiece.) (2002)

Heart Jewel The essential practices of Kadampa Buddhism. (2nd. edn., 1997)

How to Solve Our Human Problems The four noble truths. (2005)

How to Understand the Mind The nature and power of the mind. (4th. edn., 2014)

Introduction to Buddhism An explanation of the Buddhist way of life. (2nd. edn., 2001)

Joyful Path of Good Fortune The complete Buddhist path to enlightenment. (2nd. edn., 1995)

Living Meaningfully, Dying Joyfully The profound practice of transference of consciousness. (1999)

Mahamudra Tantra The supreme Heart Jewel nectar. (2005)

Meaningful to Behold Becoming a friend of the world. (5th. edn., 2007)

Modern Buddhism The path of compassion and wisdom. (2nd. edn., 2013)

The New Guide to Dakini Land The Highest Yoga Tantra practice of Buddha Vajrayogini. (3rd. edn., 2012)

The New Heart of Wisdom Profound teachings from Buddha's heart (An explanation of the *Heart Sutra*). (5th. edn., 2012)

The New Meditation Handbook Meditations to make our life happy and meaningful. (5th. edn., 2013)

Ocean of Nectar The true nature of all things. (1995)

The Oral Instruction of Mahamudra The very essence of Buddha's teachings of Sutra and Tantra. (2nd. edn., 2016)

Tantric Grounds and Paths How to enter, progress on, and complete the Vajrayana path. (1994)

Transform Your Life A blissful journey. (2nd edn., 2014)

Universal Compassion Inspiring solutions for difficult times. (4th. edn., 2002)

Sadhanas and Other Booklets

Venerable Geshe Kelsang Gyatso Rinpoche has also supervised the translation of a collection of essential sadhanas, or ritual prayers for spiritual attainments, available in booklet or audio formats.

Avalokiteshvara Sadhana Prayers and requests to the Buddha of Compassion.

The Blissful Path The condensed self-generation sadhana of Vajrayogini.

The Bodhisattva's Confession of Moral Downfalls The purification practice of the *Mahayana Sutra of the Three Superior Heaps*.

Condensed Essence of Vajrayana Condensed Heruka body mandala self-generation sadhana.

Condensed Long Life Practice of Buddha Amitayus.

Dakini Yoga The middling self-generation sadhana of Vajrayogini.

Drop of Essential Nectar A special fasting and purification practice in conjunction with Eleven-faced Avalokiteshvara.

Essence of Good Fortune Prayers for the six preparatory practices for meditation on the stages of the path to enlightenment.

Essence of Vajrayana Heruka body mandala self-generation sadhana according to the system of Mahasiddha Ghantapa.

Feast of Great Bliss Vajrayogini self-initiation sadhana.

Great Liberation of the Father Preliminary prayers for Mahamudra meditation in conjunction with Heruka practice.

Great Liberation of the Mother Preliminary prayers for Mahamudra meditation in conjunction with Vajrayogini practice.

The Great Mother A method to overcome hindrances and obstacles by reciting the *Essence of Wisdom Sutra* (the *Heart Sutra*)

A Handbook for the Daily Practice of Bodhisattva and Tantric Vows.

Heartfelt Prayers Funeral service for cremations and burials.

Heart Jewel The Guru yoga of Je Tsongkhapa combined with the condensed sadhana of his Dharma Protector.

The Kadampa Way of Life The essential practice of Kadam Lamrim.

Keajra Heaven The essential commentary to the practice of *The Uncommon Yoga of Inconceivability.*

Lay Pratimoksha Vow Ceremony.

Liberating Prayer Praise to Buddha Shakyamuni.

Liberation from Sorrow Praises and requests to the Twenty-one Taras.

Mahayana Refuge Ceremony and Bodhisattva Vow Ceremony.

Medicine Buddha Prayer A method for benefiting others.

Medicine Buddha Sadhana A method for accomplishing the attainments of Medicine Buddha.

Meditation and Recitation of Solitary Vajrasattva.

Melodious Drum Victorious in all Directions The extensive fulfilling and restoring ritual of the Dharma Protector, the great king Dorje Shugden, in conjunction with Mahakala, Kalarupa, Kalindewi and other Dharma Protectors.

Offering to the Spiritual Guide (*Lama Chopa*) A special way of relying upon a Spiritual Guide.

Path of Compassion for the Deceased Powa sadhana for the benefit of the deceased.

Pathway to the Pure Land Training in powa – the transference of consciousness.

Powa Ceremony Transference of consciousness for the deceased.

Prayers for Meditation Brief preparatory prayers for meditation.

Prayers for World Peace.

A Pure Life The practice of taking and keeping the eight Mahayana precepts.

Quick Path to Great Bliss The extensive self-generation sadhana of Vajrayogini.

The Root Tantra of Heruka and Vajrayogini Chapters One & Fifty-one of the *Condensed Heruka Root Tantra*.

The Root Text: Eight Verses of Training the Mind.

Treasury of Wisdom The sadhana of Venerable Manjushri.

The Uncommon Yoga of Inconceivability The special instruction of how to reach the Pure Land of Keajra with this human body

Union of No More Learning Heruka body mandala self-initiation sadhana.

The Vows and Commitments of Kadampa Buddhism.

Wishfulfilling Jewel The Guru yoga of Je Tsongkhapa combined with the sadhana of his Dharma Protector.

The Yoga of Buddha Amitayus A special method for increasing lifespan, wisdom and merit.

The Yoga of Buddha Heruka The essential self-generation sadhana of Heruka body mandala & Condensed six-session yoga.

The Yoga of Buddha Maitreya Self-generation sadhana.

The Yoga of Buddha Vajrapani Self-generation sadhana.

The Yoga of Enlightened Mother Arya Tara Self-generation sadhana.

The Yoga of Great Mother Prajnaparamita Self-generation sadhana.

The Yoga of Thousand-armed Avalokiteshvara Self-generation sadhana.

The Yoga of White Tara, Buddha of Long Life.

To order any of our publications, or to request a catalogue, please visit www.tharpa.com or contact your nearest Tharpa office listed on pages 393–394.

Study Programmes of
Kadampa Buddhism

Kadampa Buddhism is a Mahayana Buddhist school founded by the great Indian Buddhist Master Atisha (AD 982-1054). His followers are known as 'Kadampas'. 'Ka' means 'word' and refers to Buddha's teachings, and 'dam' refers to Atisha's special Lamrim instructions known as 'the stages of the path to enlightenment'. By integrating their knowledge of all Buddha's teachings into their practice of Lamrim, and by integrating this into their everyday lives, Kadampa Buddhists are encouraged to use Buddha's teachings as practical methods for transforming daily activities into the path to enlightenment. The great Kadampa Teachers are famous not only for being great scholars but also for being spiritual practitioners of immense purity and sincerity.

The lineage of these teachings, both their oral transmission and blessings, was then passed from Teacher to disciple, spreading throughout much of Asia, and now to many countries throughout the Western world. Buddha's teachings, which are known as 'Dharma', are likened to a wheel that moves from country to country in accordance with changing conditions and people's karmic inclinations. The external forms of presenting Buddhism may change as it meets with different cultures and societies, but its essential authenticity is ensured through the continuation of an unbroken lineage of realized practitioners.

Kadampa Buddhism was first introduced into the West in 1977 by the renowned Buddhist Master, Venerable Geshe Kelsang Gyatso Rinpoche. Since that time, he has worked tirelessly to spread Kadampa Buddhism throughout the world by giving extensive teachings, writing many profound texts on Kadampa Buddhism, and founding the New Kadampa Tradition – International Kadampa Buddhist Union (NKT-IKBU), which now has over 1200 Kadampa Buddhist Centres worldwide. Each Centre offers study programmes on Buddhist psychology, philosophy and meditation instruction, as well as retreats for all levels of practitioner. The emphasis is on integrating Buddha's teachings into daily life to solve our human problems and to spread lasting peace and happiness throughout the world.

The Kadampa Buddhism of the NKT-IKBU is an entirely independent Buddhist tradition and has no political affiliations. It is an association of Buddhist Centres and practitioners that derive their inspiration and guidance from the example of the ancient Kadampa Buddhist Masters and their teachings, as presented by Venerable Geshe Kelsang.

There are three reasons why we need to study and practise the teachings of Buddha: to develop our wisdom, to cultivate a good heart, and to maintain a peaceful state of mind. If we do not strive to develop our wisdom, we will always remain ignorant of ultimate truth – the true nature of reality. Although we wish for happiness, our ignorance leads us to engage in non-virtuous actions, which are the main cause of all our suffering. If we do not cultivate a good heart, our selfish motivation destroys harmony and good relationships with others. We have no peace, and no chance to gain pure happiness. Without inner peace, outer peace is impossible. If we do not maintain a peaceful state of mind, we are not happy even if we have ideal conditions. On the other hand, when our mind is peaceful, we are happy, even if our external conditions are unpleasant. Therefore, the development of these qualities is of utmost importance for our daily happiness.

Venerable Geshe Kelsang, or 'Geshe-la' as he is affectionately called by his students, has designed three special spiritual programmes for the systematic study and practice of Kadampa Buddhism that are especially suited to the modern world – the General Programme (GP), the Foundation Programme (FP), and the Teacher Training Programme (TTP).

GENERAL PROGRAMME

The General Programme provides a basic introduction to Buddhist view, meditation and practice that is suitable for beginners. It also includes advanced teachings and practice from both Sutra and Tantra.

FOUNDATION PROGRAMME

The Foundation Programme provides an opportunity to deepen our understanding and experience of Buddhism through a systematic study of six texts:

1 *Joyful Path of Good Fortune* – a commentary to Atisha's Lamrim instructions, the stages of the path to enlightenment.

2 *Universal Compassion* – a commentary to Bodhisattva Chekhawa's *Training the Mind in Seven Points*.

3 *Eight Steps to Happiness* – a commentary to Bodhisattva Langri Tangpa's *Eight Verses of Training the Mind*.

4 *The New Heart of Wisdom* – a commentary to the *Heart Sutra*.

5 *Meaningful to Behold* – a commentary to Bodhisattva Shantideva's *Guide to the Bodhisattva's Way of Life*.

6 *How to Understand the Mind* – a detailed explanation of the mind, based on the works of the Buddhist scholars Dharmakirti and Dignaga.

The benefits of studying and practising these texts are as follows:

(1) *Joyful Path of Good Fortune* – we gain the ability to put all Buddha's teachings of both Sutra and Tantra into practice. We can easily make progress on, and complete, the stages of the path to the supreme happiness of enlightenment. From a practical point of view, Lamrim is the main body of Buddha's teachings, and the other teachings are like its limbs.

(2) and (3) *Universal Compassion* and *Eight Steps to Happiness* – we gain the ability to integrate Buddha's teachings into our daily life and solve all our human problems.

(4) *The New Heart of Wisdom* – we gain a realization of the ultimate nature of reality. By gaining this realization, we can eliminate the ignorance of self-grasping, which is the root of all our suffering.

(5) *Meaningful to Behold* – we transform our daily activities into the Bodhisattva's way of life, thereby making every moment of our human life meaningful.

(6) *How to Understand the Mind* – we understand the relationship between our mind and its external objects. If we understand that objects depend upon the subjective mind, we can change the way objects appear to us by changing our own mind. Gradually, we will gain the ability to control our mind and in this way solve all our problems.

TEACHER TRAINING PROGRAMME

The Teacher Training Programme is designed for people who wish to train as authentic Dharma Teachers. In addition to completing the study of fourteen texts of Sutra and Tantra, which include the six texts mentioned above, the student is required to observe certain commitments with regard to behaviour and way of life, and to complete a number of meditation retreats.

A Special Teacher Training Programme is also held at KMC London, and can be studied at the centre or by correspondence. This special meditation and study programme consists of six courses spread over three years based on the books of Venerable Geshe Kelsang: *How to Understand the Mind*; *Modern Buddhism; The New Heart of Wisdom; Tantric Grounds and Paths*; Shantideva's *Guide to the Bodhisattva's Way of Life* and its commentary, *Meaningful to Behold*; and *Ocean of Nectar*.

All Kadampa Buddhist Centres are open to the public. Every year we celebrate Festivals in many countries throughout the world, including two in England, where people gather from around the world to receive special teachings and empowerments and to enjoy a spiritual holiday. Please feel free to visit us at any time!

For further information about NKT–IKBU study programmes or to find your nearest centre visit www.kadampa.org, or please contact:

NKT-IKBU Central Office
Conishead Priory, Ulverston,
Cumbria LA12 9QQ, UK
Tel: +44 (0) 01229-588533
Email: info@kadampa.org
Website: www.kadampa.org

or

US NKT-IKBU Office
KMC New York
47 Sweeney Road
Glen Spey, NY 12737, USA
Tel: +1 845-856-9000
Fax: +1 845-856-2110
Email: info@kadampanewyork.org
Website: www.kadampanewyork.org

Tharpa Offices Worldwide

Tharpa books are currently published in English (UK and US), Chinese, French, German, Italian, Japanese, Portuguese and Spanish. Most languages are available from any Tharpa office listed below.

UK Office
Tharpa Publications UK
Conishead Priory
ULVERSTON
Cumbria, LA12 9QQ, UK
Tel: +44 (0)1229-588599
Web: tharpa.com/uk
E-mail: info.uk@tharpa.com

US Office
Tharpa Publications US
47 Sweeney Road
GLEN SPEY, NY 12737, USA
Tel: +1 845-856-5102
Toll-free: +1 888-741-3475
Fax: +1 845-856-2110
Web: tharpa.com/us
E-mail: info.us@tharpa.com

Asian Office
Tharpa Asia
1st Floor Causeway Tower,
16-22 Causeway Road,
Causeway Bay,
HONG KONG
Tel: +(852) 2507 2237
Web: tharpa.com/hk-en
E-mail: info.asia@tharpa.com

Australian Office
Tharpa Publications Australia
25 McCarthy Road,
MONBULK VIC 3793
AUSTRALIA
Tel: +61 (0)3 9752 0377
Web: tharpa.com/au
E-mail: info.au@tharpa.com

Brazilian Office
Editora Tharpa Brasil
Rua Artur de Azevedo 1360
Pinheiros, 05404-003
SÃO PAULO, SP, BRASIL
Tel: +55 (11) 3476-2330
Web: tharpa.com.br
E-mail: contato.br@tharpa.com

Canadian Office
Tharpa Publications Canada
631 Crawford St.,
TORONTO, ON M6G 3K1
CANADA
Tel: (+1) 416-762-8710
Toll-free: (+1) 866-523-2672
Fax: (+1) 416-762-2267
Web (Eng): tharpa.com/ca
Web (Fr): tharpa.com/ca-fr
E-mail: info.ca@tharpa.com

French Office
Editions Tharpa
Château de Segrais
72220 SAINT-MARS-
  D'OUTILLÉ, FRANCE
Tél/Fax : +33 (0)2 43 87 71 02
Web: tharpa.com/fr
E-mail: info.fr@tharpa.com

German Office
Tharpa-Verlag Deutschland
Mehringdamm 33, Aufgang 2,
10961 BERLIN, GERMANY
Tel: +49 (030) 430 55 666
Web: tharpa.com/de
E-mail: info.de@tharpa.com

Japanese Office
Tharpa Japan
KMC TOKYO, JAPAN
Web: tharpa.jp
E-mail: info@kadampa.jp

Mexican Office
Tharpa México
Enrique Rébsamen Nº 406
Col. Narvate, entre Xola y
  Diagonal de San Antonio
MÉXICO D.F., C.P. 03020,
MEXICO
Tel: +52 (55) 56 39 61 86
Tel/Fax: +52 (55) 56 39 61 80
Web: tharpa.com/mx
E-mail: info.mx@tharpa.com

Portuguese Office
Publicações Tharpa Portugal
Rua Moinho do Gato, 5
Várzea de Sintra
2710-661 SINTRA,
PORTUGAL
Tel: +351 219231064
Web: tharpa.pt
E-mail: info.pt@tharpa.com

South African Office
26 Menston Rd., Dawncliffe,
Westville, 3629, KZN,
REP. OF SOUTH AFRICA
Tel: +27 (0)72 551 3429
Fax: +27 (0)86 513 3476
Web: tharpa.com/za
E-mail: info.za@tharpa.com

Spanish Office
Editorial Tharpa España
Calle Manuela Malasaña 26
local dcha, 28004 MADRID,
SPAIN
Tel: +34 917 55 75 35
Web: tharpa.com/es
E-mail: info.es@tharpa.com

Swiss Office
Tharpa Verlag Schweiz
Mirabellenstrasse 1
CH-8048 ZÜRICH
SWITZERLAND
Tel: +41 44 401 02 20
Fax: +41 44 461 36 88
Web: tharpa.com/ch
E-mail: info.ch@tharpa.com

Index

The letter 'g' indicates an entry in the glossary

A

absorption of cessation 313–315
absorption without
    discrimination 27–29
actions. *See also* karma
  pure 292, 306
  virtuous/non-virtuous
    271–274, 284
ageing 280–282
aggregates, g. *See also* five
    aggregates
  contaminated 121, g
  inherently existent 141–142
  pure 121
aggression 150
alertness 87, 106, 162
all-accompanying mental factors
    14–15, 19–35
Amitabha, Buddha 59
analogies
  bird leaving nest 262
  bird shot down 279
  blind turtle 258–259
  bucket in a well 142–143
  candle flame 15
  child named 'Buddha' 140–141
  cutting down tree 294
  dreaming 10, 311
  fire in the house 278
  magician's illusion 104

  painting Buddha image 221
  peacock 310
  putting hand into fire 119–120
  rope mistaken for snake 142
  son of a childless woman 313
  thorn bush 285
  toy snake 124, 131, 140
analysis 169–170
anger 25, 98, 117–120, 150–151,
    156, 237
  at inanimate objects 69, 117
  causes of 103–104, 105
  conceived object 239
  destroying merit 307
  faults of 67–68, 118–119
  intellectually-formed 234–235
animals 61, 274, 275, 293
  rebirth as 258, 264, 267, 288,
    296
  suffering of 275, 301
appearing object 181, 231
apprehended object 181
Asanga 80, g
asceticism 145–146, 189
aspiration 37–41, 47, 57, 60, 82
  four types 38–39
  twofold division 39–40
aspiring bodhichitta, g. *See also*
    bodhichitta
attachment 26, 64–67, 98, 113–116,
    152, 156, 158, 159, 219